Math for All

Math for All

Differentiating Instruction, Grades 3–5

Linda Dacey &
Jayne Bamford Lynch

Math Solutions Publications
Sausalito, CA

To our first teachers, our mothers:
Maureen Flynn Schulman
Mildred Jane Bamford

Sadly, we lost them both while we were writing this book.
We will always be grateful for their love.

Math Solutions Publications
A division of
Marilyn Burns Education Associates
150 Gate 5 Road, Suite 101
Sausalito, CA 94965
www.mathsolutions.com

Library of Congress Cataloging-in-Publication Data

Dacey, Linda Schulman, 1949–
   Math for all. Differentiating instruction, grades 3/5 / Linda Dacey and Jayne Bamford Lynch.
      p. cm.
   Includes bibliographical references and index.
   ISBN-13: 978-0-941355-78-0 (alk. paper)
   ISBN-10: 0-941355-78-0 (alk. paper)
   1. Mathematics—Study and teaching (Primary) 2. Mathematics—Study and teaching (Elementary)
I. Lynch, Jayne Bamford. II. Title. III. Title: Differentiating instruction, grades 3/5.
QA11.2.D328 2007
372.7′049—dc22

2007014902

Editor: Toby Gordon
Production: Melissa L. Inglis
Cover design: Jan Streitburger
Interior design: Joni Doherty Design
Composition: ICC Macmillan Inc.

Printed in the United States of America on acid-free paper
11   10   09   08   07   ML   1   2   3   4   5

A Message from Marilyn Burns

We at Math Solutions Professional Development believe that teaching math well calls for increasing our understanding of the math we teach, seeking deeper insights into how children learn mathematics, and refining our lessons to best promote students' learning.

Math Solutions Publications shares classroom-tested lessons and teaching expertise from our faculty of Math Solutions Inservice instructors as well as from other respected math educators. Our publications are part of the nationwide effort we've made since 1984 that now includes

- more than five hundred face-to-face inservice programs each year for teachers and administrators in districts across the country;
- annually publishing professional development books, now totaling more than sixty titles and spanning the teaching of all math topics in kindergarten through grade 8;
- four series of videotapes for teachers, plus a videotape for parents, that show math lessons taught in actual classrooms;
- on-site visits to schools to help refine teaching strategies and assess student learning; and
- free online support, including grade-level lessons, book reviews, inservice information, and district feedback, all in our quarterly *Math Solutions Online Newsletter*.

For information about all of the products and services we have available, please visit our website at *www.mathsolutions.com*. You can also contact us to discuss math professional development needs by calling (800) 868-9092 or by sending an email to *info@mathsolutions.com*.

We're always eager for your feedback and interested in learning about your particular needs. We look forward to hearing from you.

Math Solutions.
PUBLICATIONS

Contents

Preface

The idea for this book began four years ago when I started to think about how few ideas related to differentiating instruction were integrated into the mathematics education literature. I felt strongly that a book focused on differentiating instruction in mathematics was needed and first turned to Rebeka Eston to join me in writing one at the primary level.

To more effectively reach teachers' specific grade-level needs, our idea for one book grew into a two-book series, one for grades K–2 and the other for grades 3–5. Jayne Bamford Lynch agreed to work on the grade 3–5 with me. Jayne is a seasoned teacher, tutor, math coach, and consultant who brings great enthusiasm to her work. There is significant overlap between the two books, though each is tailored to its particular grade span. The classroom vignettes differ, of course, as well as most of the teacher reflections and some teaching strategies and techniques. Sometimes particular stories and reflections were relevant across the grade levels and we made only those changes necessary for the intended audience.

Trends and buzzwords come and go in education, but the need for differentiated instruction is constant. Our students deserve to have their individual learning needs met in their classrooms. Throughout the book we suggest that teaching this way is a career-long goal, one part of our professional journey. We know that this is true for us, and we are eager to share our current thinking with you.

—LINDA DACEY

Acknowledgments

This book features stories and student work from a number of classrooms. Numerous colleagues, workshop participants, and children have informed our work. We are profoundly thankful for their time, insights, and contributions. We are particularly grateful to the Massachusetts students and teachers in public schools in Cambridge, Lincoln, Melrose, Peabody, Somerville, and Tyngsboro.

Linda would like to acknowledge Lesley University and the Russell Foundation for their support of her work. Jayne remains grateful to the students, parents, teachers, and administrators who welcome her into their schools as their math coach. Together, we would like to express appreciation for Rebeka Eston Salemi who helped shape this work. Also, our families and our friends fuel our spirits and we are always thankful for their patience, flexibility, and love.

We thank our editor, Toby Gordon, for her interest and guidance in this project from its earliest inception, and Marilyn Burns for her direction and support. Thank you, too, to Joan Carlson and Melissa Inglis and the many other talented people we have encountered at Math Solutions Publications.

Chapter 1
Thinking About Differentiation

This year David, a third-grade teacher, is worried about a student who seems to care only about getting the right answer. The student seems uninterested when other students share how they solved a problem and is resistant to representing her ideas on paper. David knows from his contact with her family that they, too, focus on whether their daughter is getting the correct answers. When given an open-ended problem she seems to lack the confidence or initiative to just give it a try. Instead, she persistently asks, "What am I supposed to do? Can't you just show me?" When David asks a series of questions beginning with, "What's one thing you can tell me about this problem?" he can often get her to tell one idea about how to begin the task. David is particularly troubled about how she will perform on state-mandated tests. He's concerned that she won't have the confidence to try the open-ended response questions and so the results won't really reflect what she knows.

Jesse teaches fourth grade and worries most about a student in her class who has difficulty processing visual information. The student reverses numbers, confuses mathematical symbols, and miscopies information. Jesse tries to make sure that a verbal description accompanies everything that she or other students write on the board so that this student will receive auditory as well as visual input. As he is known to jump from one problem to another without completing his work, Jesse has also started to give him only one problem at a time. She is hopeful that this technique will help him to focus. Though Jesse is clear that this student struggles with visual input, she sometimes thinks that the level of mathematical challenge is also a factor. The student does do better when he works with another student who can read the problem aloud and record their work. Jesse is worried that this student is falling further and further behind and that he is beginning to get frustrated more quickly. The other day Jesse overheard him say, "I just can't do math."

Ali, a fifth-grade teacher, is concerned about a student whose mathematical ability is exceptional. It is difficult to keep the student interested in class investigations. Yesterday, Ali noticed that the student groaned when asked to explain her thinking. When Ali queried her, the response was, "It's just something I know." She finishes her work very quickly and then can be distracting to her peers. Ali would like to have the student work on the same concept as the other students, but at a deeper level or in a more sophisticated manner. This goal has become more difficult as the year has continued and Ali worries about how rarely this student is truly challenged in math. Ali wishes she had more time right now to explore some mathematical ideas herself.

These three teachers are like most teachers of elementary school children. They want to provide for the needs of all of their students. They want to recognize the unique gifts and developmental readiness each child brings to the classroom community. These teachers also realize that addressing the variety of abilities, interests, cultures, and learning styles in their classrooms is a challenging task.

Variations in student learning have always existed in classrooms, but some have only been given recent attention. For example, our understanding of intelligence has broadened with Howard Gardner's theory of multiple intelligences (Gardner 2000). Teachers are now more conscious of some of the different strengths among students and find ways to tap into those strengths in the classroom.

Brain research has given us further insight into the learning process; for example, it has shown us that there is an explicit link between our emotional states and our ability to learn (Jensen 2005, Sprenger 2002). Having a sense of control and being able to make choices typically contributes to increased interest and positive attitudes. So we can think of providing choice, and thus, control, as creating a healthier learning environment.

At the same time that we are gaining these insights, the diversity of learning needs in classrooms is growing. The number of English language learners (ELLs) in our schools is increasing dramatically. Classroom teachers need to know ways to help these students learn content, while they are also learning English.

Different values and cultures create different learning patterns among children and different expectations for classroom interactions. In addition, our inclusive classrooms contain a broader spectrum of special education needs and the number of children with identified or perceived special learning needs is growing. On a regular basis, classroom teachers need to adapt plans to include and effectively instruct the range of needs students present.

How can teachers meet the growing diversity of learning needs in their classrooms? Further, how do teachers meet this challenge in the midst of increasing pressures to master specified content? Differentiated instruction—instruction designed to meet differing learners' needs—is clearly required. By adapting classroom practices to help more students be successful, teachers are able to both honor individual students and to increase the likelihood that curricular outcomes will be met.

This book takes the approach that differentiated mathematics instruction is most successful when teachers:

- believe that all students have the capacity to succeed at learning mathematics;
- recognize that multiple perspectives are necessary to build important mathematical ideas and that diverse thinking is an essential and valued resource in their classrooms;
- know and understand mathematics and are confident in their abilities to teach mathematical ideas;
- are intentional about curricular choices; that is, they think carefully about what students need to learn and how that learning will be best supported;
- develop strong mathematical learning communities in their classrooms;
- focus assessment on gathering evidence that can inform instruction and provide a variety of ways for students to demonstrate what they know; and
- support each other in their efforts to create and sustain this type of instruction.

We like to think about differentiation as a lens through which we can examine our teaching and our students' learning more closely, a way to become even more aware of the best ways to ensure that our students will be successful learners. Looking at differentiation through such a lens requires us to develop new skills and to become more adept at:

- identifying important mathematical skills and concepts;
- assessing what students know, what interests them, and how they learn best;
- creating diverse tasks through which students can build understanding and demonstrate what they know;
- designing and modifying tasks to meet students' needs;
- providing students with choices to make; and
- managing different activities taking place simultaneously.

Many teachers find that thinking about ways to differentiate literacy instruction comes somewhat naturally, while differentiation in mathematics seems more demanding or challenging. As one teacher put it, "Do we have to differentiate in math, too? I can do this in reading, but it's too hard in math! I mean in reading, there are so many books to choose from that focus on different interests and that are written for a variety of reading levels." While we recognize that many teachers may feel this way, there are important reasons to differentiate in mathematics.

There are several indications that we are not yet teaching mathematics in an effective manner, in a way designed to meet a variety of needs. Results of international tests show U.S. students do not perform as well as students in many other countries at a time when more mathematical skill is needed for professional success and economic security. There continues to be a gap in achievement for our African American, Native American, and Hispanic students. Finally, we are a country in which many people describe themselves as math phobic and others have no problem announcing publicly that they failed mathematics in high school.

In response to these indicators, educators continue to wrestle with the development and implementation of approaches for teaching mathematics more effectively. The scope of the mathematics curriculum continues to broaden and deepen. There are shifts in emphasis. For example, current trends stress the importance of algebra and, as a result, the elementary curriculum is shifting its focus to include early algebraic thinking. The way we teach math has changed, requiring students to communicate their mathematical thinking, to solve more complex problems, and to conceptually understand the mathematical procedures they perform. And, all of this is happening at a time when our national agenda is clear that "no child is to be left behind."

Even though teachers strive to reach all of their students, learners' needs are ever increasing and more complex to attend to in the multifaceted arenas of our classrooms. Considering the ways differentiation can assist us in meeting our goals is essential. Carol Tomlinson, a leader in the field of differentiated instruction, identifies three areas in which teachers can adapt their curriculum: *content, process,* and *product* (Tomlinson 1999, 2003a, 2003b). Teachers must identify the content students are to learn and then judge its appropriateness to make initial decisions about differentiation. The first step in this task is to read the local, state, or national standards for mathematics. A more in-depth analysis asks teachers to be aware of the "big ideas" in mathematics and then to connect the identified standards to these ideas. A decision to adapt content should be based on what teachers know about their students' readiness. Thus, the teacher needs to be aware of or to determine what students already know. Taking time to pre-assess students is essential to differentiated instruction. Based on this information, teachers can then decide the level of content that students can investigate and the pace at which they can do so.

Differentiation Within a Unit

Let's consider fifth graders who are beginning a mini-unit on number theory. One of the standards of this content area is that students be able to identify and apply concepts of number theory. The classroom teacher knows that making connections among concepts and representations is a big idea in mathematics. She wants all of her students to be able to represent and connect number theory ideas. For example, she wants her students to represent square numbers visually by making squares on graph paper as well as to connect those representations to the symbolic notation $y = x^2$. She believes if students "owned" this connection, they wouldn't have so much trouble remembering the formula for finding the area of a square.

The teacher will incorporate this idea into the unit, but first, she wants to informally pre-assess her students to find out how they might classify numbers. She wants to know whether they can readily identify "classes" of numbers, such as square numbers, even numbers, prime numbers, and multiples. In lieu of just giving them lists of numbers and having them extend or identify the types of numbers in the lists, she'll launch the unit with a problem-solving activity. The activity will allow her to get a feel for her students' common understanding and to identify students who may need more or less support in this area. She'll observe her students carefully as they work and make notes about their thinking and writing. She'll be able to use the data to inform the lessons that follow.

She asks students to get out their math journals and pencils and gather in the meeting area. She writes the numbers *4, 16, 36, 48, 64,* and *81* on the whiteboard and asks the students to copy these numbers in their journals. She then writes:

> *Which number does not belong?*
> *4, 16, 36, 48, 64, or 81*

She then says, "Use your journal to jot down your ideas. I want everyone to have some time to think. Please don't share until we have a green light." As the teacher says this she points to the depiction of a traffic light next to the whiteboard and places the Velcro®-backed star on the red signal. Students are given time to work independently while the room is quiet.

"It's the four!" Sheila calls out immediately after the teacher moves the star to the green signal. The teacher thinks about asking how many other students agree with Sheila, but as she wants them to eventually find more than one candidate, she decides not to have them commit to this thinking. Instead she asks, "Does anyone think they know why Sheila might think that the four does not belong?" Several hands are raised and others are nodding their heads.

She calls on Tara who explains, "It's only one number. The rest are two."

Dewayne adds, "It's the only number less than ten, the rest are between ten and one hundred."

"It's only one digit; the rest are two-digit numbers," says Marybeth.

"Wait," says Melissa, "I got another number answer, too. It's eighty-one."

"Hmm, interesting, I want you to hold on to that thought," says the teacher. "Right now, please write in your journals any other reasons why a number doesn't belong in this group. Like Tara, Marybeth, and Dewayne, you might find different reasons for why a particular number does not belong. Like Melissa, if you change the rule, you might find a different number that does not belong. You will have about ten minutes. You can work on your ideas the whole time, or, if you finish early, find a partner who has finished and share. Some of you might find rules to eliminate each of the numbers, one at a time."

Already, the teacher has heard minor variations in the students' thinking. Tara seems to recognize a visual difference in the numbers, while Marybeth uses more formal language to describe this attribute. Dewayne refers to the value of the numbers and Melissa is willing to verbalize another possibility. The teacher looks around and sees everyone has spread out a bit and begun to think and write. After a couple of minutes, she notices that a few of the students have stopped after writing about the number four. She quietly asks them if they remember Melissa's number. Some do and others need to be reminded, but with a bit of coaching, all are able to identify eighty-one as different because it is an odd number.

After almost ten minutes the teacher notices that all but two of the students are talking in pairs about their work. She gives them a one-minute warning and when that time has passed, they huddle more closely and refocus as a group. The teacher asks them to draw a line under what they have written so far, and then to take notes about new ideas that arise in their group conversation. As the students share their work, several ideas related to number theory terms and concepts are heard. Jason identifies the square numbers in order to distinguish forty-eight from the other numbers. Judy also refers to square numbers when she eliminates sixteen as "the only number that is the square of another number in the list." Naomi tells the class that eighty-one is different because it is not divisible by four. Most interesting to the teacher, Naomi also says, "All of the other numbers are even, but they have to be if they are multiples of four." After each comment there is a short conversation. Sometimes the teacher asks another student to restate what has been heard, or to define a term, or to come up with a new number that could be included in the list to fit the rule.

Each time, the teacher makes sure there is time for students to take some notes and that the majority of them agree that the classification works. She secures their agreement as she points to each number in the list and says, for example, "Is this a multiple of four?" Sometimes students suggest ideas that don't hold true. Robert identifies eighty-one as the only prime number until a friend reminds him that nine times nine is eighty-one. No one mentions that three and twenty-seven are also factors of eighty-one, but one counterexample is enough. Claire suggests that thirty-six is different because "it has a sum of nine," but this is refuted when eighty-one is tested.

Two students use arithmetic to find a number that is different. Benita's work is the most complex. She identifies eighty-one as different because "you can't get there with just these numbers." She explains her work further by writing the following equations on the board:

$$64 \div 16 = 4$$
$$64 \div 4 = 16$$
$$48 - 16 + 4 = 36$$
$$64 - 16 = 48$$
$$16 \times 4 = 64$$

Two days later, Naomi surprises the class with a new equation: $(16 \div 4) + (16 \div 4) + (36 \div 4) + 64 = 81$. Benita is crestfallen at first, but then brightens as she adds "without using one of the numbers more than once" to her rule.

While students do not experience this activity as a pre-assessment task, it does give the teacher some important information that she can use to further plan the mini-unit on number theory. She can determine students' willingness to think divergently, to come up with different possibilities for the same number. She has an indication of their understanding and comfort level with concepts and terms such as *factors, multiples, divisible, primes,* and *square numbers.* With students' written work, she can determine the ideas and terms they included prior to the group debriefing. She can also gather evidence as to whether the students' notes are accurate and complete, contain their own additional ideas, or include drawings, lists, and definitions.

From this information she can decide how to adapt her *content* for different students. The complexity of ideas can vary. Some students can reinforce ideas introduced through this activity, while others can investigate additional ideas such as triangle numbers, cubic numbers, and powers. She can have some students explore ideas that will allow them to complete or create if-then statement such as "If a number is a multiple of six, then it is a multiple of _____." Divisibility rules and common multiples can be used to solve problems and relationships can be generalized through algebraic equations.

Once content variations are determined, *process* is considered. Some students can draw dots to represent square and triangular numbers so that they have a visual image of them while others can connect to visual images of multiples and square numbers on a hundreds chart. (See Figure 1–1.) The teacher can create some packets of logic problems, such as the one that follows, which require students to identify one number based on a series of clues involving number theory terminology:

1	2	3	4	5	6	7	8	9	10
11	12	13	14	15	16	17	18	19	20
21	22	23	24	25	26	27	28	29	30
31	32	33	34	35	36	37	38	39	40
41	42	43	44	45	46	47	48	49	50
51	52	53	54	55	56	57	58	59	60
61	62	63	64	65	66	67	68	69	70
71	72	73	74	75	76	77	78	79	80
81	82	83	84	85	86	87	88	89	90
91	92	93	94	95	96	97	98	99	100

x	1	2	3	4	5	6	7	8	9	10
1	1	2	3	4	5	6	7	8	9	10
2	2	4	6	8	10	12	14	16	18	20
3	3	6	9	12	15	18	21	24	27	30
4	4	8	12	16	20	24	28	32	36	40
5	5	10	15	20	25	30	35	40	45	50
6	6	12	18	24	30	36	42	48	54	60
7	7	14	21	28	35	42	49	56	63	70
8	8	16	24	32	40	48	56	64	72	80
9	9	18	27	36	45	54	63	72	81	90
1	10	20	30	40	50	60	70	80	90	100

Figure 1–1 *Visual images of multiples of 4 on a hundreds chart and square numbers on a multiplication chart.*

> *What is my locker number?*
> *The number is between 250 and 275.*
> *It is an even number.*
> *It is a multiple of 3.*
> *It is not a multiple of 5.*
> *It is divisible by 4.*
> *My locker number is _____.*

Another packet could offer brainteasers that involve clues about remainders:

> *What's the fewest number of pennies I could have? When I put them in two equal stacks, there is one penny left over. When I put them in three equal stacks, there is one penny left over. When I put them in four equal stacks, there is one penny left over.*
>
> *(You might want to get some chips to help you model the pennies.)*

Some students could write rap lyrics to help them remember the meaning of specific terms. Other students could play a two- or three-ring attribute game with number theory categories as labels; they would then place numbers (written on small cards) in those rings until they could identify the labels. A learning center on codes could help students explore how number theory is related to cryptology. The teacher could think about pairs of students who will work well together during this unit and identify subsets of students that she wants to bring together for some focused instruction.

Then the teacher must think about product—how her students can demonstrate their ability to use and apply their knowledge of number theory at the end of the unit. For example, students might write a number theory dictionary that includes representations, pretend they are interviewing for a secret agent job and explain why they should be hired based on their knowledge of number theory, create a dice game that involves prime numbers, make a collage with visual representations of number theory ideas, or create their own problem booklet.

It's not necessary, or even possible, to always differentiate these three aspects of curriculum, but thinking about differentiating content, process, and products prompts teachers to:

- identify the mathematical skills and abilities that students should gain and connect them to big ideas;
- pre-assess readiness levels to determine specific mathematical strengths and weaknesses;
- develop mathematical ideas through a variety of learning modalities and preferences;
- provide choices for students to make during mathematical instruction;
- make connections among mathematics, other subject areas, and students' interests; and
- provide a variety of ways in which students can demonstrate their understanding of mathematical concepts and acquisition of mathematical skills.

It is also not likely that all attempts to differentiate will be successful, but keeping differentiation in mind as we plan and reflect on our mathematics instruction is important and can transform teaching in important ways. It reminds us of the constant need to fine-tune, adjust, redirect, and evaluate learning in our classrooms.

Differentiation Within a Lesson

Consider the following vignette from a fourth-grade classroom. Having just taken a workshop on differentiated instruction, the teacher wants to try something different in her classroom. She is thinking about a lesson she sometimes leads this time of year and decides to make some changes. She wants to provide more choice, be more open to variations in student thinking based on readiness, and have a variety of materials available for the students to use. She feels that she is a novice in this way of teaching and is unsure of where these changes will lead her.

The teacher begins the class by introducing the students to the book, *Even Steven and Odd Todd,* written by Kathryn Cristaldi (1996). She holds the book up and asks, "What do you think this book might be about?" Several children raise their hands. John answers, "I think it is about two boys, one named Steven and the other named Todd." Madelyn continues, "I think Steven will like even numbers and things and Todd will like odd numbers and stuff like that."

The teacher begins the book and sure enough John and Madelyn are correct. Steven loves everything to be even and Todd loves everything to be odd. They are cousins and early in the story, Steven learns that Todd is spending the summer with him. It is clear that this proximity will lead to some disagreements.

At this point the teacher stops reading and asks, "Does anyone have a cousin?" All hands are raised as the students smile and look at one another. She follows up with, "Have you ever had to compromise to get along with your cousin?" Most heads nod and the students begin to tell stories.

"My cousin always likes to play sports when I visit and I don't like to play sports all the time," tells John.

Sam adds, "My cousin always likes to watch TV and get up early."

Meghan rolls her eyes and says, "My cousin always gets my bed when she sleeps over. I have to sleep on the floor."

"Well," says the teacher, "let's find out what happens to these cousins." As she reads, the students learn that when the boys order pizza, Steven orders four slices while Todd orders three. When they go to an ice cream shop, Steven orders two scoops of double-dip chocolate chocolate ice cream and Todd orders a triple nutty fudge sundae. Throughout their summer together, Todd manages to disrupt Steven's desire to have everything be even. Toward the end, Steven plants a perfectly even garden and enters it in the garden contest. Without Steven's knowledge, Todd disrupts this plan by planting an odd number of cacti, each of which has five long needles. Fortunately, just as Steven proclaims that he can no longer stand his cousin, who is just "too odd," they win the contest.

The students appear relaxed as they listen to the story and giggle during the boys' conflicts. When the teacher finishes the book, she closes it and asks, "If Even Steven and Odd Todd made a rectangular garden together, could they compromise by having an even perimeter and an odd area or an odd perimeter and an even area?"

Initially the students seem perplexed by the question. Usually the teacher would now offer a review of area and perimeter, but this time, she decides to probe the students' ideas first. She asks, "What are *area* and *perimeter*?" Kim Su raises her hand quickly and states, "Area is the middle of a box." The teacher responds, "Tell me about the box." Kim Su continues, "The box has cubes in it. Can I show you?" When the teacher nods, Kim Su walks to the board and draws a five-by-three rectangle with grid lines on the board:

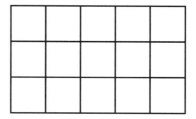

The teacher asks, "How do you know the area, Kim Su?" "Well," she says, "you just count the boxes!" It appears from the looks on the students' faces that this technique makes sense to them and helps some who may have forgotten the meaning of area. Lisa comments, "I don't like to count them all, I multiply them."

Once the class restates these ideas, the teacher redirects their thinking to perimeter. She asks, "Why might we want to know the perimeter of a garden?" "Oh I know," responds Pedro. "It's for making a fence around the garden." John then jumps up and gets permission to go to the board. He writes a *5* and a *3* on the two unlabeled sides of Kim Su's drawing and tells the class, "All you have to do is add up all of the numbers." Jill looks excited when she offers, "I remember now. The perimeter is the distance around the figure."

The teacher asks, "What is *distance*?" and Jill walks to the board and begins to count her way around the figure. She points to each intersection on the outline of the grid and arrives at the answer of sixteen. She then turns to the class and says, "See, it's sixteen." The teacher asks if the students agree with Jill and most nod their heads. She then asks, "Sixteen what?" Jill and several other students in the class shrug their shoulders.

The teacher explains that perimeter is measured in units and has the students identify the unit they counted, the distance from one intersection to another. As they counted sixteen of these, the perimeter is sixteen units. The students seem more confident about this idea and so she asks what they counted to find the area. She points to one of the squares in Kim Su's figure and "squares" is said in a chorus. The teacher responds, "Yes, squares, we measure area in square units." She them asks them to restate the area of the figure as fifteen square units.

"So back to the cousins," says the teacher. "Can they have a garden that will make both Even Steven and Odd Todd happy?" She draws a rectangle on the board, writes *garden* above it, and asks, "Does anyone have an idea of what measurements the boys might want for their garden?" Marcia replies, "I would make one side an even number and the other side an odd number, like four and seven." The teacher asks Marcia to come up to the board and label the rectangle accordingly.

"What would be the area of this rectangle?" the teacher queries. Rex responds, "Twenty-eight." The teacher repeats the twenty-eight, but in a voice that lets Rex know that she is waiting for him to identify them as square units. After he does she asks the class, "Do any of you think you know how Rex got this answer?" Dana responds, "He could have just multiplied four by seven." Christa adds, "Or he can make rows and count the squares." The teacher goes back to the board and draws a grid to highlight and connect these students' ideas. Many students nod their head with apparent understanding.

"Now what about the perimeter?" asks the teacher. "How can we find the perimeter of Marcia's garden?" Josh eagerly calls out that "you just need to add another seven and four and then add them all up." He comes to the board, records *4* and *7* along the corresponding sides, and then writes, $4 + 4 + 7 + 7 = 22\ units$ to the side of the figure. The teacher organizes the information by writing it in a list:

length = 7 units

width = 4 units

area = 28 square units

perimeter = 22 units

She waits for the students to identify the name of the units before she records them. She then pauses and asks, "Do you think both cousins would be happy? Talk it over with your neighbor."

The consensus of this group is that both cousins would not be happy because three of the four numbers are even, and that isn't fair to Todd. The teacher then wonders aloud, "Hmm, will both the area and perimeter always be an even number or an odd number of units, if the cousins make rectangular gardens?" She waits a moment and then declares, "This is what we will be investigating today during math class. I would like for you to explore the relationship between area and perimeter and lengths of odd and even numbers of units."

At this point in the lesson, the teacher makes another change. Normally she would assign rectangular figures for all of the students to investigate. This time she offers the students a bit of a choice. She posts a chart on the board with four regions, labeled *Area = 24 square units*, *Area = 21 square units*, *Perimeter = 24 units*, and *Perimeter = 21 units*. (See Figure 1–2.) Knowing that her students enjoy working together, she invites them to sign up (in pairs) for one of the investigations. She explains, "When you sign up for *Area equals twenty-four square units*, for example, you try to find out all the different perimeters you could have with that area. What do you think you do if you sign up for the perimeter that equals twenty-four units?" she asks. Once the students respond and she is assured that they understand the tasks, she invites students to come sign up on the chart one table at a time.

Figure 1–2 *A chart with task choices.*

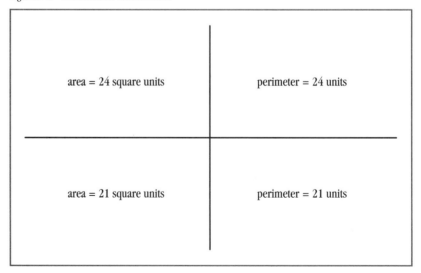

| area = 24 square units | perimeter = 24 units |
| area = 21 square units | perimeter = 21 units |

Now she is ready for another change; students will have more choice among materials. This time string, color tiles, and centimeter graph paper are available at each working station along with the traditional dot paper. The students sign up for their chosen tasks and head for a place to work. As they do so, the teacher overhears Josh talking to Pete as they stand in front of the chart. "I am not going to sign up for the perimeter problem of twenty-one because that just can't happen," Josh declares with authority. "How do you know?" asks Pete. "You see," begins Josh, "any two numbers doubled is even, so if you have seven and seven and three and three, then you would have to have an even number."

The teacher decides to ask a question: "Would this be true for all perimeters or just twenty-one units?" Josh looks off to the right for a minute while he ponders this question. Then he says, "For rectangles, the area has to be even. But I don't know about other shapes. Can I do that?" he pleads. "Sure, who are you going to work with?" the teacher asks. The teacher smiles as Josh heads off looking for a partner. She enjoys Josh, but isn't always quite sure how to manage him in a classroom setting, particularly during math time. He is quite enthusiastic about his ideas and works at a fast pace. He frequently yells out answers and can get frustrated when others do not understand his thinking or appear not to appreciate his passion for the topic. He finds it hard to sit in his seat when he gets excited and often stands alone when he works. The teacher is pleased to see Josh find a partner and begin to work eagerly.

The teacher checks in with Kim Su to make sure she is now referring to square units of area. Following this conversation, the teacher looks up and notices that all pairs of students are engaged in their investigation. She wonders if this is because they were able to choose their own problem to solve and which materials to use. Samantha and Ellen are investigating a rectangular garden with an area of twenty-four square units. Rather than using manipulatives, they make a T-chart to organize the factors of twenty-four. They decide that if they start with a factor pair they could divide one side in half and double the other side to find the next factor pair. (See Figure 1–3.)

Then these students systematically draw rectangles on a piece of dot paper, using the factor pairs. (See Figure 1–4.) When all of the rectangles are drawn, they count around each one to find the perimeter and conclude that all of the perimeters are even. Encouraged by the teacher, they explore other areas in the same systematic way, exhausting all pairs by relating to what they know about multiplication and then making corresponding figures.

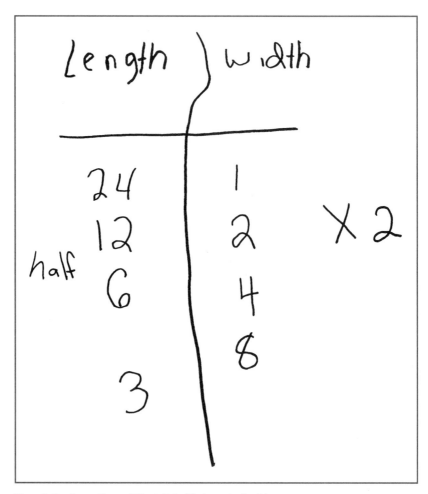

Figure 1–3 *Samantha and Ellen's list of factor pairs for 24.*

They find it interesting that all of the rectangles they make have a perimeter with an even number of units, but do not yet trust that this would happen all of the time.

Len and Marietta also use dot paper to draw rectangular arrangements of twenty-four square units. The teacher notes that they add the lengths of the sides to find the perimeters of these figures. They then count the dots on each side and notice that there is one more dot than the number of units they have recorded for length. This distracts them for a bit, but they then decide to ignore it and depend on their knowledge of multiplication to determine the length measures. The teacher notes this behavior, marveling at their ability to ignore apparent contradictory information. She realizes that they have counted both endpoints on the line and that this is why their count has increased by one. She decides to bring this up in the whole-group discussion that will follow as she is sure other students might find this distracting as well.

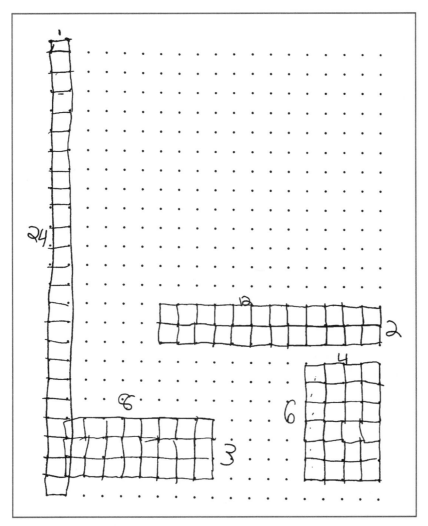

Figure 1–4 *Samantha and Ellen's drawing of rectangles that correspond to their factor pairs.*

Several pairs use manipulatives. Corey and Tim decide to experiment with the string. They cut a string twenty-one inches long to represent the perimeter. As the teacher watches them work she can see that they are forming rectangles with the string and then measuring the sides with a ruler. At first, they are not sure what to do when their side lengths do not measure a whole number of inches. Then they simply stretch the string a little to make the length "so it works." But in doing so, they change the length of the string. The corners or angles of the rectangle are slightly rounded, again making it difficult to measure accurately. The teacher recognizes the difficulty of using string and offers the pair a ten-by-ten geoboard thinking they can use the string with the board, which might help to avoid these difficulties. They are not interested in the board, however, and so their data are inaccurate.

Maggie and Katie use the color tiles to build their figures with areas of twenty-one square units. They appear to need to sort all the tiles by color before using them and this takes them a great deal of time. They form two rectangles for this area, but do not have time to explore other figures.

Two students, Matt and Kate, also use the color tiles. They have chosen to investigate rectangles with an area of twenty-four square units. They discover that all of the perimeters are an even number of units. They explore a couple of other examples on paper, discuss the properties of even and odd numbers, and conclude that the perimeter of a rectangle will always be an even number of units. Though they discuss their ideas together, their explanations show different perspectives. (See Figures 1–5 and 1–6.)

A whole-class meeting provides an opportunity for students to share their ideas. Most students are confident about their individual data, but only a few have come to any generalizations. When Matt and Kate share their ideas, some students look confused and other students challenge them. Their thinking remains firm and as they continue to explain their ideas with additional examples, more heads begin to nod in agreement. The teacher is pleased with their progress. It feels good to see students beginning to form general-izations and to have the work led by the students themselves.

This activity provided several types of differentiation. Even though the children were allowed to choose which of the four conditions they wanted to investigate, there was room for different readiness levels, including a challenge for a particularly adept student. A variety of materials was used in order to complete

Figure 1–5   *Matt's explanation of perimeter.*

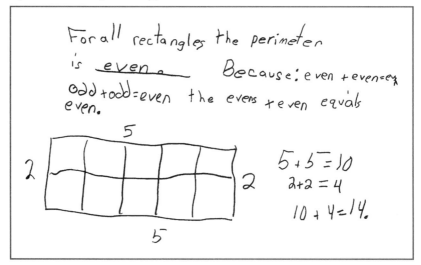

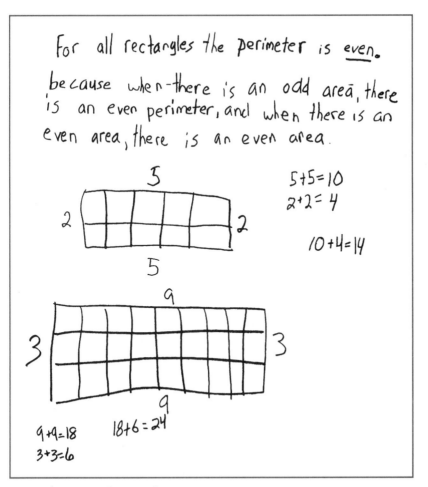

For all rectangles the perimeter is even.
because when there is an odd area, there
is an even perimeter, and when there is an
even area, there is an even area.

3

2   2

5

$5+5=10$
$2+2=4$

$10+4=14$

9

3   3

9

$9+9=18$ $18+6=24$
$3+3=6$

Figure 1–6   *Kate's explanation of perimeter.*

the tasks and different recordings were produced to demonstrate understanding.

    After the activity, the teacher reflects on what she has learned.

Teacher Reflection

Though the book about Steven and Todd is written for younger students, it only takes a few minutes to read and it really motivates this lesson. Also, I know most of my students like to listen to stories. This is a good problem for the class to work on. Many students know *area* and *perimeter* in isolation, though they sometimes get confused between the two. Also, they have not explored relationships between these measures. At first when Kim Su started talking about a box with cubes in it, I thought she was confusing area and volume. Her drawing helped me to realize that it was just an issue with vocabulary.

(Continued)

Many of these students tend to just think about the problem at hand, and not about how that problem might relate to a bigger mathematical idea. But, they have made progress this year. The range of abilities in this class speaks to the need to differentiate.

I don't think I would use the string again. I imagined them placing it around the centimeter paper and then counting the units. The string was too flexible and I think it just confused the students who used it.

I wish Maggie and Katie hadn't spent so much time sorting the tiles. Perhaps I should have refocused them, but Katie can become quite upset when she isn't allowed to finish something she has started. Perhaps I should have limited her choice of materials, but I don't like to single her out.

I was pleased with how students were on task, but because of all the different levels, a class discussion was a little hard to manage. I didn't expect the range of conclusions. Our next unit is fractions and decimals and we'll revisit this idea then. I want my students to realize that it is possible to have a perimeter with an odd number of units, for example, if a rectangle were 4.5 units by 6 units. Making conjectures and then finding when they do and do not apply is an important aspect of mathematical thinking. Overall, though, I thought the students did well.

This teacher is not as much of a differentiation novice as she may have thought. This is true of most teachers. Every day teachers are trying to meet students' needs without necessarily thinking about it as differentiated instruction. Similar to this teacher, however, seeing teaching and learning through the lens of differentiation helps us to better meet students' needs and to do so more consciously. Over time, teachers can develop the habits of the mind associated with differentiated instruction. Remember and think about the following questions as you continue reading and planning your lessons.

1. What is the mathematics that I want my students to learn?
2. What do my students already know? What is my evidence of this? How can I build on their thinking?
3. How can I expand access to this task or idea? Have I thought about interests, learning styles, uses of language, cultures, and readiness?
4. How can I ensure that each student experiences challenge?
5. How can I scaffold learning to increase the likelihood of success?
6. In what different ways can my students demonstrate their new understanding?
7. Are there choices students can make?
8. How prepared am I to take on these challenges?

Chapter 2
Changing Expectations

Some people describe mathematics as a subject that requires you to learn how to follow a series of prescribed steps in order to find the one correct answer. Such a description reflects the way mathematics is sometimes taught, but not the subject itself. Instruction that emphasizes a rule-based approach to mathematics focuses on factual and procedural knowledge. It is the way most of today's teachers were taught. Procedures for addition, subtraction, multiplication, and division, along with the associated basic facts, were almost the entire focus of the early and intermediate elementary school curriculum. Factual knowledge, such as vocabulary and basic facts, were stressed as well as specific algorithms for finding sums, differences, products, and quotients with whole numbers, fractions, and decimals. Students were expected to learn facts through memorization and to perform the same algorithmic procedures regardless of the specific numerical examples.

A common outcome of such rule-based instruction is that to find the sum of $499 + 11$, many students (and adults) mindlessly proceed with the algorithm that they were taught. They add the ones, get 10, and record *0* in the ones column and *1* in the tens column. When explaining their work, they don't necessarily mention the distinct place values in the regrouping process. Often the rule "You can't write ten here," said while pointing to the ones column, is considered sufficient. They then add $1 + 9 + 1$, find a sum of 11, and record again. Though they are now working in the tens column, the language associated with this step is often the same as with the ones column. Few of these students have any idea that there are eleven tens and that they are recording one ten, while regrouping the remaining ten tens to one hundred, allowing them to write a *1* in the hundreds column:

$$
\begin{array}{r}
\overset{1}{499} \\
+\ 11 \\
\hline
0
\end{array}
\qquad
\begin{array}{r}
\overset{1\ 1}{499} \\
+\ 11 \\
\hline
10
\end{array}
\qquad
\begin{array}{r}
\overset{1\ 1}{499} \\
+\ 11 \\
\hline
510
\end{array}
$$

Add the ones.   *Add the next column.*   *Add the next column.*
9 + 1 = 10   *1 + 9 + 1 = 11*   *1 + 4 = 5*
You can't write 10.   *You can't write 11.*
Write the 0 and   *Write the 1 and*
regroup 1.   *regroup 1.*

While these place-value relationships may have been taught originally, they are often lost in rote practice. In fact, the traditional addition algorithm is often summarized as "add each column just like they were ones." This may be an efficient generalization for those that can follow it, but it doesn't develop conceptual understanding of addition or of relationships among numbers. Most problematic, it doesn't lead to flexible thinking grounded in conceptual understanding.

More flexible thinkers use a conceptual approach; they consider the numbers and values first and then determine the most sensible way to find the sum. In this case, a simple mental computation is all they need. Thinking of 499 as one less than 500 and recognizing that 10 + 1 = 11, the student combines the 1 with the 499 to get 500 and then simply increases this number by one 10 to find the sum, 510:

Think: 499 is one less than 500.
10 + 1 = 11   *Split 11 into 10 and 1.*
1 + 499 = 500   *Add the 1 to 499.*
500 + 10 = 510   *Add the remaining 10.*

There are several mathematical concepts embedded in this method:

- Numbers can be split into parts without changing the sum.
- Numbers can be added in any order without changing the sum.
- Numbers ending in zeroes are easier to work with, so it makes sense to combine numbers to reach such landmarks.
- Ten ones are equal to one ten. So increasing the tens digit by one is the same as adding ten ones.

Similar thinking can be applied to operations with fractions. Consider the example $\frac{3}{4} + \frac{7}{8} + \frac{1}{2}$. The traditional approach involves finding a common denominator and then identifying equivalent fractions using that denominator. Following the several steps of this process, the problem is transformed to $\frac{6}{8} + \frac{7}{8} + \frac{4}{8}$. Now the algorithm for addition with like denominators can be applied. The sum of $6 + 7 + 4$ is identified as 17 and the improper fraction, $\frac{17}{8}$, results. Finally, 17 is divided by 8 to change the improper fraction to a mixed number and identify the sum as $2\frac{1}{8}$.

This procedural approach involves several steps that each must be performed in the appropriate sequence. But most of us are fairly familiar with eighths, fourths, and halves, allowing for more flexible, conceptual thinking. For example, a fifth-grade student found the sum of $\frac{3}{4} + \frac{7}{8} + \frac{1}{2}$ through the following mental arithmetic approach:

> *I know that $\frac{1}{2}$ is equal to $\frac{4}{8}$ and that I can add the numbers in any order. So I'll use the eighths where I need them. I'll use two with $\frac{3}{4}$ to make 1 and I'll use one with $\frac{7}{8}$ to make another 1. There's one left over, so the sum is $2\frac{1}{8}$.*

Such rich mathematical thinking is cultivated by teachers who focus on mathematical reasoning and facilitate the development of students' ideas. As we differentiate learning activities, these priorities must remain in place for all of our students.

Along with the lack of flexible thinking, other difficulties arise when facts and procedures are taught as just rules, without conceptual frameworks. Some students begin to believe that mathematics is only a set of isolated rules that have no meaning, some lose interest in learning mathematics, and all students become underexposed to mathematical reasoning. Further, when rules and procedures are learned in isolation of concepts, misconceptions can emerge in higher grades. For example, sometimes teachers provide simple rules in hopes of simplifying a procedure for students who require more support. When working with subtraction with whole numbers, you might hear a teacher say, "You can't subtract a bigger number from a smaller one, so you need to borrow." When the students are working with the traditional algorithm for subtraction, this direction is sometimes given to students as a reminder to regroup. Later when negative numbers are involved, however, the generalization no longer holds true. You *can* subtract, for example, $4 - 7$ and get -3. This new idea may confuse some students. Further, there are always students who only remember the first portion of this phrase and make the common error shown below:

$$
\begin{array}{r}
382 \\
- 139 \\
\hline
257
\end{array}
$$

Such work does not demonstrate an understanding or a connection with the purpose of the procedure, that is, finding the difference between the two numbers.

When examples such as 31 + 234 + 6 are given to students, teachers sometimes offer the procedural rule to "line up the numbers on the right." The intent is to help students with traditional approaches to addition that require the example to be rewritten in vertical form. Students are more familiar with the way that a list of words is lined up on the left. As the arithmetic procedure conflicts with the more well-known language procedure, the rule to line up numbers on the right is given much attention. Yet later, when decimals are introduced, lining up the numbers on the right to find 3.04 + 2.1 + 5.7 will lead to an incorrect sum:

$$
\begin{array}{r}
{}^{1} \\
3.04 \\
2.1 \\
5.7 \\
\hline
38.2
\end{array}
$$

With both whole and decimal numbers, the concept that is mathematically important is that we add like values to like values: ones with ones, and tenths with tenths. It is this concept that we need to emphasize, not a procedural rule that could later lead to a misconception. As teachers, we should get into the habit of asking ourselves: Is there a mathematical concept that will help students understand what to do, regardless of the type of numbers? Am I limiting my less-advanced students' conceptual development by providing them with an oversimplified rule? Am I depriving these students opportunities to develop mathematical concepts?

Understanding Models and Representations

It's not that facts and procedures aren't important, they are, but we don't want to teach them in ways that keep students from developing the conceptual understanding that underpins their procedures and connects the facts that they know. Ideally, all three types of knowledge—*factual, procedural,* and *conceptual*—work together to build mathematical power. Let's think about fractions. Traditionally, basic terms such as *numerator* and *denominator* were taught as soon as fraction notation was introduced. Models for fractions were limited: Circular "pies" were the common visual tool. Students learned a procedure for naming a fraction: they counted the shaded parts to identify the numerator, and the number of parts in all to identify the denominator. Procedures for finding common denominators and equivalent fractions and for performing operations with fractions were also given much attention.

Today, more emphasis is placed on conceptual development before formal terminology is required. For example, students explore how the number of parts in the whole relates to the size of those parts before use of the term *denominator* is expected. More emphasis is also placed on understanding a variety of models for fractions. While circular regions remain pervasive, circles are not necessarily easy to divide into equivalent parts, nor are they the best representation for different contexts. Use of a variety of models helps students to develop a broader understanding of fractions. It is important to continue to support use of manipulatives and encourage student representations so that conceptual development deepens as students learn more complex procedures.

Let's consider the following task posed to third graders in the spring. The students have already been exposed to fractions this year and the teacher wants to review some ideas before they begin to connect fractions to decimals. The lesson begins with the following problem:

> *Imagine that you are trying to help someone understand what three-tenths means. What pictures could you draw to be helpful? You can draw more than one picture. Let's see how many different pictures we can make.*

The students are seated at tables and begin working quickly. At each table there is a basket containing several small pieces of paper. Students are instructed to draw one representation and take another piece, when they are ready to make another model. As the teacher walks around she notices that almost all of the students begin with the traditional pie showing three of ten parts shaded. She asks Mac if she can borrow his picture of this model. When Mac agrees, the teacher uses clothespins to hang up Mac's picture on the clothesline in the front of the meeting area. As she does so, she tells the class, "I would like to hang up several pictures. Does anyone have a model that looks different from this one?" Within a

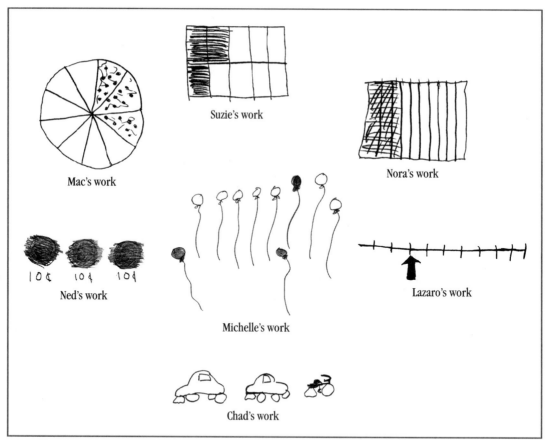

Figure 2–1 *Students showed their representations of three-tenths.*

few minutes, there are seven pictures hanging on the line. (See Figure 2–1.) The teacher asks if there are any more different ones to share. When no hands are raised, she asks each student to describe his or her representation.

Mac starts and says, "Mine is like a pizza. There were ten pieces and only three are left." He laughs and then adds, "My brother gets these and I already ate all the rest."

Suzie's is next and she says, "It was too hard for me to draw a circle. All the parts came out different. I even had to erase to make my rectangle work. Besides, I like how my grandma makes pizza on a cookie sheet. It is like a rectangle."

Nora then describes her picture. "Mine is a rectangle like Suzie's, but I don't think we cut anything this way." Carl responds, "Maybe bread," and Nora nods in agreement.

"Mine is three dimes," explains Ned as he points to the drawing he has made by rubbing his pencil on a piece of paper placed over a dime three times. "This is three-tenths of a dollar." The teacher notices some confused looks from some of the other students, but doesn't want to interrupt the flow of this initial sharing. She was anticipating that some students would get confused by others' representations, but knew that this was part of the process of helping them to think about fractions in different ways.

Then Michelle describes her picture. "I made ten balloons and colored three of them red."

Lazaro's picture is hanging next. He has drawn a line with ten marks and placed an arrow at the third mark.

Chad has the final picture. It shows two cars and a bicycle. Each of the vehicles has a flat tire. "We got a flat tire this weekend," Chad tells his classmates. "I helped my dad fix it."

After giving students the opportunity to describe their own pictures, the next step is to refocus their thinking on the mathematical aspects of the representations. Now that she has honored their individual work, the teacher wants to help them see that the essential mathematical features of their models are the same, that is, each picture suggests three parts out of a whole with ten equivalent parts. The teacher says, "All of you who shared your pictures said that you were showing three-tenths. Are these representations the same or are they different?"

"I think Suzie's and Nora's are alike," says Ryan.

"Can you tell me more?" prods the teacher.

Ryan responds, "They're both rectangles."

"Mine looks like Mac's, too," suggests Suzie. "There aren't any spaces between our parts."

Mac adds, "All of our tenths touch together, but maybe Lazaro's do, too." The teacher asks what the others think about Mac's idea. Some agree that Lazaro's model is similar, while others disagree claiming that his picture "doesn't really have full parts."

"Is there any way that your models are like Michelle's?" the teacher asks.

Janice replies, "Well, I guess so. I mean there are ten things with three of them being special, but hers is more like Chad's tires."

"But Ned's is different," says Marcus. "He only has three things. Why is that three-tenths?"

"Does anyone have an answer for Marcus?" the teacher queries.

"I think ten dimes should be there," suggests Carmen, "with a circle around three of them. It would be easier to see."

Several heads nod when this idea is shared.

"Or maybe," says Washington, "we could draw a dollar bill underneath the dimes. Then you would know that it's all the money."

Again heads nod, so Ned explains his thinking further. "Ten dimes make a dollar. So one dime is one-tenth of a dollar and three dimes is three-tenths. You don't need the dollar. You just need to know it."

Marcus replies, "Oh, OK, I get it, three dimes is three-tenths of a dollar," but Carmen stands firm and says, "You have to see the whole or say it's out of a dollar. I didn't get it until I heard about the dollar."

Throughout this unit, students will expand their thinking about models for fractions. They will consider area models for fractions where the specific shapes of the parts differ, but their area remains the same (an example of a $\frac{5}{8}$ area model follows). This type of model is not always recognized by students or by teachers as a legitimate mathematical representation.

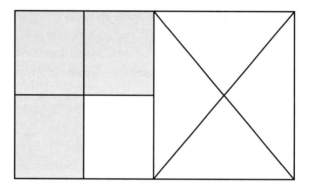

The teacher hopes that more than a few students begin to create images involving length models. She also wants her students to explore fractions as ratios. Today, however, the teacher wanted her students to begin with their own thinking and with their own representations. As you will learn from her reflection, she also wanted them to focus on what was the same about their differing models, to focus on the important mathematical ideas, and to expand their comfort level with a variety of representations.

Teacher Reflection

Recently I've been trying to vary the models I use for fractions. It is amazing how many students only think about pies, but given time, my students did create some different representations. We did a similar task earlier with a simpler fraction, one-fourth. Now I am less hesitant about challenging my students and I want to start them thinking about tenths. It was interesting to discover what they identified as different models. They didn't see the examples of set models as the same if the setting was quite different. I was pleased with how the students reflected on their models, especially about Ned's coins, and surprised by how many of them commented on connections between their depictions and real-world experiences. I think of fractions as a difficult topic for students, but it is a concept they use in their everyday life. I'd like to think some more about how I can build on these connections. Earlier in the year when we were about to start a unit on multiplication, we looked for equal groups. We made a bulletin board showing what came in threes, fours, and so on. Maybe I should try something like that for fractions.

When I first began encouraging students to create their own representations of mathematical situations, I was so impressed with their different thinking. I just wanted them to share their work. I wanted to respect their individual ideas and learning preferences while helping them become aware of the different ways we can think about mathematics. Now I want more than sharing. I want them to see the similarities as well as the differences in their work. I think this helps them identify critical mathematical concepts. This is a new idea for me and I am still working on it, but it feels like the next step in my voyage as a teacher.

This teacher's words help us to think about teaching as a journey. For many, it is a continuous growing process where new ideas and teaching strategies are developed to address current concerns. Over time, these strategies lead to the discovery of new questions and the further adaptation of our practices. Such has been the case with changes in the way we teach mathematics.

Investigating Mathematical Ideas

Recent reforms in mathematics education emphasize that learning mathematics is an active process, one that involves students in exploring ideas, making and investigating conjectures, discovering relationships, representing ideas, and justifying thinking. Such activity often results when students pursue real mathematical problems or explore open-ended tasks, that is, problems for which they don't already recognize a procedure that will lead them to a solution or tasks that may be completed in a variety of ways. When exploring these types of problems, students wrestle with ideas and are less likely to follow the same solution paths. Allowing for different approaches to mathematical tasks can lead to rich discussions that help students establish and agree on facts, construct and utilize procedures, and develop and solidify concepts. This way of teaching has two advantages: It supports deeper mathematical thinking and it supports alternative learning preferences.

Teaching with this mind-set is part of our changing expectations of mathematics instruction. Teachers facilitate mathematical discourse, rather than delineate specific steps and demonstrate how to follow these prescribed procedures. Teachers focus on questions such as: Why do you think so? What are you thinking? How do you know? When teachers engage in this approach, they often are surprised at the range of what their students are thinking. The teachers come to recognize differences in readiness levels; in approaches to tasks; in the ways students describe their work; in the connections students make among ideas; and in the ways they model, represent, and describe their thinking.

Needing to address the differences we discover

In fact, many teachers who begin to teach in ways that allow these differences to surface are truly amazed at what they see and hear. Teachers recognize that they have uncovered information about their students that they had never known before. Focusing on the development of mathematical ideas and on making links among factual, procedural, and conceptual knowledge is a significant transformation in the teaching of mathematics, and it has raised two essential questions:

1. Once we reveal the wonderfully different ways our students think about mathematics, what do we do with what we learn?
2. How do we support differentiated thinking about mathematics while still focusing on unified mathematical ideas?

Let's consider a vignette from a fourth-grade classroom. It is October and the students are working on fractions. With denominators of ten or less, the students can identify or represent fractions that are shown as congruent parts of a region, parts of a region with the same area, or as parts of a group. With common fractions such as halves, fourths, eighths, many of the students can identify and represent equivalent relationships, but the teacher feels they do so in a rote manner and would like them to have more experience applying the ideas. The students easily integrate fractions into their real-world activities demonstrated with comments such as "I only ate half of my lunch" or "It's quarter after one, is it time to go to music?" The teacher believes the students are ready to explore less familiar aspects of fractions. She wants to help her students develop better number sense with fractions and to become more comfortable with length or linear models of fractions. She wants them to be able to use their conceptual understanding of fractions to compare them and to place them on a number line between zero and one.

Development of visual models of numbers is vital. Studies have indicated the importance of the visual cortex in mathematical thinking (Sousa 2001). Activities that explicitly help students further develop their visual perceptions of numbers provide students with additional visual models to use. Students can reference, manipulate, and think about these models when solving problems.

To begin this area of study, the teacher wants to know, in an informal way, her students' varying abilities. Earlier in the week they held a schoolwide metric Olympics day, so she gathers her students around the rug to pose a question about a race. A student reads aloud the problem posted on chart paper:

> At Olympics Day, two friends are running in a race. One friend is $\frac{5}{8}$ of the way to the finish line and the other friend is $\frac{3}{4}$ of the way. Who is winning?

After the reading the teacher asks the students to close their eyes and visualize the race. When her students have had time to create visual images, she asks if they understand the question. There are lots of nods of agreement and so the teacher sends her students to their tables asking that they use pictures, numbers, and words to represent their thinking.

This is a routine they are familiar with and the students are eager to get started. They know that since they haven't been told otherwise, they are free to work alone or with partners. The teacher realizes that some of her students prefer to work alone. When they have ideas, they want to work on their solutions before they share their thinking. Other students find it easier to talk to a partner and come up with a plan together. When a new idea is being investigated, such as this problem, she likes to let them choose their preference. This way, they are working in their preferred manner as they wrestle with the challenges of new ideas.

There is a buzz in the room as some students quickly draw solutions on their papers and others look off to the side, tapping their pencils as they create a plan. After a bit more time most students are writing, but as the teacher looks about the room, she notices that Isabelle and Kara have not yet recorded anything. She sits down next to them and listens to their conversation.

"I think the three-fourths kid is winning," says Kara.

"I think five-eighths is winning," Isabelle argues.

The teacher encourages them to explain their thinking to each other.

Kara starts with, "Three-fourths is closer to the finish line because three and four are littler numbers, but in fraction math the little number is the highest number and five-eighths is the lowest."

Isabelle looks confused and states, "I don't agree. I think that five-eighths is closer because three-fourths is still near the beginning. We want big numbers." Both girls look toward the teacher for direction or approval. The teacher asks them to write and draw their ideas on paper so she can better understand their thinking. She also believes that drawing images of fractions may initiate a change in their thinking.

The teacher continues around the classroom looking for evidence of understanding or need for help. She checks in with a few more sets of partners to get a better sense of the levels of thinking about the fraction problem. Many students agree with Kara; they identify the runner that is $\frac{3}{4}$ of the way to the finish line as winning. (See Figure 2–2.) They note the importance of three and four being less than five and eight.

Some students explain this choice further by reasoning that the greater the denominator, the smaller the pieces will be. (See Figure 2–3.) Though their answer is correct, these students seem

Figure 2–2   *Kara's work focused on the size of the numbers.*

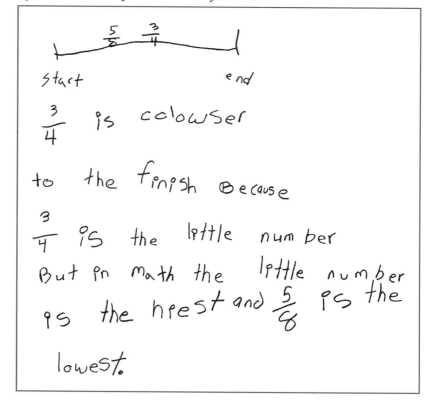

to disregard the numerator and its relationship to the denominator or to the whole.

Some students who identify $\frac{3}{4}$ as the greater fraction provide models that illustrate equivalent fractions. Though Manny does not use words to further explain his thinking, his drawing shows proportional models of fourths and eighths. (See Figure 2–4.) Janice and Quinn use length models. In fact, Quinn uses a ruler to make his drawing. (See Figure 2–5.) Janice identifies equivalent fractions correctly, but has some difficulty placing them on her model of the race. (See Figure 2–6.) Note that she records the quarters in the spaces rather than at the end of that distance. This common misconception is recognized as an endpoint problem. Many students have a similar misconception when using a ruler.

Figure 2–3 *Explanation that focused on the size of the numbers and a generalization.*

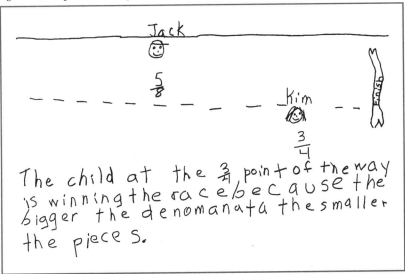

Figure 2–4 *Manny's work included proportional drawings of eighths and fourths.*

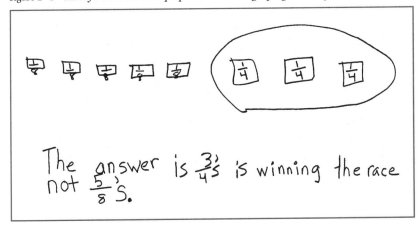

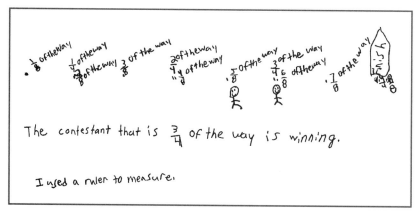

Figure 2–5 *Quinn used a ruler to make his model of the race.*

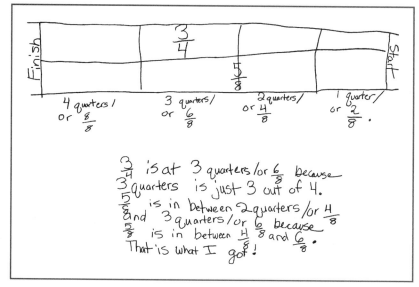

Figure 2–6 *Though not placed correctly, Janice's work included equivalent fractions.*

Xavier makes a region and a length model to represent his thinking. Note that while his pie drawing correctly depicts the relationships between fourths and eighths, the linear model does not. (See Figure 2–7.) His written explanation, however, clarifies his understanding and he gives his teacher a verbal explanation as she stops by his desk. He summarizes his ideas by saying, "Three-fourths is bigger because two-eighths is equal to one-fourth and there are five-eighths, and if two-eighths equals one-fourth, then five-eighths would only be two-fourths and one-eighth."

Some students believe that the friend who is $\frac{5}{8}$ of the way is the winner. They make a drawing of the race that coincides with their

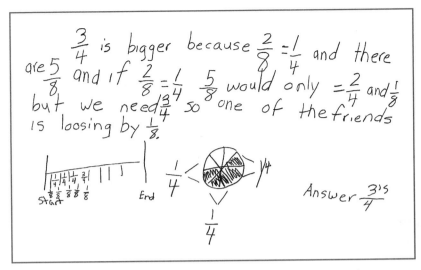

$\frac{3}{4}$ is bigger because $\frac{2}{8} = \frac{1}{4}$ and there are $\frac{5}{8}$ and if $\frac{2}{8} = \frac{1}{4}$ $\frac{5}{8}$ would only $= \frac{2}{4}$ and $\frac{1}{8}$ but we need $\frac{3}{4}$ so one of the friends is loosing by $\frac{1}{8}$.

$\frac{1}{4} < \frac{1}{4}$

Answer $\frac{3's}{4}$

Figure 2–7   *Xavier's work included a region and a length model to compare the fractions.*

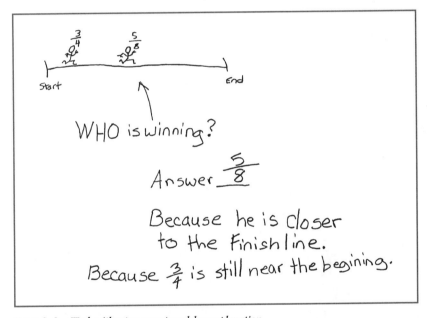

WHO is winning?

Answer $\frac{5}{8}$

Because he is closer to the finish line.
Because $\frac{3}{4}$ is still near the begining.

Figure 2–8   *Work without a correct model or explanation.*

thinking, but do not model the fractions and their explanations contain only a restatement of the relationship between the two fractions. (See Figure 2–8.)

Other students make a model of the fractions, but then only attend to the numerators or don't use the same unit to create the fractional parts. By disregarding the denominators or by changing the unit, they are actually only comparing three and five, and so identify $\frac{5}{8}$ as their answer. (See Figure 2–9 and Figure 2–10.)

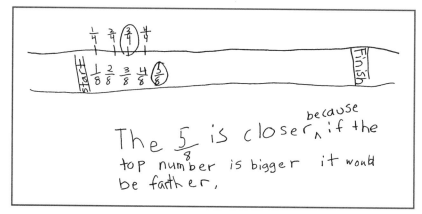

The $\frac{5}{8}$ is closer $\wedge$ because if the top number is bigger it would be farther.

Figure 2–9   *This student focused on only the numerators while making this linear model.*

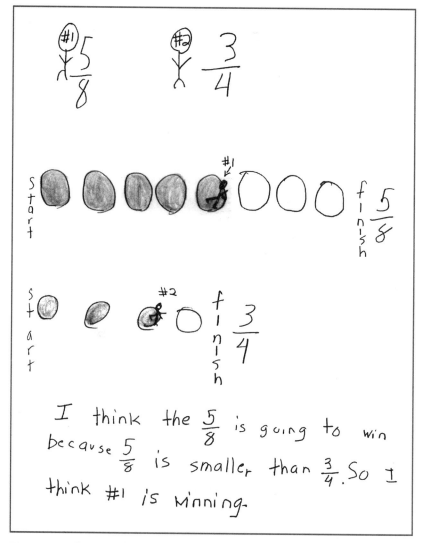

I think the $\frac{5}{8}$ is going to win because $\frac{5}{8}$ is smaller than $\frac{3}{4}$. So I think #1 is winning.

Figure 2–10   *This student used a set model, but focused only on the numerator even though he identified that five-eighths is less than three-fourths.*

The classroom is getting louder as the students reach some agreement among themselves. The teacher claps her hands and the students pause and look up as she announces, "In two minutes we will be sharing solutions. Start thinking about what you want to say about your work."

The students gather back on the rug to share their solutions. Most of the initial conversation focuses on the size of the numbers three and four versus five and eight. Then a couple of the students who thought in terms of equivalent fractions begin to explain their thinking.

Janice begins, "The second friend is winning because for them to be equal the first friend would have to be six-eighths of the way to the finish line." Liam nods in agreement. The teacher asks the students if they understand Janice and Liam's thinking and hears a common initial response from Trevor, "I don't get it."

The teacher asks Trevor, "What would make it easier for you to understand?"

"Could you draw a picture?" asks Trevor.

The teacher holds out chalk to Janice and Liam and they walk to the board. The two students confer briefly and gesture toward their individual drawings. Then Liam draws four short vertical lines on the board. Next Janice draws eight similar lines on top of Liam's, but hers are clustered closer together. They work together to draw arrows from the four lines on the bottom to pairs of the eight lines above. Once the drawing is completed they take turns explaining their work. Liam tells his classmates that the bottom four lines show three-fourths and then he draws a ring around three out of the four lines. Janice continues explaining that for each one-fourth, you have to draw two lines for eighths. She then draws a ring around six of her lines to show that $\frac{6}{8}$ would be the same as $\frac{3}{4}$. Without pausing, Janice then concludes, "So five-eighths is only five-eighths not six-eighths. So he is losing and three-fourths is winning." (See Figure 2–11.)

The teacher looks at the group of students, who seem quite impressed with their friends' thinking, even if they were not necessarily clear about all of the ideas. The teacher decides that enough has been done for today. She thanks Janice and Liam for their work and tells the class that they will continue to think about these ideas over the next few days.

When the teacher designed this lesson she was thinking about models of fractions she was hoping to see. Fractions as parts of a region, as parts of a set, and on a number line are three models these students have experienced. She wondered if they would

$3/4 = 5/8$

$\frac{2}{8} = 1/4$

$\frac{4}{8} = 2/4$

$\frac{5}{8} = \frac{2\frac{1}{2}}{4}$

The second friend is winning because for them to be equal the first friend would have to be $\frac{6}{8}$ of the way to the finish line.

Figure 2–11 *Liam and Janice's explanation of five-eighths versus three-fourths.*

see the race as a length or linear model and use a number line to represent the fractions or if they would use the more familiar circular regions. She found it interesting that many did create length models, but that others created region or set representations. In general it surprised her that many of the students who used a length model placed the fractions incorrectly on the line.

At the end of the day the teacher looked at the students' representations more closely. She found that she could separate them into three piles. There was a group of students who did not demonstrate an understanding of $\frac{3}{4}$ and $\frac{5}{8}$ as fractions or used incomplete rules to compare these fractions. There was a group of students who knew the correct answer but could not fully explain their thinking or whose single representation needed revision. And finally, there was a group of students who identified the correct answer and demonstrated a clear understanding of the situation using at least one model.

She decided that she would introduce a simpler, similar problem the next day, but that this time, she would help the students to think about the problem by comparing the fractions to 0, $\frac{1}{2}$, and 1. This way, students who already could do comparisons by creating equivalent fractions would gain an additional technique, while other students could continue to develop their understanding of fractions. After the problem, she would introduce a game.

She starts the next lesson by asking, "If two children are running a race and one friend is one-half of the way to the finish line and the other friend is three-quarters of the way there, who is winning?" This time she draws a line on the board labeling start and finish and asks, "Who can answer this question?"

Many hands are raised. After asking the students to whisper their answers to each other, the teacher asks Brandy to share her answer with the class. Brandy identifies the friend that was three-quarters of the way as winning and the teacher asks her to come up to the board and use the line to explain her thinking. Brandy writes $\frac{3}{4}$ near the finish line. The teacher then asks her to put one-half where it belongs and Brandy carefully draws a line down the middle of the line and writes $\frac{1}{2}$ below it.

The teacher, noting that Brandy did not divide the line in fourths, asks the class, "How did Brandy know that three-fourths was closer to the finish line than one-half?" Kevin raises his hand and states, "One-half is in the middle and three-fourths is more than that." When the teacher asks him how he knows that, Kevin just shrugs his shoulders. The teacher asks if someone can help Kevin out and Xavier walks up to the board. He draws two same-sized rectangles and divides one into two equal parts and one into four equal parts. The teacher recognizes that Xavier could explain his thinking further, but wants to keep the other students involved, so she quickly asks them, "Who can tell me how we might use Xavier's drawing?"

Hailey raises her hand and suggests, "We could color in the one-half and then two on the other rectangle."

"Why two?" asks Isabella.

"You would color in two so it would be one-half," explains Hailey.

"Oh, I get it," adds Trevor. "One-half takes two of the fourths."

"So it is less than three-fourths," concludes Xavier.

The teacher is pleased to watch her students building mathematical ideas together. She records $\frac{1}{2} = \frac{2}{4}$ on the board and asks, "What if the one-half were being compared to a fraction with a denominator of six, eight, or ten? What would we do?"

Quinn explains, "We'd find half by making the number on top half the number on the bottom."

The teacher pauses for her students to process what Quinn has said and then asks if anyone can restate his idea. Janice responds, "To be half, the number on the top has to be half the number on the bottom."

"Is this always true?" the teacher asks. There is a loud "yes" in response and she is delighted with the students' confidence. From experience, however, she knows that this is still a new idea for many of them and she wants to simulate further thinking. She asks, "What if there is a nine on the bottom as the denominator? What would be the numerator or the number on top?" The room becomes silent and then the students begin to fidget. Some call out four and some suggest five. Then Peggy yells out, "Four and one-half!" Everyone looks at Peggy; then they look at the teacher. The teacher asks Peggy to explain and she says, "It's like the others. Half of nine is four and one-half." The teacher writes $4\frac{1}{2}$ over 9 on the board. She knows that all of her students are not comfortable with this notation, but thinks it is important that they are at least exposed to this less common representation.

Then the teacher introduces the game. She asks for two students to come to the front of the room, divides a deck of cards (fifty cards made up of five sets of the numbers one through ten) into two equal stacks and hands each child a pile. She draws a number line on the board and labels one end *0* and the other end *1*. She tells the student to the left that he will stand for zero and the student on the right that she will stand for one. She has each child turn over the top card and asks them to make a fraction with the numerator less than the denominator. The students announce that their fraction is five-sixths. The teacher further explains the game by saying, "Your job is to decide if five-sixths is closer to zero or to one. The person representing the whole number to which it is closer, gets the cards. So, who is the winner of this round?"

The two students at the board confer and the teacher asks the other students to discuss this as well. She can tell by the looks on their faces that a couple of them are uncertain as to how to proceed, but she is pleased to hear several references to three-sixths among other students. With discussion, the students agree that five-sixths is closer to one and so the student representing one gets the cards. As a whole class they play a few more rounds. In the process they decide that if the fraction is equal to one-half, then each person gets one card since it is not closer to zero or one; it is equidistant.

So far students have been able to participate in the same activities by thinking about the mathematics in different ways. Some students are able to reason more abstractly while others continue to use models to compare fractions. Two students continue to have misconceptions. So although most students appear to be somewhat comfortable with the game, the teacher feels that it is time to differentiate the instruction. She begins by identifying the students for whom the game seemed just about right. In many ways what they need is just more time to work with these ideas, time to practice placing fractions on a number line and to become more at ease using benchmarks.

Next she thinks about the handful of students who seem to depend heavily on the region model of fractions. She decides they need more small-group instructional time where they can connect region models of fractions with linear ones and become more familiar with the use of benchmarks. The teacher knows they aren't able to follow all of the ideas shared in the large group, but hopes that more modeling and practice will help them to connect these two representational forms. In an ideal situation there would be another adult in the room who would allow someone to give full attention to these students, but she is hopeful that other students will be able to sustain their work until she can get these few students to a place where they can work independently.

Then she thinks about the students for whom the game is relatively easy. They may be challenged by a particular fraction, but in general they have developed ways of approaching the task that make sense to them and the game will quickly become routine. It is time for them to compare more than one fraction to the benchmarks.

When the next math period begins, the students recall their work from yesterday. Then the teacher turns over the top page of the chart pack revealing a list of three groups of students, with partners indicated. She gives the first group of students decks of cards and releases them to sit in pairs at their desks. This group is at ease with this activity. She believes that it is best for them to play the game the same way as demonstrated in class. She has the jacks, queens, and kings of the decks ready if needed. These cards can represent elevenths, twelfths, and thirteenths and will help to ensure that the appropriate level of challenge is maintained. The students move easily and begin to play the game.

The teacher then asks the second group of students to go to the large table in the back of the room, talk in pairs about the materials she has left in front of each seat, and complete the "warm-up questions." The teacher knows she can't leave this group on their own too long, but is comfortable that she has provided them work that they can do in pairs and that will get them ready for the what she has in mind once she joins them.

As these students move to the table, the teacher organizes the third group of students who will remain in the working area. She gives each pair a bin containing a deck of cards, some tape, several small pieces of paper, a strip of adding machine tape with a line drawn down the middle of its length, and a direction sheet. The directions modify the game a bit for these more ready students. This time, the students are to write 0 at one end of the line and 1 at the other. After they decide who wins a round, they are supposed to write the fraction on one of the pieces of paper and tape it along the line to show where it is in relation to zero and one. As their play continues, they will need to compare each number they form to both the benchmarks and to other numbers already on the line. The teacher realizes that the students would rather just write along the number line, but she wants them to use more flexible materials. By recording the numbers on paper and using the tape, the students can adjust the positions of the numbers as the play continues and their thinking changes.

The teacher stays for a bit to make sure that these students understand the task and to get some insight into their thinking. They spread out around the area and are quickly engaged in the activity. She notices that Kyle and Liam immediately fold their long strip in half and record $\frac{1}{2}$ at this point in the line.

She then joins the group at the back of the room. As requested, they are looking at the copies of fractions strips and fraction pies that have been left for them and exploring the warm-up questions. The teacher reviews one of the questions with them by asking how the circular model of thirds could help them figure out whether two-thirds was closer to zero or one. The students agree quickly that two of the thirds are more than half of the circle. When asked how they could prove that to her, they use their hands to cover up half of the circle and tell her, "There's more left over." She then asks the same question using the strip model and the students appear to agree that it is more than "half the way."

The students review the rules of the game. The teacher has already split the decks of cards in half and the first four cards in each deck have been arranged so that the initial fractions will be one-fourth, seven-eighths, one-sixth, and four-fifths. The teacher is hoping that these examples will be easier for these six students and help to build their confidence.

As the students begin to play the game, the teacher shows Nicole how she can use a view window to help her. Nicole has some difficulty with visual perception and so the teacher has cut out a circle at the top and a strip at the bottom of a piece of heavy paper. By using the "viewer," Nicole can look at just one fraction circle or one fraction strip at a time. The teacher sits with Nicole and her partner for two rounds to make sure she is comfortable with the device. Then the teacher scans the group to see how the others are doing. She notices that one of the pairs is using both the fraction strips and pies, but that Isabelle and Elise seem to be playing without reference to the models and without much conversation. Once a fraction is made, one of them claims it and the other agrees quickly to that decision. The teacher decides to intervene by asking, "Can you tell me why Elise gets three-fifths?" Both girls look at her blankly and so the teacher tries another approach, "Is there something you could show me to convince me?"

Isabelle replies, "I think we are supposed to use those things [pointing to the strips], but I'm not sure how."

The teacher takes a copy of the fraction strips and places it so that they can both see it and asks, "Do either of you see anything here that might help us to think about three-fifths?"

"Well, these are fifths," offers Elise.

"So, maybe, we should look at three of these," suggests Isabelle and counts three of the regions.

"But how do we know what's closer?" asks Elise as Isabelle looks up with questioning eyes.

The teacher is beginning to understand the conceptual difficulty and asks the girls to tell her where zero would be. Both Elise and Isabelle look perplexed at first and there is silence that the teacher chooses not to fill. Then Isabelle says, "Well, if it's nothing, I guess it's just before the first fifth." The teacher asks Elise if that makes sense to her and after she nods tentatively, the teacher asks Isabelle to record a *0* on the left edge of the first fifth. Then she asks the girls where one would be and Elise slowly places her hand at the end of the fifths. When Isabelle agrees, the teacher has Elise record *1* on the diagram. Then Isabelle's eyes get wide and she exclaims, "So it's closer to one!" The teacher is pleased with the connections these girls have made and asks them to share them with the rest of the group. She then asks the pairs to continue play as she checks in with the other students.

She starts at the meeting area and notes that Kyle and Liam also added one-fourth and three-fourths to their line with markers and use these numbers as benchmarks as well. When seven-eighths is formed, Kyle says, "Seven-eighths is one more eighth than three-fourths and one-eighth is half of a fourth. So, seven-eighths will be halfway between three-fourths and one." Liam nods and Kyle writes $\frac{7}{8}$ on one of the pieces of paper and places is correctly on the number line. The next fraction they form is five-sixths and they need to decide how this number compares to seven-eighths. They easily agree that both numbers are close to one, but are not immediately sure which of the two is greater. Then Liam shares an important insight when he says, "Wait, I think we should look at the missing parts, the one-sixth and one-eighth. If we think about them, then we can find the shortest distance to the one." Kyle builds on this idea by saying, "Oh, I get it. One-sixth is greater than one-eighth, so it's more away from one!" The teacher asks the students to explain their thinking again, both to make sure that she understands it and to help them remember this multistep procedure.

The other students are also involved in serious conversations, though they have only included one-half as a benchmark number between zero and one, and are depending more on equivalent fractions. The teacher encourages Kyle and Liam to share their thinking. She knows that most students will not be able to completely follow their new ideas during this first exposure, but is confident that with continued experience, some will begin to adopt this approach as their own.

The teacher wants to be sure that her "middle" group also gets some of her attention, so she approaches a pair of these students and asks them how they are making their decisions about the fractions. They have just formed the fraction two-sevenths. Casey responds, "I would draw seven circles and color in two and not a lot would be colored so that would be closer to zero."

"How do you see it Ben?" the teacher asks. Ben replies, "I see it like we did on the board. Half of seven is between three and four and two is less than three, so it goes to the zero." Satisfied that both students have developed techniques that work for them and provide for accuracy, she checks in with a few other partners. Then she feels a tapping on her arm and turns to Jim who asks, "Is it better to be the zero or the one?" The teacher turns around wondering about the question and asks Jim what he means. "Well Jamie thinks it would be better to be the one because more fractions are closer to one. The teacher and Jim make their way back to Jamie and she listens for a few minutes as they talk. Before too long the math session needs to end for the day. Although time did not allow for Jamie and Jim to reach a conclusion, the teacher is interested in and surprised by this question.

Teacher Reflection

After the first day, I realized my students were at many different levels of thinking about fractions. I decided I wanted to help them begin to use benchmark numbers zero, one-half, and one to compare numbers. But I also knew that they needed to work at different levels.

When I can, I like to differentiate by having students involved in a very similar activity, but in a slightly different manner. This way, I can maintain my focus better while providing for individual differences.

Over time, I have become more respectful of the different ways my students think about mathematical ideas. A couple of years ago I would have just told them to always use a linear model for this problem. Now I realize that they have strong preferences for which model they use and try to spend more time connecting the various representations they make. But I still miss some things, like realizing that some students need to concretely connect the fraction strips with the number line by adding zero and one to the strips. I am eager to return to a race car problem and see if the students apply these ideas to this situation.

Many times the students take me in directions I would not have thought about. I was really surprised about Jim and Jamie's question about whether ·zero or one was better. I wonder how other students would respond to it. Also, Kyle and Liam's thinking was much more sophisticated than I ever expected. There are so many rich ideas to talk about!

Identifying attributes of a worthwhile task

The race and fraction game activities led to a lively exploration of mathematical concepts. Relationships were discovered, affirmed or reaffirmed, a variety of ideas emerged, misconceptions were uncovered, symbolic notation was connected to visual representations, and students were eager to explain their thinking. What type of task yields such results? While it is easier to recognize a specific task as being one that will be worthwhile when explored with a specific group of students, some general attributes of a worthwhile task can be identified.

It focuses on significant mathematical ideas.

The task should be connected to big ideas in mathematics and be problematic, that is, the solution should not be apparent immediately or a variety of outcomes should be possible. In this case, number sense and connecting visual images to fractions are the big ideas. When instruction emphasizes significant ideas, students are more likely to make connections across mathematical strands or to pursue related ideas on their own. For example, a couple of weeks after Jim and Jamie thought about whether more fractions were closer to zero or one, they started talking about whether there were more whole numbers closer to zero or infinity.

It is developmentally appropriate.

For elementary school students, this means that ideas are within reach both from a cognitive level and an experiential one. Students should be encouraged to construct their own strategies or ideas and be prodded to connect their intuition and natural language to their mathematical experiences. Concrete materials, visual models, and drawing materials should be available for use at all times to support their work. As was demonstrated in the exchanges about fractions, asking students to explain their ideas or make comparisons among representations often extends students' thinking.

It is contextualized.

Presenting mathematical ideas in connection to literature or shared events (such as field races) can help students enter mathematical activities. Situating mathematical tasks within everyday contexts also helps capture students' interests and gives them insights on how to begin open-ended tasks.

It offers an appropriate level of challenge.

To be worthwhile, a task must offer a cognitive challenge that requires decisions to be made and new ideas to be explored, and yet not be so challenging as to feel overwhelming. When a task has multiple entry points, it is possible to engage students with a broad range of readiness.

It encourages multiple perspectives.

An interesting task stimulates a variety of strategies, representations, and mathematical ideas and thus encourages students to engage in mathematical discourse in which they explain and justify their thinking. When students shared the different ways they *drew* a fraction, other students were able to extend their visual representations of fractions as well.

Note that these characteristics of a worthwhile task serve two purposes. They provide attributes of a task that build broader and deeper mathematical ideas and that support differentiated instruction. That is, a task that is contextualized is developmentally appropriate, offers an appropriate level of challenge, encourages multiple perspectives, makes room for a variety of learners, and supports a variety of learning needs. While a variety of tasks are available in published materials, teachers often find that they are more successful with tasks they adapt or create themselves. Whether using tasks as written, adapting them, or creating them from scratch, teachers first need to assess where their students are in comparison to the goals of the curriculum.

Chapter 3

Getting to Know Our Students
Places to Start

*B*ack when we were in school, teachers assessed our mathematical work in the same way that our spelling tests were scored. We wrote our answers in a list and they were marked as either right or wrong. The number of incorrect responses was written at the top of the page, followed by an *x*. Teachers considered this number of incorrect or correct answers evidence of our learning and then they kept these scores in a record book for future reference. Feedback was limited to these scores. Little or no attention was given to analysis of our work and process was seldom valued.

Thankfully, this is no longer the status quo in most of today's elementary classrooms. As our expectations for teaching mathematics have changed, so have the ways in which we gather evidence of learning. In recent years, teachers have begun to examine their students' mathematical thinking more closely. They observe students as they work individually or in groups, use manipulatives, and tackle more complex tasks. They keep anecdotal records of these observations. Daily work, in which students are often expected to write or draw to communicate and represent their mathematical ideas, is looked at intently and provides assessment data that inform instructional decisions. As well as correctness, teachers look at the work in relation to curriculum standards, developmental readiness, strategy choices, misconceptions, and conceptual thinking.

More focused assessment tasks may be given at both the beginning and the end of units. Mathematical portfolios may be kept that include samples of work completed during different times of the year and across curriculum strands. Interviews may be conducted with individual students. Together, these assessment techniques allow teachers to get to know their students as individual mathematical thinkers and thus teachers can more effectively match instructional practices to their students' various needs. As described by this teacher in the following reflection about the analysis of student work, these assessment practices require more time. But when teachers make the commitment to value their students' work, the results are informative and rewarding.

Teacher Reflection

Sometimes I'm overwhelmed by my students' work. It can take a long time to analyze their recordings. I think about what the work is or isn't telling me about my students' understandings, their misconceptions, or their connections. When I think back to when it took very little time and effort to mark answers as correct or incorrect, I know I used to have a nagging feeling about this. On some level I realized that anyone could have corrected their work and that it didn't really tell me much about my students and their progress.

When I am not feeling overwhelmed, I do feel great joy while reflecting and commenting on their work. I see such possibility and get a sense of deep satisfaction about my role as a teacher. I look for patterns of thinking and use pieces of the work to help frame our next minilesson(s). I try to give authentic, purposeful feedback, too. I want the students to feel that I care about their thinking because I do! Each piece of work is evidence of learning.

This feeling is similar to how I feel when I listen to my students in class. I marvel at how students can communicate their ideas and how clever their thinking can be. I want them to feel the satisfaction that I feel, to take pride in their work and ideas.

I can remember getting worksheets handed back when I was a child. I never looked at the work again, only the red mark on the top of the page. It was the grade, not the learning, that I came to value. In contrast, I think carefully about the comments I write on my students' papers. When my students read them, or share them with a parent or family member at home, I want the students to use my comments as a way to reconnect with their thinking and to see the work as evidence of their own learning.

Though it certainly matters if an answer is incorrect, I try to see if I can figure out where any of the students got off track. For me, that's most important. When this happens I can plan instruction to help redirect the learning. If I can't make sense of their work, then I know that I need to spend more time with those students so they can help me understand what they were doing or thinking at that moment. When work is handed in that is incorrect or incomplete, I want to take the time to have students think about it again. I don't want students to feel as though their work is never finished, but at the same time, I don't want them to view each piece as a separate task that they can easily discard when they hand it in saying, "Done!"

> The students' work is interesting and informative. It has great value to me; it shows me what and how my students are learning. Isn't that the heart of the matter? I know that is not how I felt about my work in math class as a child, but it is how I want my students to feel now.

This teacher has captured many of the differences between assessment practices when she was a student and those she incorporates into her classroom. While other changes in assessment and evaluation of student learning have occurred during this time as well, such as the significant attention paid to high-stakes, mandated testing, the focus here is on those assessment practices and habits of mind that support differentiated instruction on a daily basis. Such practices include formal and informal techniques for collecting data, and most likely, many are already incorporated into your classroom. Through the lens of differentiation, however, the purposes of these data-gathering strategies become more focused and refined as do the assessment tasks we want to use with our students. Like this teacher, our sights should always be set on getting to know our students better and to understanding their ways of making sense of the mathematics they are learning. Our goals are to gather evidence of learning and to gain insights into best next steps.

Pre-Assessment

To differentiate according to readiness, we need to determine what our students already know. Note that some of the earlier classroom scenarios began with an activity that allowed teachers to pre-assess their students' knowledge and level of familiarity or proficiency with the concept at hand. Many activities can serve this purpose if they include opportunities for discussion, group work, or recorded responses and explanations. It is the teachers' clarity of purpose and attention to students' work that allow such activities to become sources of pre-assessment data. Let's consider another teacher's words as she reflects on pre-assessment.

Teacher Reflection

When I am thinking about pre-assessment, I know I am trying to identify children's zones of comfort and proficiency. I am looking for data that will help me answer questions such as: How familiar are my students with this new concept? What

(Continued)

working knowledge, skills, and strategies do they have in place to support them in this, supposedly, new area of learning? What misconceptions might they have? How comfortable are they with the mathematical language associated with this topic?

I try hard not to make assumptions about my students anymore. Some of them come to school with a wealth of mathematical knowledge and experience. Many students do not, and the range among them seems to be increasing each year. I want to meet each child where he or she is. It's hard to find that zone for each student, that place between where things are too hard and out of reach, and too easy and potentially uninteresting or not challenging. Though I know in reading it can be fun and good practice to read a book that is too easy, I also know that if that is all you are asked to read, you have considerably less opportunity to improve and become a more proficient, analytic reader. When a book is too hard, it can also be frustrating and lead to reluctance and lack of productivity. The same is true in math. I want to identify the tasks and investigations that will be just right for my students, that will challenge their thinking without overwhelming them. And, I want to do this quickly, so that we all feel good about what we are doing.

Many aspects of the importance of pre-assessment have been identified by this teacher. So, just how soon in the year should we begin this pre-assessment process? It is common for teachers to begin assessing students' reading abilities immediately. Teacher-developed, system-created, or standardized assessment tools may be used. The results of these initiatives allow teachers to get a broad sense of their students as a group and to begin to capture the range of their readiness levels. These data allow teachers to identify initial ways to differentiate their reading instruction. It is less common for teachers to attend to their students' mathematical readiness with the same intensity, but we believe that early assessment of mathematical readiness must also occur.

Anecdotal Records

From the first day of school, teachers have a myriad of ways to get acquainted with their new students. They are eager to learn about what their students know and their comfort levels with the various academic subjects, social interactions, and rules and routines of school. For example, third-grade teachers might begin to collect anecdotal data about their students' mathematical understandings during the first week by observing them sort geoblocks into two groups. As the students dive in, so do their teachers, who listen, watch, and often record what they see and hear:

- Max gathered all the blocks and sorted them quickly into two piles as if he were passing out cards for a game.

- Kayla picked up each block and told her partner everything she knew about the block before she began to sort. "This one has rectangles and squares on it" was her comment about each rectangular prism.
- Liam picked up a triangular prism and asked, "What is this?"
- Sophia and Manuel examined each block patiently, and then placed it in one of two piles: blocks that can roll and blocks that can't roll. They spent some time discussing what made a block roll. They both agreed that a block "rolled" if they wouldn't have to push it to make it roll from the top of a hill. Sophia suggested that "rolling blocks" have circles on them. Manuel wasn't sure he wanted to include blocks that would only roll sideways, not straight (cones with circular bases).

Anecdotal notes like these help the teacher get a feel for students' comfort level, engagement, and working knowledge. Over time, patterns of thinking or behavior might emerge for an individual as well as for the whole class that can help the teacher make more informed decisions for instruction. New information abounds during these first few days and weeks and teachers can sometimes feel overwhelmed. Recording these simple observations can help us focus and remember what we have witnessed.

In today's world of mandated testing, students enter the classroom with considerable information in their files related to mathematical achievement. For many teachers anecdotal records based on interactions in the classroom and standardized test scores are enough to get started. Other teachers do not want to consider test scores until they have gotten to know their students better or may not believe that such scores yield enough information. Interviews are sometimes conducted in which each student is asked to respond individually to a series of tasks or questions. We often listen to our students read to get a baseline on their literacy fluency and decoding skills. We also want to get an initial appraisal of selected skills associated with mathematics.

Interviews

Early assessment interviews are usually designed to help the teacher learn relatively quickly about students' abilities in relation to number and operations, including counting, place value, estimation, number sense, computation, and fractions. Often teachers construct their own interviews and use their state standards as a way to decide what kinds of questions to ask. One fourth-grade teacher uses the following questions in her interviews:

Counting actual objects

- Given a collection of about 150 counters, How many counters do you think there are? Please count to check. (Note accuracy and any grouping or keeping track strategies demonstrated. If students didn't group by tens ask: If you grouped these by tens, how many groups would there be?)

For each of these questions, observe any strategies evident and ask, "How do you figure out what comes next?"

Counting sequences

- What number comes just after 459? Just before 3,000?
- How do we write the number 1,024?
- Start at 3 and count by threes.
- Start at 4 and count by fives.
- Start at 57 and count backward by fours.

Estimation

- You have five dollars. Estimate to decide if you could buy one of each item on this list. Explain your thinking.

Book	$3.50
Eraser	$1.00
Notebook	$2.99
Pen	$2.98

Computation

- Find $146 + 237$ and explain your thinking.
- Find $508 - 199$ and explain your thinking.
- What is 5×9?

Fractions (Have pattern blocks available.)

- If the hexagon is equal to 2, what does the red trapezoid represent?
- If the yellow hexagon is equal to 1, how would you show $2\frac{2}{3}$?

These questions are not comprehensive, but they do give the teacher an initial perspective on each student's understanding of number and operations. The teacher can easily adapt the questions during the course of the interview to make sure each child experiences some success.

Many math educators, researchers, and research groups have designed more comprehensive assessment interviews. For example, the *Early Numeracy Interview Booklet* (Communications Division for the Office of School Education, Department of Education, Employment and Training 2001) is one part of a more comprehensive program that can easily give teachers in kindergarten through grade 5 a guide for some key assessment tasks. According to this program, an interview is "a powerful tool for assessing students' numeracy development during the first five years of schooling. . . . Time spent conducting the one-to-one interview is invaluable in enhancing teachers' understandings of students' mathematical understandings and the strategies they use. For this reason it is recommended that the classroom teacher administer the interview" (7–8).

Andrea Guillaume has written extensive interview protocols in *Classroom Mathematics Inventory for Grades K–6: An Informal Assessment* (2005). Referred to as CMI, this assessment program is similar to a reading inventory and is designed to be used by the classroom teacher. Protocols span across the elementary grades and include each of the content strands. Many of the assessments utilize common classroom manipulatives and there is also a section teachers can use to assess attitudes toward mathematics.

Leading mathematics educator and consultant Kathy Richardson has developed a series of assessment tasks designed for use as individual interviews. To date there are nine different assessment tasks in Richardson's *Assessing Math Concepts,* each focusing on an essential concept of mathematical understanding (Richardson 2003). Designed for use across the primary and intermediate grades, each of these tasks is tailor-made to help a teacher find the place at which a student transitions from a comfortable, grounded understanding of mathematics to a place where more practice, application, or instruction is required.

Similar to Vygotsky's zone of proximal development, our job is to challenge students' comfort level and then to help them find their next boundaries. Through assessment, we try to identify evidence for what the child knows or has mastered, areas where initial ideas are formed but additional experience with them is needed, and those concepts and skills that require further scaffolding or additional readiness development. Richardson (2003) also suggests how the teacher can make strategic decisions for future instruction based on data gained through interviews and provides ways to continue to assess students' work.

It is becoming more commonplace for schools or school districts to require some initial assessment in mathematics. We are all being asked to be more accountable. In turn, each teacher needs to determine his or her own best way to use data gathered from an assessment, be it formal or informal. There was a time when such initial data were used to determine ability groups in mathematics. Often referred to as *tracking*, these groups were thought to be homogenous in nature and tended to be a long-term assignment. That is not the goal assumed here. While we do recommend that students' instruction be differentiated based on readiness, we do not assume, nor do we recommend, that groups will always be formed, or that when groups are appropriate, that they will always be homogeneous or that their membership will remain unchanged for too long.

Open-Ended Tasks

Along with individual interviews and anecdotal records as ways to collect information about what their students know and how they represent their ideas, some teachers find it useful to give every student an open-ended task or problem. One third-grade teacher asks her students to respond to the question, *What do you know about 100?* Harry's response indicates that 100 is the same as 10×10. (See Figure 3–1.) He may also be referring to this

Figure 3–1 *Harry's response to* What do you know about 100?

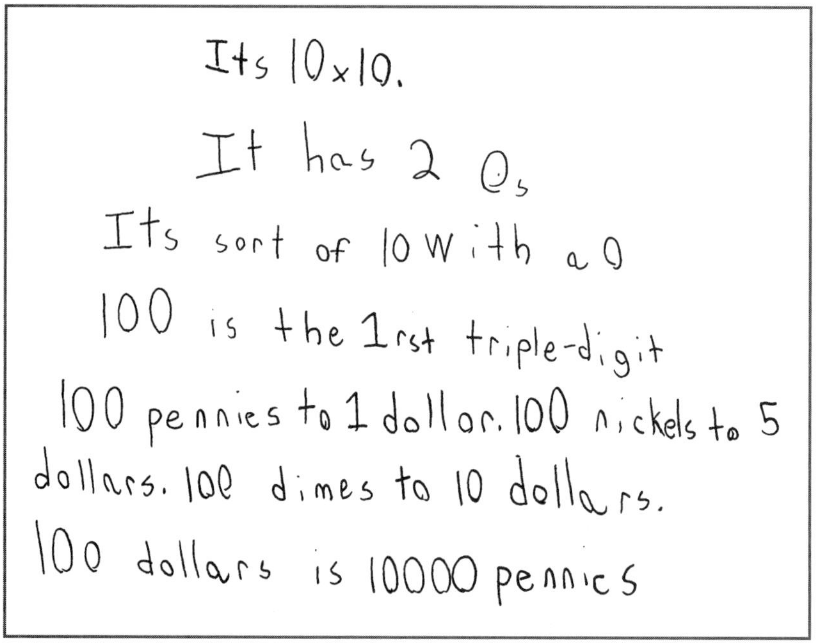

Its 10×10.

It has 2 0s

Its sort of 10 with a 0

100 is the 1rst triple-digit

100 pennies to 1 dollor. 100 nickels to 5 dollars. 100 dimes to 10 dollars.

100 dollars is 10000 pennies

relationship when he writes that 100 is *sort of 10 with a 0.* Of course he may just be responding to a visual image, but it is a connection that can lead to further ideas about place value. Harry makes many associations between money and 100 when he indicates the equivalent relationships between 100 pennies and one dollar, 100 nickels and five dollars, 100 dimes and ten dollars, and 100 dollars and 10,000 pennies. Harry also includes the statement that 100 is the first three-digit number, suggesting comfort with that mathematical vocabulary and an awareness of 100 in relation to other numbers.

Sam's response also identifies 100 as 10 × 10. (See Figure 3–2.) She indicates this relationship through repeated addition of tens as well, suggesting that she understands the relationship between

Figure 3–2   *Sam's response to* What do you know about 100?

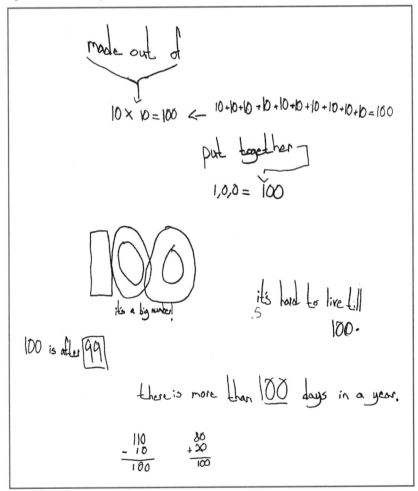

addition and multiplication. She indicates flexibility in her thinking as she connects 100 to several different ideas. She writes that it is after 99 and that it is a big number. She writes a subtraction example with 100 as the difference and an addition example with 100 as the sum. She demonstrates her number sense when she meaningfully relates 100 to the real world. She states that it would be hard to live to be a 100 and that there are more than 100 days in a year.

Teacher Reflection

I like to pose this question to my students during the first week of school. It gives me a little window of insight into their mathematical thinking. This is a question that students generally feel comfortable answering, since most feel a connection to the number one hundred. I am always amazed at the variety of the students' responses. Some students just write lots of computation examples equal to one hundred, while others provide a broader perspective than just arithmetic. I'm always saddened when a couple of students respond "I don't get it." It worries me that they are uncertain as to how to answer an open-ended mathematical question, even a fairly straightforward one.

While I encourage the use of pictures, numbers, or words to describe their thinking, some students draw beautiful pictures and get sidetracked by their attention to detail. So many of the students relate one hundred years to an old age or one hundred dollars to being a lot of money. Children use the word *gazillion* so readily, it's important to remember that at this age, one hundred still seems "big." This year a student wrote about how her grandmother would be one hundred years old next week, if she were still alive. My other students were attentive as she shared this information and it reminded me to build on the importance of numbers such as one hundred, one thousand, ten thousand, and so on. We often refer to one hundred as a landmark number in terms of computation, but it is important for number sense as well. One student wrote that one hundred is a big number and wrote it the size of the entire page. Then he wrote a very small *99* at the bottom of the page. Could this student have a misconception about the difference between these two numbers or is he just indicating how important he thinks one hundred is?

Though the range of responses is great, I don't want to read too much into them. After all, it's only one task and students sometimes need a week or two back in school before they really get going. But it is a place to begin and does help me develop some ideas about what my new students know. I don't have a specific number of responses I am looking for, though I do look for accuracy, flexible thinking, and engagement. I also check to see if there is any evidence of a child looking uncomfortable during this work. It's just an initial task, but it really helps me get to know my students better.

This teacher reminds us of the balanced way we need to think about assessment tasks. No one task can be given too much attention and yet each appropriate task does provide us with some relevant data. It is particularly important to take a similarly balanced perspective on information that is passed from grade to grade. In many schools data are shared from one grade to another by way of lists of test scores and portfolios that contain end-of-year assessment interviews or packets. Many teachers receiving this information find it to be very helpful, while others prefer to begin to make their own judgments before reviewing any of the previous data. In either case it is important to remember the significance of gathering evidence from multiple sources.

Looking Beyond Readiness

So far we have concentrated on early assessment tasks that address readiness, often the sole focus of mathematics teachers. But we also want to differentiate instructional activities according to interests, preferred learning styles, intelligences, and mathematical dispositions. We can collect this data through parent questionnaires, student input, teacher observations, and conversations with previous teachers. Collection and use of these data are ways to acknowledge that we expect our students to be different from one another and to show the children (and their parents) that we care about getting to know them as individual learners.

Questionnaires

Some teachers ask parents to complete questionnaires. While they are not always returned, when they are the information gleaned can be important. Some elementary school teachers send a questionnaire home to gather information about their students. (See Figure 3–3; see also Blackline Masters.) Questions about hobbies, collections, and activity choices in and out of school provide insight into interests students have that may connect to mathematics. Collecting coins, playing cards or logic games, doing puzzles, having an interest in sports-generated statistics, and constructing intricate block designs often relate to skills that support and utilize mathematical thinking. Children's general interests are also relevant to mathematics as they allow us to position tasks in contexts that can help capture students' curiosity and illustrate the usefulness of what they are learning. Some teachers, however, prefer to use

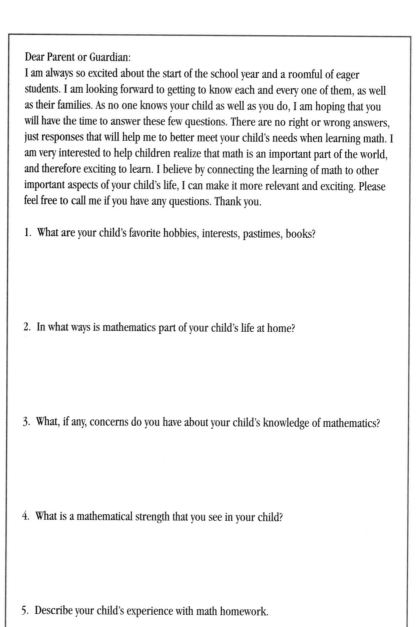

Dear Parent or Guardian:

I am always so excited about the start of the school year and a roomful of eager students. I am looking forward to getting to know each and every one of them, as well as their families. As no one knows your child as well as you do, I am hoping that you will have the time to answer these few questions. There are no right or wrong answers, just responses that will help me to better meet your child's needs when learning math. I am very interested to help children realize that math is an important part of the world, and therefore exciting to learn. I believe by connecting the learning of math to other important aspects of your child's life, I can make it more relevant and exciting. Please feel free to call me if you have any questions. Thank you.

1. What are your child's favorite hobbies, interests, pastimes, books?

2. In what ways is mathematics part of your child's life at home?

3. What, if any, concerns do you have about your child's knowledge of mathematics?

4. What is a mathematical strength that you see in your child?

5. Describe your child's experience with math homework.

Figure 3–3 *Parent or guardian questionnaire.*

forms that do not require narrative responses. (See Figure 3–4; see also Blackline Masters.)

The following reflection shows us how one teacher has gained respect for the information parents can provide.

Dear Parent or Guardian:

This first day has been a wonderful start to the school year. I am excited about getting to know each of my new students. I am hoping that you will help me by completing this questionnaire about mathematics. There are no right or wrong answers! Please feel free to call me if you have any questions. Thank you.

1 = agree
2 = somewhat agree
3 = somewhat disagree
4 = disagree

My child will stick with a math problem, even when it is difficult.	1	2	3	4
My child lacks confidence in mathematics.	1	2	3	4
My child has strong computational skills.	1	2	3	4
My child's favorite subject is mathematics.	1	2	3	4
My child becomes frustrated solving math problems.	1	2	3	4
My child does math homework independently.	1	2	3	4
As a parent, it is my job to help my child with math homework.	1	2	3	4
Math is talked about at home and is part of our everyday life.	1	2	3	4
I do not always understand the way my child thinks about math problems.	1	2	3	4
Math is taught better today than when I was in school.	1	2	3	4

Comments:

Figure 3–4 *Alternative parent or guardian survey.*

Teacher Reflection

When I first started teaching I thought my job was to teach children, that only primary teachers had to focus on families. I didn't give much thought to the parents of my students and what my relationship would be with them. How quickly I learned! Now in my fifth year of teaching, I have made progress in finding ways to connect with my students' caregivers.

(Continued)

At the beginning of the year I send home a parents and guardians survey, which asks questions about how their child learns and about their attitudes toward learning mathematics. I ask for these to be returned prior to the first open house at the end of September. I gather this information to use as a guide when I am addressing the parents or guardians. I am as surprised by the variety among the parents and guardians as I am by the variations in my students! I have parents who feel strongly that their role is to help their child with homework as well as parents who feel it is solely the child's responsibility. Likewise, I have many parents who support the recent changes in math education and several who think, "The way I was taught was fine. Why are we changing the rules?"

In addition to the survey, I share with each parent or guardian their own child's survey done in class. Often how a child answers the questions surprises the adult. One child wrote, "excellent," in response to the question, How do you feel about division? Her mother was shocked, but happy, and told me, "Last year my daughter always cried while doing her homework. I tried to help her, but I think she got more confused. She was not comfortable with me helping because she said I don't do division the right way. I am glad to see that she is liking division now." It's so easy for all of us to hang on to a perception that may no longer be true. It was important for Wanda's mother to realize that her daughter was now comfortable with division. I think this knowledge will help her mother to treat her as someone who is successful in math, which will in turn reinforce that idea in Wanda.

When it comes to talking about math, parents or guardians frequently tell me that they were not successful in or didn't like math. Sometimes I worry that these parents don't hold high enough expectations for their children. Other parents tell me how much they excelled at math and how they want the same for their children. They tell stories of how their child has impressed them at an early age and identify family traits and interests they share: "We love to look at the football stats in the newspaper." "We play cards all the time and race to see who can add up the points first." These comments give me a perspective on how the families view mathematics and how mathematics is embedded in their daily lives. I can't believe how much more I learn about my students now that I have built family connections.

Questionnaires can also be used to gather helpful data from students, such as a general interest survey given to fourth-grade students early in the fall. (See Figure 3–5; see also Blackline Masters.) Students can also tell us about how they learn best, for example, whether they like to work in groups or alone, the levels of challenge they prefer, the noise level they find comfortable, and where they like to work in the classroom. Asking children about these preferences helps them realize that we care about how they learn best. It also allows them to reflect on their learning preferences. (See Figure 3–6; see also Blackline Masters.) As the following teacher's words suggest, knowing our students' interests and preferences can help us relate to them more deeply and to better meet their needs.

What Interests You?

1. What activities do you like to do after school?

2. What are your favorite sports or games?

3. What do you like to do at indoor recess?

4. If you could plan a field trip, where would the class go?

5. Who is your favorite character from a book or a video?

6. Which of these things do you like most? Put a 1 there.
   Which of these things do you like second best? Put a 2 there.

____ music	____ reading
____ sports	____ nature walks
____ acting	____ drawing or art projects
____ being with friends	____ building things
____ science experiments	____ field trips to historical places

Figure 3–5   *General interest survey for fourth graders at the beginning of the school year.*

Teacher Reflection

I really like learning as much about my students as I can, as soon as possible. I like to know how they spend their time when they are not in school and who their favorite characters are. Yesterday I shared a baseball statistic with Melissa and asked Conrad to imagine what Harry Potter might do in a particular situation. I could tell that they were surprised I had remembered what they had written. September is such an exciting time of year. It holds such promise as we all get to know each other and form our classroom community. I love my summers, but this excitement and wonder really helps me make the transition to fall.

I have only recently asked my students to complete a questionnaire about their own learning preferences. When I first did so, I was surprised at how firm their opinions were. This year all of my students have communicated a preference for working alone or with a partner. I like to do a lot of group work. Maybe I should start with partner work and move a bit more slowly to small groups. I never would have thought about this if I hadn't collected these data.

Who Are You as a Learner?

1. If you could learn about anything at school, what would you choose?

2. What do you know a lot about?

3. How do you work best in school?

 __ alone __ partner __ small group __ large group

4. Where do you like to work at school?

 __ desk __ table __ hallway __ floor __ library area __ other

5. Do you learn best when your classroom is

 __ quiet __ somewhat quiet __ somewhat noisy __ noisy

6. Do you like school work to be

 __ easy __ somewhat easy __ somewhat hard __ hard

7. What else helps you to learn?

8. What makes it hard for you to learn?

Figure 3–6 *A learning survey for fifth graders at the beginning of the school year.*

It is also worthwhile to gain insight into students' mathematical dispositions, or their attitudes toward mathematics. As all teachers know, positive attitudes contribute greatly to successful learning. Ideally, all students enjoy mathematics, have positive mathematical learning experiences, think of themselves as successful learners and users of mathematics, and view mathematics as a useful tool in their lives. Simple observations, such as noting how a child sits or looks during mathematical activities can often provide quite a bit of information. Does her body language suggest that she is tense? Do his eyes indicate that he is disinterested? Is the position of her shoulders a sign that she is confident? Is the angle of his upper body an implication of eager anticipation? These behaviors

What Do You Think About Mathematics?

1. Math is important to learn because . . .

2. When I am learning math I feel . . .

3. One thing I am good at in math is . . .

4. One thing I am not good at yet in math is . . .

5. This year in math I want to learn about . . .

Figure 3–7 *Student math interest inventory.*

can often be observed during the first week of school and can alert the teacher to those students who might need closer attention.

Again, questionnaires can be used, such as a form used to collect data from third- through fifth-grade students about their mathematical dispositions. (See Figure 3–7; see also Blackline Masters.) Student responses suggested a variety of beliefs about mathematics. For example, when asked *Why is math important to learn?* some students indicated its relevance to their daily lives with comments such as "it is everywhere," or "in life you need to be smart in math or you will lose money." Other responses were school-based; they contained expressions of concern about their future education with comments such as "you need it for middle school," or "to go to college."

Responses also revealed how students felt about math. Many students gave short positive answers such as "really happy," "smart," "great!," "cool," or "excited." Unfortunately, even in elementary school, difficulties and ill feelings were also suggested with responses such as "nervous," "like I'm thinking so much that my head will pop off," "confused," "sad, because I don't do math well," or "like I want to hide."

Interestingly, naming an arithmetic operation was the most common response to what a student was good at, was not good at, or wanted to learn more about. All of the students were able to identify something they were good at with "adding and subtracting" being the most common response among those who identified negative feelings when learning mathematics. As students advance, fractions are more frequently identified as something they are not yet good at. Teachers who collected the data were pleased that some of the students identified "doing problems" or "learning different ways to do problems" as either their strength or as something they wanted to learn. They also recognized that their students' responses alerted them to feelings that could potentially impact learning, both positively and negatively.

Some teachers ask their students to write their mathematical autobiography, integrating the assignment with an English and language arts unit on personal narratives. A fourth-grade teacher, for example, offers a variety of questions in her assignment to help students brainstorm ideas and make connections, but she does not require them to respond to each question as she thinks it might feel oppressive or repetitive to them. (See Figure 3–8; see also Blackline Masters.)

Mia suggests that she is "not so good at math," yet she makes many positive statements about mathematics and is able to identify mathematical strengths (See Figure 3–9.) Dino begins his response by declaring that he likes math, though his later comments suggest otherwise. (See Figure 3–10.)

Getting to know our students does not happen overnight, nor is it accomplished in the first few weeks of school. Most important, this information is not static; attitudes, interests, and readiness change throughout the year. Thus it is daily routines and lessons that provide teachers with the greatest source for assessment data for the greatest number of students. Teachers are always gathering data within their normal classroom activities and adjusting lessons accordingly. Probing questions (How do you know? Can you tell me more? Can you restate what she just said?) allow teachers to gain a better understanding of what their students know and how they think about mathematical ideas. Asking students to record their thinking with words, numbers, or drawings also provides mathematical artifacts that teachers can compare over time. Conversations at recess or lunch can update teachers on their students' current interests or concerns.

Your Mathematics Autobiography

Directions: Write an autobiography that focuses on your experiences with mathematics. Use the following questions to guide your thinking. Be sure to explain your answers. You don't need to answer every question, but comment on at least five of them.

1. How do you feel about yourself in math classes?
2. What is your first memory of using mathematics?
3. What do you remember about learning to count or using numbers?
4. What kinds of things have your math teachers done to help you enjoy math?
5. What is your favorite area in mathematics (geometry, computation, logic, problem solving)?
6. What kind of math equipment, tools, or games do you like to use when learning mathematics? Why?
7. What are two examples of when you have used math outside of school?
8. When solving problems, do you prefer working alone or in a group? Why?
9. What area of math is a strength for you?
10. What area of math do you find the most challenging?

Figure 3–8 *Mathematics autobiography assignment.*

Post-Assessment

Open-ended problems or tasks can also be given as post-assessment tasks. Three colleagues, a third-grade teacher, a fourth-grade teacher, and a fifth-grade teacher, have each chosen to assign such a task at the end of their units on geometry. The teachers designed the question so that a broad range of responses could be captured:

> *What do you know about shapes?*
> *Write and draw to communicate your ideas.*

Due to the open-ended nature of the task, students can control some of the difficulty level themselves, for example, by limiting their consideration to only a few shapes or by focusing exclusively on two-dimensional shapes. Similarly, students may choose to use drawings, charts, or diagrams to communicate their ideas or they may rely more on prose. This task gives teachers an opportunity

> I feel that I am not so good at math. I have always felt this way. I remember that by the age of 2 ½. I leared to count to 10 at the age of 4. I could subtract 1 digit numbers. I like Problem Solving becuse I have fun and learn at the same time. I also enjoy using the computer becuse it makes math dynamic. Playing jacks makes me good at math too. I Love the fact that I can always check myself to see if I am right in subtraction. My favorite thing to do is math is 1-digit multiplacation
>
> I can concentrate better when I work alone. The areas in math which are my strengh are addition, subtraction and multiplacation I find divison and fractions to be more difficult than other area of math I enjoy reading the graphes in my father's newspaper.

Figure 3–9 *Mia's autobiography.*

to discover what their students choose to include, perhaps because it is what they know best, or what they believe is most important, or what they find most interesting.

Before setting their students off, the teachers talk with them about task expectations. In the fourth-grade classroom the students create the following list to guide their work:

- Focus on shapes.
- Use words and drawings to explain what you know.
- Use geometry vocabulary.
- Organize your ideas.
- Give several examples.
- Think about real-world connections.

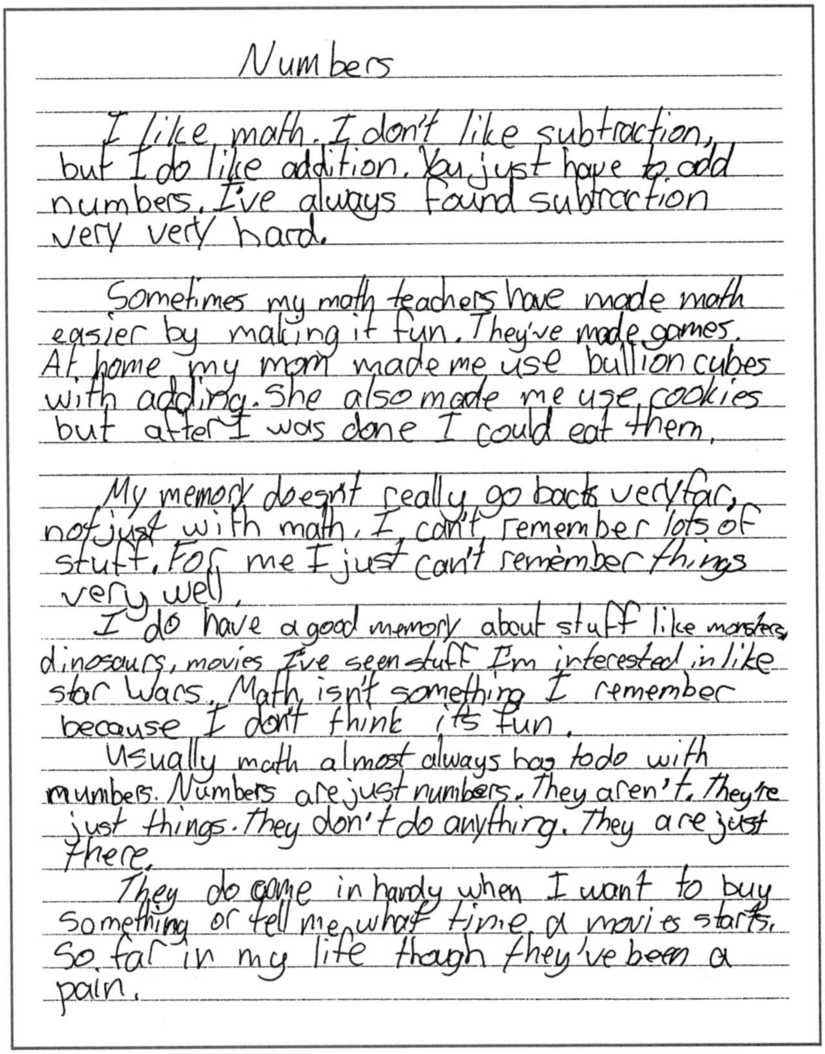

Figure 3–10 *Dino's autobiography.*

After these brief conversations, the students are eager to begin the task. Some students use shape templates, while others prefer drawing freehand. Most students begin by drawing a shape on their paper and then writing some words above or below it. A few students begin by writing an idea or the name of a shape, which they then illustrate.

Lisa, Nick, and Ben are third-grade students. Lisa's response focuses on two-dimensional shapes. (See Figure 3–11.) She classifies shapes by their number of sides and provides the correct name for three-, four-, five-, six-, and eight-sided shapes. Though she does not name the shapes that she draws within her quadrilateral category, she does include a trapezoid, a square, and a parallelogram.

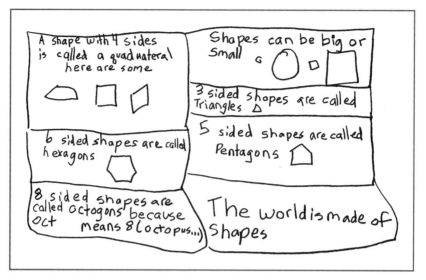

Figure 3–11 *Lisa focused on classifying two-dimensional shapes.*

She provides one example of a triangle, a pentagon, and a hexagon. Note that the sides within these figures have approximately the same length and that the figures are drawn with a base parallel to the bottom of the page. Such orientations are common; in fact, many students do not identify some of these figures when their sides are not congruent or when they are not placed in traditional positions.

Nick identifies several figures, though he makes no attempt to classify them or to associate their names with the number of sides in the figures. (See Figure 3–12.) His statement, "They all are different and sim[i]lar in lots of ways," suggests that he may know more than he is indicating in this task and his teacher decides to follow up with him orally. She laughs as she reads, "Shapes rock!" Nick is an enthusiastic student who genuinely enjoys learning.

Ben's response intrigues his teacher. (See Figure 3–13.) He does not begin with the usual drawings of common shapes, but does illustrate some important geometric concepts. He shows that shapes can be composed of other shapes and connects two-dimensional and three-dimensional figures. Ben also addresses the issues of shapes not shown in their most common position. Below a drawing of four triangles with their bases parallel to the top of the page and their third vertices pointing down, he acknowledges that shapes can look slightly different and still have the same name.

Responses by fourth- and fifth-grade students are much more complex and illustrate how many geometric terms and ideas

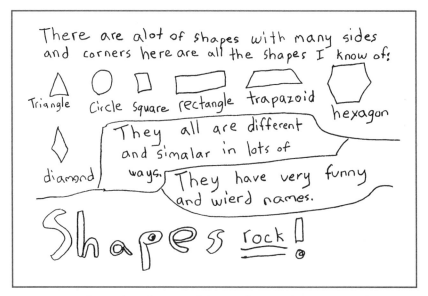

Figure 3–12   *Nick named two-dimensional shapes and expressed a positive attitude toward geometry.*

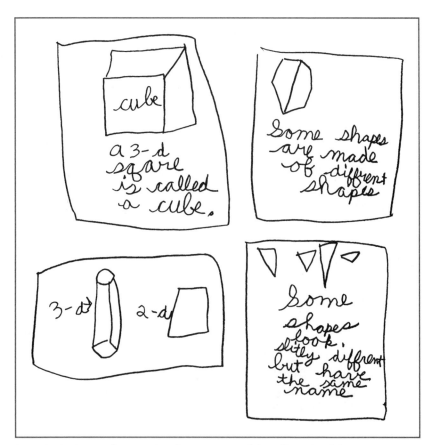

Figure 3–13   *Ben made connections between two- and three-dimensional shapes.*

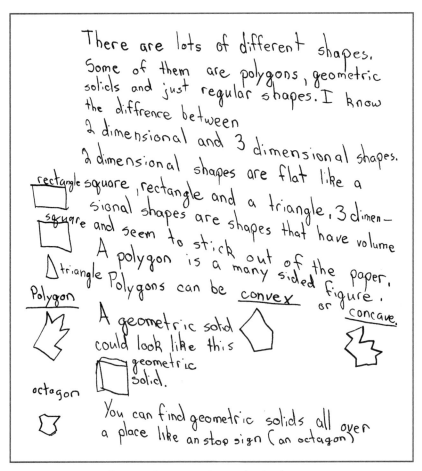

There are lots of different shapes. Some of them are polygons, geometric solids and just regular shapes. I know the diffrence between 2 dimensional and 3 dimensional shapes. 2 dimensional shapes are flat like a square, rectangle and a triangle, 3 dimensional shapes are shapes that have volume and seem to stick out of the paper. A polygon is a many sided figure. Polygons can be convex or concave. A geometric solid could look like this geometric solid. You can find geometric solids all over a place like an stop sign (an octagon)

rectangle square
square
triangle
Polygon
octagon
convex
concave
geometric solid

Figure 3–14 *Nancy, a fourth grader, gave much more detail in her response.*

upper-elementary school students are exposed to today. Nancy, a fourth grader, begins her response by writing about what she knows. (See Figure 3–14.) Her description of three-dimensional shapes as those that "have volume and seem to stick out of the paper" suggests that she has found a personal way to make meaning of this idea. Yet, her teacher finds it interesting that Nancy identifies a stop sign as a geometric solid. While a stop sign does have width and is in fact three-dimensional, most children and adults think of it solely as an octagon, a two-dimensional shape. Nancy's teacher wants to talk with her about this and he wonders what she will say.

Tai, another fourth-grade student, includes references to concave shapes and polygons, and makes connections between two-dimensional and three-dimensional figures. (See Figure 3–15.) He also introduces pyramids, right angles, and the term *parallel*. He is excited as he works. He records one idea and then his eyes light

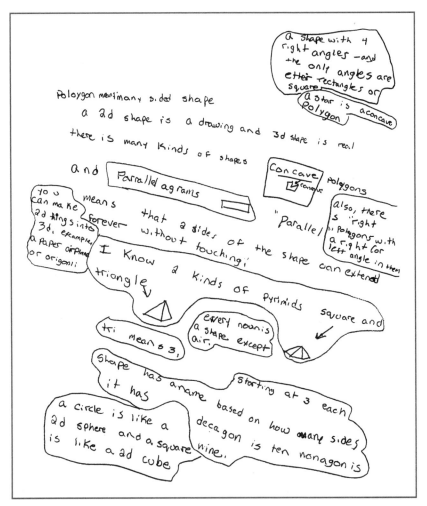

Figure 3–15 *Tai, another fourth grader, included several geometric terms to describe lines, angles, and shapes.*

up as he thinks of another. As these ideas are not necessarily related, he often records a thought and then draws a ring around it to separate it from his other recordings.

Emily and Felicia are both in the fifth grade and use templates to draw their shapes. Their teacher wonders if their attention to two-dimensional shapes results from using templates or if it reflects the recent curricular emphasis on angle measures and circumference. Emily draws several shapes, illustrates right, acute, and obtuse angles, and then gives detailed lists of the properties she associates with each figure she drew. She does not, however, classify the shapes or make connections among them. (See Figure 3–16.) Felicia begins by listing what she knows. For example, she writes, "Perimeter is the same as circumference except it's for non-circular

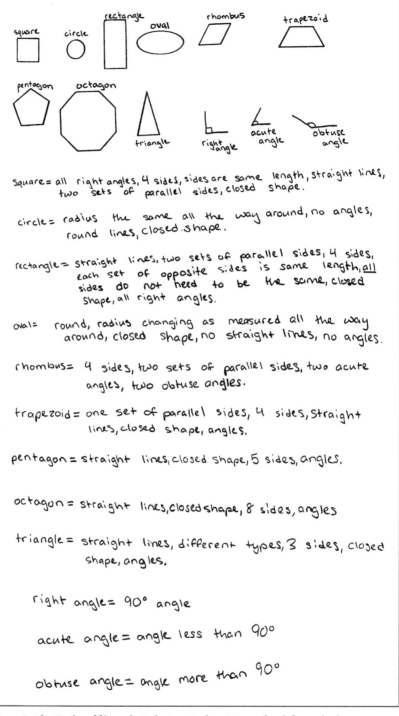

Square = all right angles, 4 sides, sides are same length, straight lines, two sets of parallel sides, closed shape.

circle = radius the same all the way around, no angles, round lines, closed shape.

rectangle = straight lines, two sets of parallel sides, 4 sides, each set of opposite sides is same length, <u>all</u> sides do not need to be the same, closed shape, all right angles.

oval = round, radius changing as measured all the way around, closed shape, no straight lines, no angles.

rhombus = 4 sides, two sets of parallel sides, two acute angles, two obtuse angles.

trapezoid = one set of parallel sides, 4 sides, straight lines, closed shape, angles.

pentagon = straight lines, closed shape, 5 sides, angles.

octagon = straight lines, closed shape, 8 sides, angles

triangle = straight lines, different types, 3 sides, closed shape, angles.

right angle = 90° angle

acute angle = angle less than 90°

obtuse angle = angle more than 90°

Figure 3–16 *Emily, a fifth-grade student, wrote descriptions of each figure she drew.*

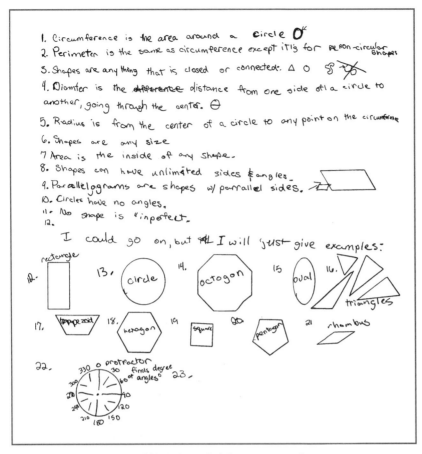

1. Circumference is the area around a circle O
2. Perimeter is the same as circumference except it's for ~~person~~ non-circular shapes
3. Shapes are anything that is closed or connected. △ O
4. Diameter is the ~~difference~~ distance from one side of a circle to another, going through the center. ⊖
5. Radius is from the center of a circle to any point on the circumference
6. Shapes are any size
7. Area is the inside of any shape.
8. Shapes can have unlimited sides & angles.
9. Parallelograms are shapes w/ parrallel sides.
10. Circles have no angles.
11. No shape is "inperfect.
12.

   I could go on, but ~~AL~~ I will just give examples:

rectangle 13. circle 14. octogon 15 oval 16. triangles
17. trapezoid 18. hexagon 19 square 20 pentagon 21 rhombus
22. protractor 330 0 30 finds degree 300 60 of angles° 23. 270 90 240 120 210 180 150

Figure 3–17   *Felicia, another fifth grader, included a protractor in her response.*

shapes." She then draws and labels several shapes, along with a picture of a protractor. (See Figure 3–17.)

The fifth-grade teacher found Rafael's response particularly interesting. Rafael is a strong visual learner. He often makes diagrams to summarize the events in a story and his language often reflects his visual preference. Just this morning the teacher was listening to Fred explain to Rafael why they should play soccer this afternoon instead of going on a bike ride. After Rafael heard Fred's reasoning he replied, "OK, I *see* what you mean." Along with illustrating and labeling many geometric shapes and concepts, he draws tools that he associates with geometry. Note his two representations connect metric and English units along with the geoboard, compass rose, and protractor. (See Figure 3–18.)

The three teachers share their students' work and are amazed at the differences across the grade levels. The third-grade teacher was surprised by how much more complex the students'

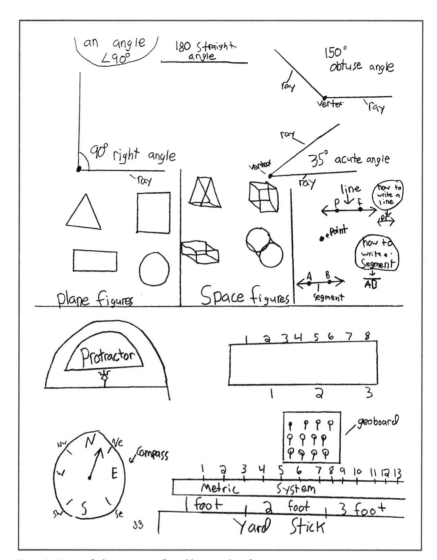

Figure 3–18 *Rafael's response reflected his visual preference.*

responses were in the upper grades. They decide to include this work in the students' portfolios. Next year, they want the students' teachers to have these artifacts to help them determine readiness for future work in geometry. They also are interested in watching the evolution of the students' work over time. Perhaps they could repeat the assignment later in the year and next year they might use it as both a pre- and a post-assessment.

Pre-assessments, post-assessments, interviews, questionnaires, and observations—so what do we do with all these data? Many teachers comment that they get overwhelmed by the amount of information they collect. In a professional development course, one teacher bemoaned, "Sometimes I feel like I am drowning in paperwork. Every piece is important; I don't want to give it back to the student in case I need to refer to it in some way. It's all so interesting, but I'm beginning to want to find a way to figure out what I need to know versus just what is nice to know."

One recommended practice is to take a few minutes a day to write two to three items about what you know about five students. The idea is to have focused on each student by the end of the week. Over time, teachers begin to see patterns among their students that can be useful to understanding developmental sequences. Furthermore, these notes can serve as summative statements of what teachers feel confident that their students understand. Or, the notes can provoke the next questions to guide instruction, such as "Can you tell me more about three-dimensional shapes?" or "Tell me why we use protractors." Throughout this process, teachers are frequently asking: What more do I need to know about my students to offer them an effective and engaging math program? Creating thoughtful rubrics and checklists can also help teachers to assess student work in a more expedient manner.

Teacher collaborations

Sometimes teachers experience uncertainty or confusion in regard to particular students. No matter how much data they collect, they feel that they still have not gathered information that allows them to figure out how to best reach these students. Some teachers who face this situation have learned the benefit of turning to each other for assistance.

Jessica and Leah are two experienced third-grade teachers who have worked together for the past fifteen years. They worked as teaching partners until Jessica accepted a grade-level change. This year Jessica is teaching fifth grade for the first time. Although Jessica and Leah are comfortable with teaching the third-grade mathematics curriculum, Jessica wishes she had more support for learning the fifth-grade curriculum. No professional development is planned for mathematics this year; the system adopted a new program three years ago and everyone in her school received grade-level training then.

Jessica wishes she could turn to Leah, someone she trusts and respects, to help her think about her new challenges. Her class is larger than she is used to and the levels of abilities seem to be more varied then ever. Although the other fifth-grade teachers have been friendly and helpful, she would like her trusted colleague to help her decide how to better meet her students' needs. When they both taught third grade, they planned together and often combined their classes for joint projects. Jessica often provided more leadership in language arts and reading, while Leah often led the way in mathematics and science. A few times when they were trying something new, they would assist each other when one of their classes was at gym. Jessica is enjoying the challenge of fifth grade, but wonders if she made a mistake in leaving Leah.

In the teacher's room, they learn about a professional development plan two second-grade teachers have developed. They agree to meet once at the beginning of each unit to review the material. Then they visit each other's classroom once during each unit and look for *evidence of learning,* a term their professional development presenter used when they were looking at student work. They also meet before the visit to review the mathematics in the lesson and any particular concern they might have. Finally, they meet to debrief the lesson. After listening to this plan, Jessica timidly asks Leah if they could try it too, even though they no longer teach the same grade. To her relief, Leah misses Jessica's support as well and is interested in learning more about the curriculum in the upper grades.

Today's visit is in Jessica's classroom. Jessica has twenty-four fifth-grade students with many different levels of mathematical understanding. The unit is data analysis and the students are working on developing a conceptual understanding of a mean average. In the lesson the students will examine data in a line plot and then use a physical model to find the mean. The students have a solid understanding of how to find a median or mode, but have only a rote approach to finding the mean.

In their preconference, Jessica shares that she would like Leah to watch as students use Unifix cubes to model a leveling concept of the mean, a conceptual model that is described in her textbook. As Jessica explains, "You build a tower for each piece of information. Then you try to decide how many blocks each tower would get if they were all the same level. It's as if you have all the blocks to work with and then redistribute them so that each gets the same amount." Leah immediately recognizes how well this model maps onto the algorithm that students learn for finding the mean. She says, "Oh, I get it. Using them all is like adding all of the numbers up and leveling is like dividing." The students have worked with the model in yesterday's lesson and Jessica wants to make sure they can "see" all three models for average: mode, median, and mean in their towers. Jessica and Leah are excited about this new idea and practice with the cubes before the lesson.

Jessica asks Leah to pay particular attention to Katie and Nathan, two students who were having a bit of difficulty in the initial lesson, and to observe David. David joined Jessica's classroom last month and she does not quite understand his mathematical thinking yet. He usually arrives at correct answers, but she can not always follow his reasoning. Yesterday, his work looked very different and she is not sure that he understood the model.

As the lesson begins Jessica asks the students what they like to eat at parties. Students respond quickly, mentioning ice cream, cake, tacos, hot dogs, hamburgers, pizza, and candy. Then she asks them if they have ever had bite-size or mini pizzas. Heads nod as she shows them a line plot. (See Figure 3–19.) She tells the students, "This plot shows the number of mini pizzas each child ate at a party. We are going to model the data to show how to find the typical number of mini pizzas each child ate. How could we use the Unifix cubes at your tables to show these data?

Several hands raise and she calls on Bobbi. "We show the numbers with the cubes," she offers. "Someone else tell me more about how we could show the numbers," Jessica says to the other students. Dillon suggests, "We would build them. So we put two together four times." Kim adds, "Just like towers." Confident that the students understand what they are to do, Jessica gives each pair time to make eleven towers of cubes to show the data. (See Figure 3–20.) She has also left other data sets at each table for later exploration.

Once the towers are built, the teacher asks about the mode. Derek says, "We know that the mode is two because it has four towers and that is the most." When asked about the median, Marietta demonstrates how she starts with her right pointer finger on the eight and her left pointer finger on the first tower of two. She explains, "Then I walk my fingers in until they meet at the

Figure 3–19   *A line plot.*

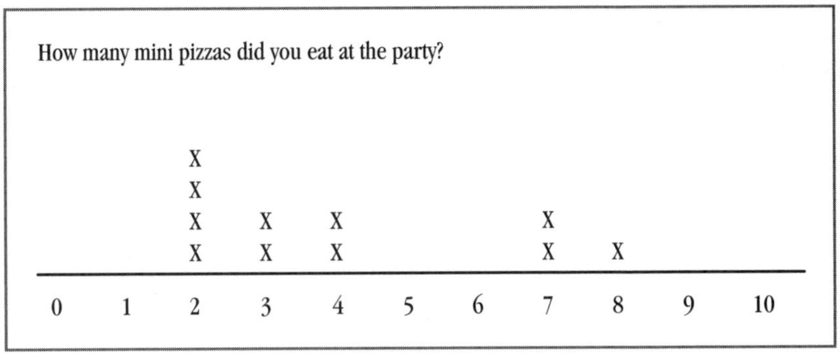

How many mini pizzas did you eat at the party?

```
          X
          X
          X     X     X                 X
          X     X     X                 X     X
    ─────────────────────────────────────────────────────
    0     1     2     3     4     5     6     7     8     9     10
```

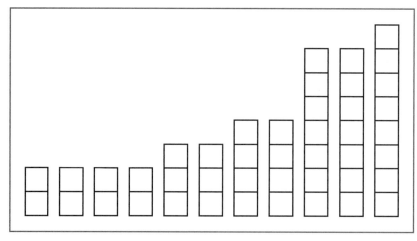

Figure 3–20 *A representation of data with cubes.*

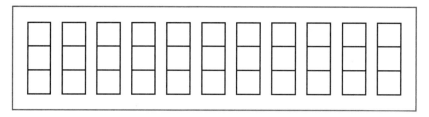

Figure 3–21 *An even distribution or leveling model of mean.*

tower of three." Then Jessica asks the students to work in pairs to find the mean or arithmetic average of these data.

As the students work, Leah sits near Katie and Jonathan. Katie moves some blocks to try to level the eight-tower with some of the two-towers, but then stops and looks confused. She looks up at Leah and says, "I'm trying to even them out, but I can't remember whether I am coming or going." Leah thinks about her third-grade students who sometimes have a similar difficulty when modeling word problems. "Let's rebuild the towers," she suggests, "and use different colors for towers near each other." As Katie and Jonathan rebuild their towers, Leah glances around the class and notes that many of the students have redistributed their cubes correctly so that they have eleven towers with four cubes in each tower. (See Figure 3–21.) She wanders over to where David is working with Camille. David is explaining his thinking to Camille using cubes on top of the line plot. He has made a larger line plot without the Xs, and placed one cube to represent each X. Leah catches Jessica's attention and motions subtly for her to come over as well. She also glances back at Jonathan and Katie to make sure they are still progressing.

"Can we listen, too?" Jessica asks. "Sure," David responds, "I'm just starting over to show Camille, again. We're trying to even it out so they could all have the same number of slices, right?" Camille, Leah, and Jessica nod. David continues. "So each person who had two slices could have one more, if the person who had eight slices had four less." As David says this, he moves the four cubes above the two over to the three. He also moves the cube above the eight over to the four. He then looks at Camille and says, "So how could we get some others closer together?" Jessica and Leah stifle their reaction to David's imitation of a teacher and watch Camille, who with some hesitation moves one of the cubes above the seven to the six, and then moves one of the threes over to the four. "You got it!" exclaims David. "It's like we have to balance everything in the middle." The teachers watch as David and Camille continue to move the blocks toward the center until all eleven blocks are above the four. (See Figure 3–22.) Leah and Jessica continue asking questions until they feel comfortable with their understanding of David's thinking and then they move on to other pairs of students who are exploring the additional problems Jessica has made available.

During their postconference, the two teachers talk about how making towers of different colors seemed to help Katie and Jonathan and then they discuss David's thinking. Leah remembers learning that the mean was a balance point when she took statistics in college. Together they explore both models for mean with other sets of data. They agree that making the towers even leads better to a computational approach for mean, but that David's balance method does show conceptual understanding.

Teacher Reflection

Interesting, just when I thought I understood a physical model for the mean, my students challenge me to think in a different direction. At first, I didn't think David understood what he was doing; it looked so different. I am so glad Leah was there to hear his thinking. I don't think I ever would have remembered what he did, but together we were able to re-create it. I was worried about whether this approach would always work. Trying it with some other sets of numbers and hearing Leah connect it to a college math class helped me feel better about that.

I know that a few years ago I would not have taken the time to understand students with a different approach. I would have just assumed it wasn't right and led them to the way I wanted them to see it. What am I thinking? Years ago I would have only shown them the computation model of adding all

(Continued)

of the numbers up and dividing by eleven. I would have thought I taught a great lesson and many of my students would have learned a basic skill, but only on a surface level. These students could not have explained what a mean was or why they were adding and dividing.

Having Leah to talk with helped me allow David to follow his different path to understanding the mean. She also helped me with Katie and Jonathan. I think of these students as so much older than my third graders were. I don't always recognize that they sometimes need simpler concrete models as well. I hope my knowledge of the fifth-grade curriculum can be helpful to her when I visit her class.

Figure 3–22   *David's balance model for mean.*

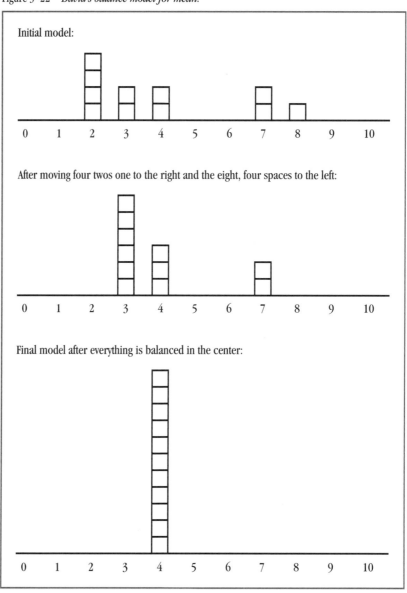

This example helps us to remember to take the time to understand our students' thinking and not to assume that different is incorrect. It speaks to the importance of differentiating mathematical models within assessment tasks and instruction and to recognize that even older children may need more obvious concrete models. It also reminds us to constantly adjust our lenses as we look for evidence of student understanding.

We believe that getting to know each student is at the heart of differentiation. By using a wider variety of assessment practices and specially designed data-gathering techniques, teachers can have a greater understanding of each student as a unique learner and, as a result, have a deeper and broader view of the learning trajectory for each student. Making decisions about for whom, why, and when to differentiate becomes clearer when it is based on what we know about our students and our curriculum. Information about students' readiness, learning preferences, and interests enables teachers to offer different ways for students to develop and to demonstrate their mathematical knowledge. Ways to match, adapt, or create curriculum in order to meet a variety of learner needs is the focus of the next two chapters.

Chapter 4
Casting a Wider Net for Readiness

*T*hrough assessment we uncover many of the similarities and differences among our students' thinking. It offers us an opportunity to look for patterns in our students' learning, both as individuals and as a group. Inevitably, assessment data for any classroom reveal a range in students' experiences, interests, and readiness. In response to these differences, teachers work diligently to delineate standards for all learners, to build inclusive classroom environments, and to vary their teaching styles in order to address these differences. Yet, no matter how carefully learning outcomes are identified, habits are developed to encourage community, or diverse instructional strategies are employed, teachers remain most concerned about the range, great or narrow, of student readiness. Consider the following words of this third-grade teacher.

Teacher Reflection

I often wonder how I am going to meet all of my students' needs. Just yesterday our class was talking about factors. We discovered that a factor can be determined by skip-counting. We decided that if you want to find the factors of 20, then you think about numbers that you could skip-count by and land on 20. The students were working in groups when Max called me over. He was working on finding all of the factors of 16. Max was confused, "This will go on to infinity!" he exclaimed. When I asked him what he meant he replied that, "There are so many factors of sixteen, like one-half, one-fourth, one-eighth, one-sixteenth." He was so excited I could hardly understand what he was saying. He continued, "Well, if you skip-count by halves, then after thirty-two times you land on sixteen. Right?"

I have never had a third-grade student ask such a question. Many of my students are still struggling to count by numbers other than ones, twos, fives, and tens and a couple of my students still count only by ones. It will be simple to refine the definition of a factor with him, but how am I going to continue to interest Max in our curriculum? Should I challenge him to count to sixteen by fifths, give him a much greater number to explore such as 320, or have him explore prime numbers?

Max is always surprising me. He often quotes records from the *Guinness Book of World Records* or some other fact he has read in the newspaper. The other day we were talking about ways to earn money and one of the students told us about her lemonade stand. Max shared that there was once a lemon that weighed 11 pounds, 9.7 ounces. He just always seems to have numerical data to bring to the conversation, no matter what the topic is. He's very comfortable finding sums and differences mentally, while others are still refining their paper-and-pencil techniques when three- and four-digit numbers are involved. He multiplies and divides accurately and efficiently, though as a class, we are still exploring basic facts. He really could begin to learn operations with fractions and decimals, but then what will he do later? Is there a way to enrich my curriculum or should he have opportunities to explore more advanced topics?

Max does appear to be particularly strong in math, maybe even one of those students who would get involved with national programs for the gifted, but there are always some students in my class who are beyond parts of my curriculum. When this happens in reading, I don't feel as lost. It's so much easier to just find another book for a child to read. And when I do so, I won't be disrupting the curriculum that the student is supposed to follow next year.

Max may very well be the student who represents the more advanced students in his third-grade class this year. Perhaps he is not alone. More than likely there are classmates whose profiles are dramatically different. A fourth-grade teacher provides us her thoughts on a student who is less ready for math challenges.

Teacher Reflection

One of my students, Ryder, really concerns me. We're putting on a class play and I thought it provided an opportunity for some of my students to review their mathematical skills. The entire school is invited to the play and so the students were working in groups to solve problems related to planning for refreshments. Ryder was working in a group who had the responsibility of finding the number of students in the school. They decided to visit each class to find the number of students in that class. Ryder was assigned the classrooms in our wing of the building. He returned with his data: 17, 22, 21, 23, 23, 18. The numbers were written randomly on a small scrap of paper. Fortunately, his group leader knew

(Continued)

that there were only five classes in this wing and noticed that Ryder had written six numbers. They decided that he had written twenty-three twice. This may or may not have been the source of the error, but they both seemed satisfied. Ryder's lack of organization often results in his making errors.

Ryder's next task was to find the sum of the five numbers to determine the total number of fourth graders. His sum would then be checked by another member of his group. When we were consistently working with addition and subtraction, Ryder was fairly proficient. He would look for combinations of ten or split numbers into parts in ways that made sense to him. As Ryder began to find this sum he became agitated. He erased several times. There were several tally marks written on his paper. Basically, he was trying to count on by ones. His final answer was eighty-nine.

What bothers me the most is that Ryder used to be able to do these basic tasks. I review with him fairly often, but it never seems to be enough. I wish I knew how to help him hold onto his ideas.

If I had an assistant in the classroom during math time, I could work with him more often. I have a reading specialist in my room twice a week who works with the readers that struggle the most. That special time for them really makes a difference. My school system provides extra materials for reading and I have lots of books in my classroom that less-advanced readers can enjoy. But, I don't have these materials in math and can't just repeat the same problems he did last year.

Considering ways to manage and meet the range of readiness in our mathematics classes is no easy task. Most elementary teachers feel much as these teachers do. What we take on as a rudimentary challenge in literacy becomes seemingly impossible to many, when it comes to mathematics. We're often not sure how to challenge those students who are beyond grade level, and sometimes it feels as if the students who are less ready can slip easily through our grasps. At times, nothing feels just right or appropriate.

But how do we define *appropriate*? It is a word used frequently in the educational arena. Too often, we aim for the middle or average group and just hope the others will manage. Referring to Vygotsky's zone of proximal development helps us think more clearly about what is appropriate for each student. It is that "area" that provides challenge, without going beyond the student's comfort zone or edges, that is, without being too easy or too hard. We can't possibly provide a separate curriculum for each of our students, nor would that be advisable. The social interaction and exchange of ideas among students is too important a component of learning. So how do we expand our curriculum so that it is appropriate for students whose grasp of mathematics differs greatly from that of the majority of students?

Transforming Tasks

Choosing mathematical tasks is one of the most important decisions that we can make. While it is difficult for one task to be appropriate for all learners, most tasks can be transformed to be more inclusive, to allow a greater number of students access, and to provide additional students with possibilities for more expansive thinking. When we do this, we are casting a wider net that can "catch" a broader range of students. Our goal then is to transform or modify tasks, to meet a wider range of readiness. (See Figure 4–1.) Note that the range of learners does not change, nor the field that is deemed *appropriate*; rather, the tasks themselves are stretched to be better aligned with our students' needs. To do this, we begin with the tasks in our curriculum and consider how they can be modified.

Teachers have discovered a variety of ways in which tasks can accommodate different levels of readiness. One adaptation a teacher can make is to allow students to have some control over the difficulty level. This, for example, can be done with word problems. Instead of the standard format where all the numbers are provided, a word problem may be written without numbers and the student asked to provide them. For example, students may be asked to write numbers in the following word problem so that it makes sense:

> *Nora had _____ stamps in her stamp book. There were _____ stamps on each page. Then Nora's uncle came to visit and gave her enough stamps to fill _____ more pages in her book and add _____ stamps to the next page. Now Nora has _____ stamps.*

Figure 4–1   *Tasks can be transformed to meet a wider range of readiness.*

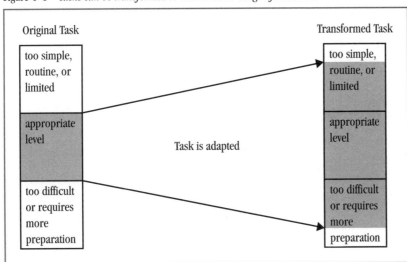

Students can choose numbers according to their comfort levels, but *must* recognize the mathematical relationships among their chosen numbers. This is an important point. Whenever we expand tasks in order to allow more access, we never want to do so in ways that undermine the integrity of the mathematical challenge. All students must have access to tasks that require mathematical thinking, not just rote learning or less complicated thinking.

Students can also make choices within simple practice assignments. Imagine a standard list of ten division examples. By changing the directions, *Complete exercises 1–10*, students can make choices according to their readiness. Consider the following alternatives:

Pick five of these examples that have a quotient that is less than twenty and tell how you know that will be so.

Pick one example and write four different division examples that will have the same remainder.

Pick one example and find the quotient. Then write a word problem that could be solved with this computation.

Another approach is to open up a problem so that there is more than one answer. Problems with more than one answer allow room for expansion. Some students will be quite satisfied with finding one answer and it may take them some time to do so. Other students may find one solution quickly, but be able and interested to find more possibilities. By removing information or by creating a greater number of choices, many problems can be adapted to allow for multiple answers. Examples of such problems include:

How might you shade three-eighths of this figure?

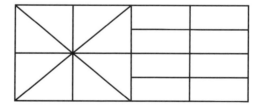

Jocelyn and Bryce each have some pencils. Together, they have fewer than sixteen pencils. If Bryce gives Jocelyn three of his pencils they will each have the same amount. How many pencils could each student have?

Use graph paper. Draw six different quadrilaterals with an area of six square units.

Here are the answers: 42, 2, 294, $3\frac{1}{2}$*
What could be the questions?

Number Story:
Sabina and Mike ran each day this week. Each day Sabina ran 3 miles in 30 minutes. Mike ran 6 miles in 72 minutes every day.

Possible responses: (Students may provide one or more questions for one or more answers.)

42: How many more minutes did Mike run than Sabina each day?
How many fewer minutes did Sabina run than Mike each day?
How many miles did Mike run this week?
At this rate, how many miles would Sabina run in two weeks?

2: On average, how many more minutes does it take Mike to run a mile than Sabina?
On average, how fewer minutes does it take Sabina to run a mile than Mike?

294: How many more minutes did Mike run than Sabina this week?
How many fewer minutes did Sabina run than Mike this week?

$3\frac{1}{2}$: How many hours did Sabina run this week?

Other choices for answers are possible, but it is usually best to limit the list to four or five possibilities.

Figure 4–2   *Example of students' answers to* What's the question?

Standard tasks can also be transformed by providing students with a "number story" and with "answers." Then students are asked to create questions within the given context that will yield the answers provided. Students can make choices about which questions they provide; they may also identify more than one question for some of the answers. (See Figure 4–2 for an example of such a problem, along with possible questions.)

Some tasks have multiple solutions in that there are a variety of ways to respond to them. The problem in Chapter 3, which required students to describe what they knew about shapes, is an example of such a task. Teachers usually create these tasks by thinking about the topic and identifying a broad question that taps into what students know, see, or recognize. Examples of open-ended probes include:

Write and draw to tell about fractions.

Your friend divided 3,208 by 8 and got the answer 41. What would you write and draw to show you friend what is wrong with this answer?

How would you describe a cube to someone who has never seen one?

What are some patterns you see on the hundreds chart?

How might we write numbers if we didn't have zeroes?

How is measurement used in your home?

Materials

Teachers have long recognized that children operate on a variety of levels in terms of their needs for concrete models. Therefore, the types of materials available may make the difference as to whether a problem is accessible. Consider the problem that follows:

> *Leah and Noelle have a large pepperoni pizza. Leah eats some of the pizza. Noelle eats $\frac{3}{8}$ of the pizza. Now $\frac{1}{4}$ of the pizza is left. How much pizza did Leah eat?*

Teachers can make a variety of materials available to children when solving this problem, including drawing materials, Cuisenaire rods, fraction strips, fraction pies, and a laminated picture of a pizza cut into eight slices. This is not to say that all students would choose to use these materials; many students might prefer abstract thinking. As we learn from the following teacher's reflection, however, having a range of materials available can provide students with access to this type of thinking.

Teacher Reflection

When I first began teaching fifth grade three years ago I thought my students would no longer need to use manipulative materials. I started my teaching career at grade 1 and so, of course, I expected my students to use concrete materials at that level. Over the years I've come to recognize that mathematical models are important at any age. This really hit home when I was taking a professional development course. We were solving a problem about twenty-seven small cubes arranged in one large $3 \times 3 \times 3$ cube. The question was about how many cubes had one, two, or three faces showing. I saw some people making drawings and some others apparently able to figure this out in their heads. There was no way I would be able to do that! I was so grateful for the small cubes that the professor had made available. At first I was embarrassed to need them, but then I saw other teachers starting to build with them, too. From that moment on I vowed that I would always have different kinds of materials available for student use.

During the past year I've tried to pay closer attention to which kinds of materials my students prefer. I noticed that some of them use base ten blocks when we are working with decimals, some find the decimal squares easier to use, and others prefer to draw their own models. In the fall some of my students were reluctant to use materials of any kind. I encouraged them to try concrete models and kept a variety of manipulatives available. If I see a student really struggling I will bring materials over and suggest we work together. But, I try to only intervene when necessary. I want my students to realize that ultimately they are in charge of their own learning and responsible for making choices that help them to succeed.

Tiered Activities

Sometimes even open-ended tasks need to be differentiated in order to be successful with a wide range of student readiness. In this case, tiered activities can be used or created. Such activities allow students to focus on the same general concept or skill, but to do so according to their levels of readiness. Consider the following example from a fourth-grade classroom.

The teacher begins the lesson by rolling out a walking number line that begins on zero and ends on one hundred. She asks for a volunteer and Rita comes to the front of the room. The teacher then shows the students a bicycle helmet that has been covered with aluminum foil. "I want you to imagine that Rita is a robot," the teacher says as she offers the helmet to Rita, who puts it on immediately. "Now Rita is a very special kind of robot," the teacher continues to explain. "She only takes steps that are five spaces long. We'll call her a five-stepper. When Rita begins at zero, where will she land first?" the teacher asks. The teacher is met with a chorus of "five," and Rita takes a step starting at zero, and landing on five. The teacher believes that students have an initial understanding of the context. To be sure, she asks students to talk with their neighbors in their whisper voices about the next three numbers on which the robot will land. Rita then demonstrates the walk.

Next a couple of other students take the opportunity to be a five-stepper robot. Roberto starts on two and makes five steps, with the students calling out the landing numbers (7, 12, 17, 22, 27 . . .) as he walks. Then Maria dramatizes the robot, beginning at four. The students enjoy being the robot; they wear the helmet as they demonstrate and walk in a stiff manner, without bending their knees.

Believing that the students are now ready to investigate this situation further, the teacher shows the students' names listed in three groups on a piece of chart paper. Within each group the students are free to form partnerships or to work alone. Each group is also color-coded to correspond to the folder in which students will find copies of tailor-made direction sheets for their group. Red is associated with the first level of the task, blue with the second, and green with the third. (See Figure 4–3; see also Blackline Masters for individual tasks identified by color.)

The teacher is thrilled by how seriously each group takes up its challenge. She is happy that the students are so engaged and delighted that they are getting a lot of practice with computation. The task also provides them an opportunity to identify patterns, think about how to organize their data, and explore relationships between addition and multiplication. A few students will also explore algebraic thinking. She wonders what her students will do when they come across some patterns that are not as obvious as the patterns that occur when the robot is a "five-stepper." The teacher is also curious to see how students will compute. She expects to observe a wide range of strategies including counting on, paper-and-pencil techniques, and mental arithmetic. She believes she will see some of these behaviors across the three groups. That is, some students who are ready to work with greater numbers may sometimes rely on less complex strategies, while students not ready to work with greater number may occasionally feel enough comfort and familiarity with the particular numbers chosen to use more advanced strategies.

The students assigned to the red (first) tier task take a bit of time to collect paper and pencils and focus on the task. Once they begin, however, they maintain their attention to the work. Kara and Leslie sit together, though each works separately. They both record *3* and then Kara uses a number line to find the next numbers and Leslie counts up on her fingers. They work at a similar pace and check with each other every four numbers or so. They continue in this manner until Kara stops at seventy-eight and Leslie stops at eighty-three. When they compare, they notice this disparity and Kara suggests that they, "Just count to check." She places a finger on each number she has recorded while counting by ones. She is at fifteen when her finger reaches seventy-eight. She turns to Leslie and says, "See fifteen. We stop at seventy-eight." Lesley agrees and erases the eighty-three even though in actuality, eighty-three is where the robot would land after the fifteenth step. Kara has included the starting number, three, in her count.

Red Group

The five-stepper robot starts on the number 3 and takes a walk.
- On what numbers will the robot land when it takes fifteen steps?
- Write the numbers.
- Make a list of the patterns you see in the numbers.
- Think about:
  patterns in the ones place
  patterns in the tens place
  even and odd number patterns
  patterns in the sums of the first and second number, the third and fourth number, the fifth and sixth number, and so on

Start the robot at a different number.
- On what numbers will the robot land when it takes fifteen steps?
- Which patterns stay the same?
- Which patterns change?

Blue Group

The five-stepper robot is going for a walk.
- Pick the number on the line where the robot starts.
- On what numbers will the robot land when it takes fifteen steps?
- Pick a different start number.
- On what numbers will the robot land when it takes fifteen steps?
- Write about patterns you find in your lists.

Now do the same with a four-stepper robot.
- What patterns do you find?

Green Group

Imagine that you have several robots: a two-stepper, a three-stepper, a four-stepper, all the way to a nine-stepper.
- Pick the number on the line where the robots will start.
- Explore the walks of four different robots.
- Try at least two start numbers for each robot.
- Write about the patterns you find in your lists.

Choose a robot that you have not yet explored. Try to predict how many steps it will take for the pattern in the ones place to repeat. Explain your thinking and then check your prediction.

Figure 4–3 *Task descriptions for tiered fourth-grade robot stepper problem.*

The girls appear to believe they have finished, when the teacher reminds them to look back at the task directions. They read and look at the digits in the ones place. Leslie is excited to notice that the threes and eights alternate. Together they realize that the digit in the tens place is repeated twice and then increases by one. Though they do not use this language, their recognition is demonstrated when Kara says, "Look, it goes one, one, then two,

two, then three, three." Leslie joins in on the second three and they continue through their list. Leslie records that every other number is even, and then works hard at finding a pattern in the sums of adjacent numbers. (See Figure 4–4.) They do not have time, today, to start the robot on another number, nor do they seem to realize that the pattern could have helped them to identify the next numbers. They have found several patterns, though, and their sums are accurate.

Chan and Zane are working nearby. Chan has limited English usage, though he clearly understands the task from the class introduction and demonstration. Zane is less clear about what they are supposed to do. He looks at Chan and shrugs his shoulders. Chan records *3* and *8* quickly. Then he points to the three and holds up his left hand. He puts down one finger at a time until he has a closed fist and then points to the 8. Zane's face registers understanding and he counts aloud to thirteen as Chan lowers his fingers. Chan records *13* and, as they lack computational fluency, they continue in this manner until they reach eighty-three.

The students assigned to the blue (second) tier seem to find the materials they need and begin the assignment more quickly. Coincidently, there are several boys in this group of eleven students and many begin by drawing a robot. Unlike most of the other students working on the first two levels of this task, Jake and Lenny record their data vertically. They list numbers and then count to see if they have fifteen steps, making check marks as they do so. Through conversation they decide that their start number is not a step and cross it off. They explore patterns with a five-stepper robot and as Jake says, "We don't have to really do the math. We just follow the patterns. It's always every other." The teacher asks why that might be so and they look confused at first. Then Lenny says it's

Figure 4–4 *Leslie's recordings.*

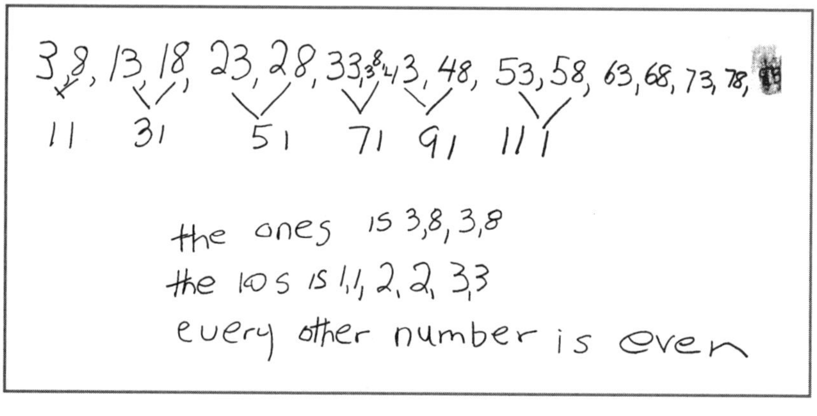

Math for All: Differentiating Instruction, Grades 3–5

always like five, then zero, when you count by fives, so the other is the same, but just up two." The teacher recognizes that they are beginning to make connections, but don't yet see that by adding two fives, they are adding ten, and thus the ones digit will be the same every other time. But this is enough for now and they are eager to begin working with a four-stepper to see if it will be the same.

As they begin to record the four-stepper Jake announces, "Wow, this is different. We have to do the work." They once again cross off the start number and then continue making their list, counting every so often to see how many more steps they have to record. When they are finished, they sigh and put down their pencils. Then Lenny points to the written task description and says, "But there must be a pattern because we're supposed to look for one." Jake replies, "Look they're all different, seven, one, five, nine, three, seven, one, five, nine, three, seven, oh, oh, look." With excitement he then draws lines under each number that ends in three and shows Lenny the pattern in the ones place. "I wish we saw that earlier," replies Lenny. (See Figure 4–5.)

Figure 4–5 *Jake and Lenny's work about a four-stepper robot.*

Rita, Colleen, and Amy are working together and Rita assigns each a role. She declares, "Colleen you can be the robot because I've already done that. Amy, you tell Colleen where to walk and I'll write the numbers." They follow this system carefully and record two sets of data for a five-stepper. Their process, however, requires more time than other methods and they don't have much discussion about the patterns. Rita announces that the numbers alternate and the other two girls confirm her idea. The teacher notes that she wants to make sure Colleen and Amy record numbers as well when they work again so that they, too, can focus on the data.

Michael is working alone. He continues the five pattern all the way to 393. When the teacher asks about his work he replies, "It's an easy pattern and so I wanted to keep going. It feels good." She comments on how many numbers he wrote and asks him to choose a different robot to try.

There are six students assigned to the green (third) level tier. They are able to work independently of the teacher, checking with each other if they have any questions. Though they record their ideas separately, there is much group conversation in the beginning. They seem to enjoy the freedom to begin wherever they want on the number line. After a brief discussion of choices, it is decided that Jon and Todd will begin on −1. They draw a number line to decide on where the first jump will land. They create tables for the two-, nine-, eight-, and four-steppers and then explore a 4.1-stepper. (See Figure 4–6.)

Lisa and Mike are intrigued with negative and decimal numbers. The teacher hadn't expected this and is quite surprised by this interest. They explore several starting numbers for different steppers. They discuss their lists and Lisa decides, "Sometimes the patterns work and sometimes they don't." Mike nods and adds, "Like the negative ones." Ironically, because these students are so interested in choosing and exploring different numbers, they are just beginning to discuss patterns when it is time to come back together as a class.

While students don't meet as a whole class each day, this teacher believes it is important for students to share their work at some point in a tiered activity. Students from the red group (first tier) report first. They explain the patterns they found with the five-stepper. The teacher notices that the students in the green group (third tier) are paying close attention and looking at their lists of numbers. She wonders if they are trying to discover more patterns themselves.

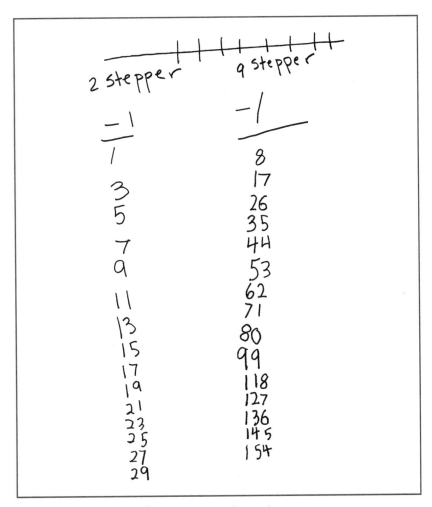

Figure 4–6   *Lists for two- and nine-steppers, starting at –1.*

Next the teacher asks Jake and Lenny to begin the blue group (second tier) report so that they can be the first to show their use of a vertical list. After they report, she asks the students whether they think it is easier to see the patterns when they write across the page or when they write down the page. Some of the students who wrote horizontally say they would like to try a vertical list next time. Other students think that listing that way takes up too much paper.

Finally the students in the green group report. "We started at negative one," Jon begins. "Does anyone have a question about that?" Rita raises her hand and so Jon assumes the role of teacher. He says, "Imagine I'm a robot at zero. Would I step forward or backward to get to negative one?" Kristen responds, "Backwards," and Jon asks if everyone agrees. Rita shakes her head and then says, "No, it would be two steps." Jon looks perplexed for a moment and then says, "Oh, I get it. You think there is a negative zero." Rita nods and asks if she can draw a number line on the board. She then proceeds to draw a line that contains both 0 and −0. Jon erases the negative zero explaining, "There's the right side and the left side. Zero is just itself in the middle." Rita seems satisfied with this explanation.

During indoor recess the teacher notices that two of the students from the green group, Meagan and Brooke, are off in a corner working intently. The teacher listens for a while and learns that they are still exploring the robot task, but this time they are not working with negative or decimal numbers. They begin with a three-stepper that starts at four. (See Figure 4–7.) Then they decide to add the digits in each of the landing numbers and find the repeating pattern of 4, 7, 1 in these sums. When they get their first double-digit sum (10) Brooke says, "No we want the pattern to be

Figure 4–7 *Brooke and Meagan explored several patterns and then developed a generalization.*

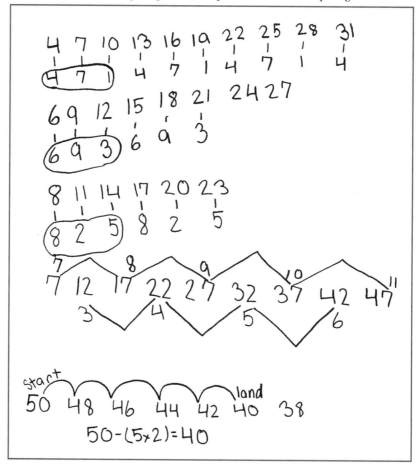

the same. If we just keep adding, we get one." Meagan agrees and erases the 10 and replaces it with 1. The students are excited by this simple pattern and decide to try another three-stepper. This time they start at 6 and they again find a pattern in the sum of the digits: 6, 9, 3. Meagan gets very excited at this point and tells Brooke, "Look it's just like our other pattern, but it's two more and our start number is two more."

They try another starting number and then decide to consider a five-stepper. They are drawn to what they call the "every other pattern" and decide to find the sums of these digits. At this point, the teacher intervenes and asks about their thinking. Brooke responds, "We wanted to find patterns like the first group. Our numbers were more fun for adding, but not for patterns." When recess ends the students put their work away, but find another opportunity to work that afternoon. This time they focus on "backward steppers" and develop a generalization to represent the relationship between the "start and land numbers." The teacher looks forward to the students sharing their work tomorrow, after others have had the opportunity to do more investigation as well.

Teacher Reflection

The math consultant for my district encouraged me to try this problem with my students. I have never tried a tiered task before, but have been concerned about the broad spectrum of learners in my classroom. I was surprised that so many of the students wrote their numbers across the page. We have been playing Guess My Rule games recently and recording the data in a table. I just assumed they would write vertically. I guess the way we read and write is just too persuasive for most students to think about recording in a different manner. I was also surprised by how many students drew robots. Were they just hesitant to think about the task or did the drawing help them to focus on the context and make a plan?

My biggest surprise was that the third-tier students did so little pattern finding initially. I could really see how the way the first-tier task was written helped those students to find patterns. Did the other tiers need more help to get started? I think I would offer them a bit more support next time. I liked the fact that the third-tier students paid attention to the first-tier report and that it simulated their thinking. They were just so excited about collecting the data and working with less ordinary numbers that they couldn't step back. As Meagan and Brooke showed me, this is such a rich problem and there is so

(Continued)

much more that the students can discover. Maybe I will put some graph paper out and see if anyone decides to make a line graph of the results.

It was wonderful to observe how well the students stayed on task. I could really see the power of tiered tasks. The students were willing to work so long because they were challenged at just the right level. Too often some of my students who have difficulty give up too easily and some of my better students just rush through things sometimes. Also, I never would have expected the conversation about −0. That never would have come up at all if the students hadn't been able to choose the robot's starting positions. It was so much fun to watch Jon be a teacher and to see Brooke and Meagan spend their recess on this!

The story from this fourth-grade classroom demonstrates the effectiveness of tiered assignments. This is usually the case when the teacher has a clear rationale for creating the assignment and makes sure that the activities include mathematical ideas at varying complexities so all students can be challenged appropriately. Simultaneously, the teacher made sure that the task could be approached from a variety of entry points and was thus accessible to all students. Finding the right combination of accessibility and challenge is the goal of a tiered approach. In this case, some additional support may have led the most ready students to focus more on pattern finding. (See the three Blackline Masters; note that the task has been adjusted slightly to prod more pattern thinking in all of the groups.)

Creating tiered assignments

So how do we create tiered assignments? As always the first step is to identify the important mathematical ideas. Consider third graders studying geometric shapes, focusing on three-dimensional shapes such as rectangular and triangular prisms, cylinders, and pyramids. They are also reviewing quadrilaterals (as a general name for all four-sided figures), identifying rectangles, squares, trapezoids, and parallelograms as particular types of quadrilaterals. Teachers can use "shape critter" tasks to reinforce these content goals while also providing students with opportunities for deductive reasoning and problem posing. The shape critter tasks ask students to identify similarities and differences among critters made of shapes. It often helps to begin with the middle level, focusing on what you would expect most of your students to be able to do. (We will call this level, or tier, blue.) A shape critter card can then be developed for that audience. (See Figure 4–8; see also Blackline Masters.)

Each of these is a whirly do.

None of these is a whirly do.

Which one of these is a whirly do?

Describe the characteristics of a whirly do:

Make up a name for these critters and write it in the blank.
1. Each of these is a _____.

Draw one more critter. Be sure it fits the rule.

2. None of these is a _____.

Draw one more critter. Make sure it doesn't fit the rule.

Describe the characteristics of this critter.

Figure 4–8   *Blue tier shape critter card for grade 3.*

The blue card begins with "whirly do figures," three-dimensional figures with a curlicue. Three-dimensional figures without the curlicue do not fit the rule, nor do two-dimensional figures with a curlicue. Students then are asked to complete a critter series by naming the critter and adding a figure to each section. In both tasks, the students are asked to write about the characteristics of the critters.

Two other tiers can then be developed by adjusting the middle (blue) tier. For example, in a simplified version (red), all of the whirly do figures in the top half of the card have curlicues, so the student does not have to consider this characteristic; they need to focus only on figures with three dimensions. The second half of the card is the same as the blue tier except that students talk about the characteristics rather than write about them. (See Figure 4–9; see also Blackline Masters.)

In a more challenging version (green), the whirly do figures on the top half of the card are the same as the blue tier, requiring students to attend to both characteristics. In the second half of the card, however, students completely create the critters and accompanying drawings. (See Figure 4–10 on page 102; see also Blackline Masters.)

A tiered task for data collection and analysis requires students to conduct a survey, represent and interpret results, and compute costs related to the data. (See Figure 4–11 on page 103; see also Blackline Masters.) In the simplified (red) tier, students plan a class trip. Four choices are provided for the trip in order to make the data more manageable. The computation will most likely involve multiplying to find the total admission fee and then adding the cost of a bus. The more challenging (blue) tier requires students to collect data to make recommendations to an athletic store about sneaker preferences. It does not restrict the data and the computation is also more complex, perhaps necessitating finding averages. The most challenging (green) tier asks students to prepare for a luncheon with their kindergarten buddies. They are responsible for planning the lunch and the activities, and again, the choices are not limited. At least one of their graphs must be a double bar graph and the computation is far more complex, requiring them to first decide on the quantities of food they will need to purchase, analyze the caloric and sodium content of the food, and estimate the total cost of the food.

A tiered task involving pattern finding and algebraic reasoning shows how broad the tiers can be, reaching a wide range of readiness. All tiers involve the same growing pattern of arches for which

Each of these is a whirly do.

None of these is a whirly do.

Which one of these is a whirly do?

Talk with your partner about what makes a whirly do.

Make up a name for these critters and write it in the blank.
1. Each of these is a _____.

Draw one more critter. Be sure it fits the rule.

2. None of these is a _____.

Draw one more critter. Make sure it doesn't fit the rule.

Talk with your partner about these critters.

Figure 4–9   *Red tier shape critter card for grade 3.*

Each of these is a whirly do.

None of these is a whirly do.

Which one of these is a whirly do?

Describe the characteristics of a whirly do:

Make up your own critters and their characteristics.
Write their name in each blank.
Draw the pictures.
Write your rule on the back.
Trade cards with a friend and find the rules.

1. Each of these is a _____.

2. None of these is a _____.

3. Which of these are _____?

Figure 4–10   *Green tier shape critter card for grade 3.*

Red Tier

Plan a Class Field Trip

1. Survey your classmates to find out the type of field trip they would like. The choices are a science museum, a historic tour, an art museum, or an aquarium.
2. Prepare a report of what you learn. In your report include:
   - the choices each person made
   - a table of your data
   - a bar graph of your data
   - your recommendation for a class trip
3. Consider the cost of the class trip. Your jobs are to:
   - brainstorm possible costs (remember four parent helpers)
   - use the computer or make calls to collect data
   - find the total cost

Blue Tier

Consult to a Business

The local athletic store wants to know more about students' preferences for sneakers. The owners are interested in learning more about the number, color, size, and types of sneakers that they should keep in stock. You are collecting the data for our classroom and preparing a report.

1. Make sure to include raw data, tables, and graphs in your report as well as your recommendations.
2. Investigate prices of sneakers. Based on your data, how much do you think your class will spend on sneakers this year?

Green Tier

Plan a Lunch Party

We are going to have lunch with our kindergarten reading buddies. Use supermarket flyers to prepare possible choices.

1. Collect data about lunch preferences and activities for both classes. Make sure to include raw data, tables, and graphs in your report as well as your recommendations. At least one of your graphs must be a double bar graph representing data for both classes.
2. Analyze your menu. Use references to estimate total calories and sodium content.
3. Make a shopping list. Use the flyers to find the price of the items we will need to buy. Explain how to use the information to estimate the total cost of the lunch.

Figure 4–11 *Tiered activity for data collection and analysis.*

the first three models are shown: arch 1, arch 2, and arch 3. In the simplified (red) tier, students begin by physically building arch 4 and drawing arch 5. They answer specific questions about arch 6 and arch 7 and then identify the number of pieces that would be needed to build arch 8. (See Figure 4–12; see also Black-line Masters.)

Arch Patterns

Look at these arches.

It takes 4 squares, 1 rectangle that's not a square, and 4 triangles to build arch 2. So, it takes a total of 9 pieces to build arch 2.

Assume the pattern continues.

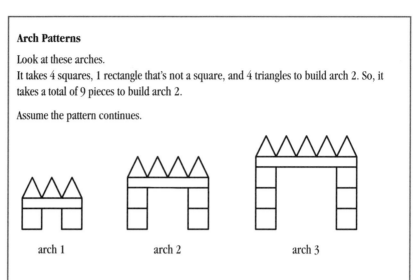

arch 1   arch 2   arch 3

Red Tier

1. Make sure you see the 9 pieces in arch 2.
2. Use the squares, rectangles, and triangles to build arch 4.
3. How many pieces does it take to make arch 5?
4. Draw arch 5.
5. How many squares are there in arch 6?
6. How many triangles are there in arch 7?
7. How many pieces does it take to make arch 10? Explain your thinking.

Blue Tier

1. How many pieces will it take to build arch 10? Explain your thinking.
2. In general, how can you use the arch number to find the number of triangles?
3. How many pieces will it take to build arch 40? Show your work.

Green Tier

1. How many pieces will it take to build arch 30? Show your work.
2. In general, how can you use the arch number to find the number of squares?
3. Rose Marie used 48 pieces to make an arch. What arch number did she make? Explain your thinking.

Figure 4–12 *Tiered activity for algebraic thinking.*

In the more challenging (blue) tier, students move to generalizations right away. While physical materials and drawings are options that they could choose to use, students are not directed to do so. The task begins with a question about arch 10. Then students are asked to create a general rule for finding the number of triangles and to identify the number of pieces in arch 40. In the most challenging (green) tier, students begin with the question about arch 40. The next question asks them to reverse their thinking; that is, they are told the number of pieces needed and are asked to identify the arch number.

Our class is going to make decorative boxes during art class to sell at the annual crafts fair.

Red Tier

Your group is going to decorate boxes that are 4-by-3-by-2 inches. You are going to cover them with the piece of wrapping paper provided. How many of these boxes can you cover? Be sure to think about different ways to put the boxes on the paper. Explain your answer.

Blue Tier

Our class is going to decorate 20 boxes that are 4-by-3-by-2 inches. We are going to cover them with wrapping paper. You can buy the paper in a roll or in sheets (see examples). What's the least amount of paper we should buy (rolls, sheets, or rolls and sheets)? Explain your answer.

Green Tier

Our class is going to decorate boxes that have a volume of 24 cubic inches. What size boxes could we have? (Each dimension is a whole number of inches.)

We are going to cover them with wrapping paper. You can buy the paper in a roll or in sheets (see wrapping paper at the back table). What's the least amount of paper we should buy (rolls, sheets, or rolls and sheets) to cover two boxes of each size? Explain your answer.

Figure 4–13   *Tiered measurement investigation.*

Measurement is a skill with obvious real-life applications. Anyone who has ever cut a piece of paper to wrap a present, only to find that the ends do not quite meet, knows the importance of spatial and measurement sense. Three tiered measurement tasks involving covering boxes with wrapping paper help students explore these challenges. (See Figure 4–13; see also Blackline Masters.) In the red tier, students are provided with the dimensions of a box and a sheet of wrapping paper, and asked how many boxes they can cover. This task requires students to think about the various ways to place the box on the sheet of paper. In the blue tier, students are asked to cover twenty of the boxes and to determine the least expensive combination of rolls and sheets of wrapping paper to buy. Along with placement, students must think about the measurements of both the sheet and the roll. In the green tier, the volume of the box is identified and students must first identify possible dimensions of the boxes. To do so, students must understand the relationship between volume and the dimensions of the box. Once the different sizes are determined, students find the number of sheets of paper needed to cover four boxes of each size. Ascertaining the best placement of the boxes is made more challenging because of the various box sizes involved.

Compacting

Along with tiered tasks, some teachers consider *compacting* content for more ready learners. This strategy recognizes that some content can be accelerated or eliminated for these learners. What remains is a more *compact* version of the standard curriculum. The process is similar to all models of differentiation: Key curricular ideas are identified, students are pre-assessed, and appropriate learning decisions are made based on that data.

Though compacting is often associated with gifted learners, it is important to remember that a variety of factors impact students' readiness. A student may have come from another school district or another country where the material was already considered. Students' interests or family culture may have already provided significant learning opportunities within a particular content area. For example, Gwen is a third-grade student whose father is a carpenter and in the process of remodeling their kitchen. Gwen often serves as her father's "assistant." She has been involved with making scale drawings of the new kitchen and measuring boards before her father actually makes a cut with the saw. Also, her father lived in France until he came to this country for college and so he uses the metric side of his measuring tools as often as the other. As a result, Gwen's exposure to standard measurement, measuring tools, and ways to reduce errors of measurement is well beyond her grade level. Though other mathematical units are well suited to Gwen, measurement is one that can be compacted.

Though compacting can serve a variety of students, teachers are sometimes reluctant to actually eliminate content from the curriculum. As we learn from this teacher, outside support for compacting can be helpful.

Teacher Reflection

Jamie seemed to walk in the door already knowing everything covered in our curriculum. Fortunately, my school system has been holding workshops on differentiated instruction. The presenter introduced me to the idea of compacting. I never thought about just eliminating some of the lessons. I was always trying to find a way for Jamie to be more involved, even if it was just to help others. I was reluctant to try compacting, but didn't know what else to do. I made an appointment with my principal and asked for her advice. She was supportive and encouraged me to try this approach.

Now Jamie and I hold a miniconference at the beginning of each unit. After pre-assessment, we look at the list of the unit's lessons together. He sees me check the ones that he is still responsible for and cross some of the others

---

out. Jamie is an independent learner and together we identify projects that he can do in lieu of participating in the other lessons. The plan is also shared with his family. Jamie is so much happier now that we have begun to compact his learning. He now offers to help his classmates more readily and looks more engaged during our class discussions. It's as if a burden has been removed from both of us. We no longer have to just make the curriculum work; we can change it more than I realized.

Additional Resources

Though this teacher has been successful with the compacting strategy, it does require teachers to monitor independent work and to have additional resources available. Teachers also need more resources for those students who need additional support. This need is felt particularly by some teachers who use nontraditional textbooks that have fewer practice exercises or problems. Exchanges with other teachers and Web sources can be helpful. The goal is to provide mathematical materials equivalent to our multilevel classroom libraries for reading.

Multilevel problem decks can provide for the broad spectrum of readiness within grades 3 through 5. Grade-level decks can be purchased and then teachers can redistribute the decks among themselves so that each class set contains cards for additional grade levels. If purchasing is not an option, problems can be found in old textbooks or in sample textbooks for each grade level. Cut out problems from lessons and paste them onto file cards of the same color. Then cut out examples of more challenging problems often included in special boxes within texts and highlighted as brainteasers or some similar title. Paste these problems onto files cards of a different color. You may want to search for problems across two, three, or four grade levels. Label the cards from each grade level with a different letter or use some other identification scheme. Then sort the problems by strand. So, for a particular strand such as geometry, you would have:

basic problems below grade level (color 1—A)

advanced problems below grade level (color 2—A)

basic problems at grade level (color 1—B)

advanced problems at grade level (color 2—B)

basic problems above grade level (color 1—C)

advanced problems above grade level (color 2—C)

This organizational approach allows students at all readiness levels to have access to more advanced problems as well as basic ones at their grade level. Though the initial creation of the deck is time consuming, teachers find that it serves their students well and can be used over many years.

Technology also offers teachers many resources. If one or more computers are available in your classroom, Webquests, applets, and practice games can help meet a variety of readiness levels. Virtual manipulatives are available at http://nlvm.usa.edu/en/nav/index.html, allowing individual access to a great variety of models, both in the classroom and at home. A worthwhile site for learning more about Webquests is http://school.discovery.com/schrockguide/webquest/webquest.html.

When students are learning new mathematical skills, they need to practice those skills. As you know, exactly when practice is needed, the length of time it is needed, and the level at which it is needed varies greatly among learners. Computer games often provide different levels of challenge and more and more practice games are available for free on the Internet. A game in which the focus is merely to practice should not be played for too long; once a skill is mastered, there is no reason to play the game. But for the brief time when a practice activity is needed, the computer game can make it readily available within a motivating format.

Each of these curriculum adaptations is a response to variation in readiness. In order to provide for a wider range of students, teachers can cast a wider net by:

1. allowing students some control over the difficulty level by having them
   - provide the numbers in the problem
   - choose exercises to complete
2. transforming problems so that they allow for
   - one or more solutions
   - a wider range of responses and understandings
3. providing multiple models such as
   - pictures of real objects or counters
   - different models of our number system such as number lines, base ten blocks, and hundreds charts
4. varying the challenge offered students through
   - tiered tasks
   - curriculum compacting
5. extending resources by
   - sharing materials with teachers at other grade levels
   - using Internet resources

Decisions to make these kinds of adaptations or to provide differentiated learning opportunities are grounded in knowledge of our curriculum and our students. As we choose among modifications we must remember that all students deserve challenging, thought-provoking problems and tasks. Too often, in the spirit of "helping," some students are provided with simplistic tasks or rules to follow that are not connected to conceptual understanding. Algorithmic steps such as divide, multiply, subtract, and bring down for division do not help the learner understand the division process. Similarly, oversimplistic statements such as "take-away means subtract" do not allow students to understand the variety of language or uses associated with subtraction.

Knowing our students and our curriculum are essential first steps, but making decisions about what content and teaching strategies are appropriate is where we begin the hard work of providing all of our students with improved access to the curriculum. It is in the conscious act of matching our students' needs with what our curriculum and pedagogy have to offer that differentiation helps us meet our instructional goals most effectively. Many times readiness is only one piece of the puzzle. This matching of tasks to learners also has to consider language, learning styles, and preferences. There is a need to develop ways to adapt tasks according to these factors as well.

Chapter 5

Breaking Down Barriers to Learning

The term *universal design* originated in the field of architecture. This philosophy of design is committed to providing inclusive environments that work better for everyone: door levers rather than knobs, curbless showers, and doors that open automatically are examples. Door levers are easier for older, arthritic hands and for anyone else carrying packages with only an elbow free for use. The idea is to build this way right from the beginning, rather than to retrofit spaces when special circumstances arise. So with this philosophy, all bathrooms would be built with wider doorways, not renovated when a family member needs to be in a wheelchair. In this type of environment, barriers to independent living are removed at the design stage. Access for people with physical disabilities is considered from the inception and everyone benefits from these decisions.

Many of our students face learning barriers in our classrooms. Students' readiness levels are not always apparent, even when conscientious teachers observe their students closely and provide tasks designed to pre-assess learning. Sometimes there are barriers that keep students from accessing prior knowledge or from demonstrating what they have learned. When not attended to adequately and respectfully, language, learning styles, sensory preferences, and anxiety can keep students from reaching their full potential as successful mathematical doers and thinkers.

Recently, educators have begun to think about a teaching philosophy that embraces universal design. What would our curriculum plans look like if we designed activities that worked for everyone right from the beginning rather than remediating or reteaching or in architectural terms, retrofitting, once original plans prove unsuccessful or inadequate?

Language

We begin with language and its impact on learning mathematics by thinking about a class of fifth graders. The students are working with three-dimensional shapes. Today they are exploring an activity called *viewpoint*. Students organize themselves in pairs and each student collects twenty-four cubes. The first task is for the partners to create structures with one of their sets of cubes. Then they make drawings of five views of the structure: top, front, back, left side, and right side. As the teacher walks around she marvels at the number of different ways the pairs interact. Mark and Russell work separately, each drawing a different view, and then agree that Mark will draw the top view. Craig and Martha work together. For some views, Craig does the drawing, for others, Martha, but they communicate as they draw. As the teacher passes their workstation she hears Craig say, "No, you need one more on the right." Pam and Trek also take turns recording the views. Trek's English is somewhat limited, but they point and shake their heads until they agree.

When the partners complete their drawings, some ask the teacher to check them. She tells them that they are ready for the next step, knowing that the second part of this activity will provide feedback on their accuracy. When the drawings are complete, the pairs of students are to cover their structures with cloth and exchange their "viewpoints" with another pair. Their goal is to use the other pair's drawings and the remaining twenty-four cubes to build an exact copy of the structure. Again, the teacher notices Pam and Trek pointing and gesturing as they work to build a structure that corresponds to the drawings. Trek beams with pride when the original structure is uncovered and found to match the one that he and Pam created.

Once all of the pairs have had the opportunity to build and check their structures with the originals, the students gather in the meeting area to discuss this activity. The teacher notices that midway through the conversation, Trek appears confused. The teacher is somewhat surprised. Though Trek is often unclear on directions and has a more limited grasp of English than many of the other students, he usually does well when concrete materials are involved. Earlier he truly seemed to enjoy his success, so why does he appear uncertain now?

Later in the day she finds time to sit with Trek and ask him about the meeting. She begins by saying, "I saw that you were able to draw the different views and to build a structure to match the drawings."

Trek sighs and say, "I think so, but no."

"What do you mean?" the teacher asks.

"Faces," Trek responds.

The teacher thinks back on the class conversation and remembers that Jonathan had introduced the idea that the structure really had six faces, but we were only drawing five of them. At the time the teacher noted that the students were using an everyday use of the term *face* in the same way that we might refer to the face of a building or a rock, as opposed to the mathematical term that explicitly identifies the flat surface of a polygon. By the mathematical definition, several of the structures had multiple faces on one of their sides. She decided not to interrupt the conversation at that point, but did notice when Ruth said, "We sometimes confused the right face with the left face" and Jason added, "We were surprised that we drew the back and front faces the same, but in the building, they were a lot different."

"Oh," the teacher said to Trek, "I should have made sure we stopped and talked about that word. I'm sorry." She picks up one of the smaller cubes that was nearby and asks Trek about its faces. Trek picks up the cube and starts drawing a happy face on one side of the cube. The teacher then begins to understand that Trek was thinking about a very different meaning for the word *face*. She places Trek's hand on his face and says, "face," she takes paper, draws a smiley face, and says, "face," and then points to a different side of the block and says, "face," again. She points to each face on the cube while counting them and says, "The cube has six faces." She repeats this procedure with a triangular prism. Then Trek counts the faces on both figures and slowly starts to smile. Tomorrow the whole class will review this term.

Fortunately, Trek's misconception was discovered because he cued the teacher to his confusion, the teacher followed up with him individually, and he was able to identify the confusing term. It would have been easy for the teacher to have missed Trek's visual cues or to have been unable to find the time to follow up on her instinct that something was amiss.

Misconceptions involving language are sometimes hidden. Learners may pretend to understand or be able to submit work that can be deemed correct in spite of their literal interpretations and misperceptions of the related mathematical terms. Students who are learning English or who have language difficulties may be reluctant to communicate their thinking. Note that the teacher first made sure to validate Trek's work. She also took some responsibility for the confusion. This stance helped Trek to feel more comfortable and to be open to clarification.

Students who are confident in their thinking are often more willing to expose their misconceptions as they are less concerned about having a different perspective. Consider Mabel, a third-grade student, who has collected data on the number of aunts each of her classmates has. After collecting the data she represents the information with Unifix cubes. The teacher reminds her to show the data in a line plot. With surprise in her voice Mabel asks, "Does each aunt have to be in the story?" The teacher is taken aback at first, but then realizes that Mabel is associating the word *plot* with creative writing. The teacher pauses and then says, "Plots are about stories. Graphs can tell stories, too. A line plot is a way to tell the story of your data." Because Mabel was comfortable asking a question immediately, the teacher could address the term right away. But as Mabel is a strong student in both language arts and mathematics, the teacher is reminded that even students such as Mabel can miss the nuances of our mathematical language.

It is common to hear teachers' concern about their students who are struggling to learn the language necessary to be successful in mathematics. The mathematics vocabulary of our elementary classrooms has increased dramatically in recent years and both teachers and students are sometimes challenged to use correct terms as they communicate their understanding of concepts. As one fifth-grade teacher explained, "These students have so many mathematical words to learn. When I went to school I had never even heard of a stem and leaf plot."

Some teachers invest a great deal of time creating word walls in their classrooms so that the students have constant access to the vocabulary related to current topics. At the beginning of the school year, one group of teachers began with words already posted on the wall and as the year went on, added more terms. Many of these teachers, however, found that several of their students did not refer to the word walls, even though doing so would have been beneficial. They found word walls did not work because they were a teacher initiative that did not involve the students.

The following year these same teachers had their students participate in the creation of the word walls. Students chose words they wished to define and illustrate and then posted their work beside the word strips. This level of involvement seems to have made the word walls more meaningful and students consulted them more regularly.

Sometimes it is difficult to separate language difficulties from mathematical ones. Naomi is being interviewed by her fourth-grade teacher late in the spring. "What is one-half of four?" the teacher asks. "One-half," she replies. Her teacher then asks, "What is one-half of two?" Again, Naomi replies, "One-half." Next the teacher asks, "If you have four slices of an orange and eat half of them, how many slices do you have left?" As he says this he points to imaginary slices of orange on the table and pretends to eat one of them. Immediately Naomi responds, "Two." When asked about eight in the same problem format, Naomi correctly identifies four as the answer. The teacher is not sure if the real-world model or the gestures were essential for Naomi to understand what to do, or if she just didn't understand the phrase, "one half of." The teacher wonders why Naomi's first response was one-half and decides to emphasize the language by saying, "Yes, one-half of eight is four." Naomi looks up at him a bit perplexed, but then her eyes widen and she says, "Oh, four and four is eight, so four is half." The teacher knew Naomi had made an important connection.

These classroom examples emphasize the important role of language in the teaching and learning of mathematics. For some students, talking about mathematical ideas can help to solidify concepts and further develop confidence. Occasionally, students such as Mabel have a minor difficulty or misunderstanding that can be addressed easily. For others, language can be a significant barrier, one that keeps them from grasping new ideas or from demonstrating what they know.

While language has always been important, today the relationship between language and mathematics is even more prominent. Now that the significance of problem solving is recognized, mathematical tasks are often presented within language-rich contexts. The once familiar phrase *show your work* is now often replaced with *explain your thinking*. These approaches to mathematics necessitate careful attention to mathematical vocabulary and to the language of mathematical reasoning so that these barriers to learning can be ameliorated.

The language of mathematics is both complex and subtle. It takes considerable experience for children to become comfortable with it. Even a mathematical term that has been discussed for several days can be more challenging than teachers realize. Students develop deep understanding of mathematical language only through several approaches that develop mathematical concepts and connections. Sometimes, when the nature of the activity changes, less than complete understanding is revealed.

Owen, a fifth grader, is identifying similar triangles. Throughout the lesson, he has been able to correctly identify the similar triangles within given examples. To challenge Owen further, his teacher has given him a cut-out triangle and asked him to make one that is similar to it. Owen picks up the triangle and turns it around, examining it from several perspectives. "Mine's tilted to the left," he announces, as he carefully looks for a piece of blue construction paper that matches the color of the triangle he was given. Owen looks at the triangle one more time before he carefully cuts out his own example.

When Owen is through cutting, he proudly shows his product to the teacher. His teacher looks disconcerted, but quickly changes her expression and says, "So tell me about your triangle." Owen holds up his original triangle and replies, "It's similar to this one. It's blue and it's tilted to the left." To probe his thinking further, the teacher asks, "So, what does similar mean, Owen?" He responds, "If the triangles are similar, they are sort of alike, like these two." After a bit more conversation, Owen agrees that the triangles would still be similar, even if he had used red paper, yet he maintains the idea that when the triangles "mostly look alike," they are similar. As we learn from the teacher's reflection, Owen's thinking came as a surprise.

Teacher Reflection

Owen had been completing the exercises so quickly, I was sure he would perform this task well. I really gave it to him because I thought he would enjoy the challenge. When I went back to look at the examples in the book, I realized how often "sort of alike" would be enough for him to choose the correct answer. At this grade level, we don't do much but identify similar figures. We talk about angle measures and length ratios, but I have to admit that I don't spend much time on this concept. I now realize that Owen was just looking at the figures to make a decision. In a way, his thinking is supported by our everyday use of the word, though he knew it applied to shape. This incident made me realize how important it is for students to create their own definitions and examples. If Owen had done so, he might have known that similar triangles must have the same angle measures and sides with proportional lengths.

We need to be sensitive to language issues. According to the 2000 census data, nearly one in five Americans speaks a language other than English at home (U.S. Census Bureau 2003). Before students are asked to complete mathematical tasks, we need to make sure that the language of the task is understood. To do this, teachers can:

- have students read the task repeatedly, as in a choral reading format;
- encourage students to dramatize word problems;
- ask students to summarize the task in their own words;
- preview specialized vocabulary;
- have vocabulary lists available when students write about their ideas;
- use pictures, models, and gestures to clarify ideas whenever possible;
- have students try out their thinking in pairs or small groups, before speaking in front of the whole class;
- make sure that symbolic notation is mapped carefully onto everyday situations and concrete models;
- speak slowly and avoid idioms and contractions; and
- pose problems in familiar contexts that students will recognize.

We also need to pay attention to particular terms that may be problematic. For example, many mathematical terms, such as *face*, *plot*, and *similar*, have a different meaning in everyday usage. One classroom teacher helps students note these different meanings through dramatizations. She begins by reading *Amelia Bedelia Helps Out* by Peggy Parish (1979). The teacher pantomimes Amelia as she dusts the crops and sows the seeds. The students giggle as Amelia misinterprets directions left by her aunt. After the story, as an example of what could happen in the classroom, the teacher dramatizes telling Amelia to make a table to show her data. Then acting as Amelia, she pulls out a hammer and nails and says she needs to find some wood. The students laugh and talk about how Amelia Bedelia makes sense of the directions. Throughout the year the teacher refers to Amelia whenever she wants to make a distinction between a mathematical and everyday meaning of a particular term. Examples of words found in the elementary curriculum that have different everyday and mathematical meanings include:

count   edge

difference   expression

face	plot
factor	point
fair	range
graduated	real
height	ruler
identity	set
left	side
mass	similar
mean	table
net	turn
odd	volume
one	yard

Homophones, or words that sound the same but have different spellings and meanings, can be similarly problematic. Again, special attention should be given to these terms and humorous examples can be helpful. One teacher tells her students about the following conversation and asks them to figure out what happened.

> *Two people leave a doctor's office when one says, "What was your weight?" The other replies, "Five minutes." "Oh," says the first. "Mine was one-hundred thirty pounds."*

Examples of mathematical words with everyday homophones include:

cents/scents	plane/plain
eight/ate	sum/some
fair/fare	symbol/cymbal
hour/our	week/weak
one/won	weight/wait
pi/pie	whole/hole

Some everyday words sound similar to mathematical terms, including *cents/sense*, *half/have*, *quart/court*, *sphere/spear*, and *tenths/tents*. Teachers should enunciate these words carefully, record them when they are first introduced, and listen deliberately to students' pronunciation of them.

As with universal design, attention to language will benefit all of our students. When we listen deliberately to our students and ourselves, and attend deliberately to the language used, students are better able to access their previous learning as well as to better understand the tasks they are asked to perform. Like all language skills, learning the language of mathematics is an important goal for all students and can remove barriers to learning mathematical ideas.

Multiple Intelligences

Along with language, students differ greatly in the ways they prefer to explore mathematical ideas. Howard Gardner emphasized the differences among students' thinking when he developed his theory of multiple intelligences. He has now identified eight intelligences: linguistic, logical-mathematical, spatial, bodily-kinesthetic, musical, interpersonal, intrapersonal, and naturalist (Gardner 2000). When lessons and activities do not tap into different ways of knowing, barriers result. As limited knowledge and facility with basic facts can also become a barrier to success with more complex computation, let's consider the goal of learning basic facts through the perspective of multiple intelligences.

Attitudes about how to best learn these basic facts has changed in recent years. Most experienced teachers first learned their basic facts through memorization accompanied by timed tests. One hundred facts were presented on a single sheet of paper and they and their fellow students were given three to four minutes to complete the items. Often this ritual was repeated on a weekly basis. In between, they might have studied the facts for one number, for example, the seven's table, or practiced with flash cards. There was little or no instruction on conceptual models that could be linked to these facts or on ways to make connections between one fact and another.

Today's teaching tends to place more emphasis on conceptual understandings to support the learning of basic facts. Shortly after being introduced to multiplication through models, students begin to recognize that changing the order of the factors does not change the product, that is, they can predict that 3×5 will have the same product as 5×3. When introduced to division, many students intuitively realize that to find $45 \div 5$, they can think, "What do I multiply by five to get forty-five?" Several fact strategies are developed. For example, doubles such as 7×7 are emphasized and then used to find 8×7.

So is this a better approach to learning basic facts? The answer is not simple. Placing an emphasis on conceptual development is definitely a better way to learn the meaning of multiplication. In the previous approach, students often memorized the facts without ever developing an understanding of what multiplication was or how it could be used. Fact strategies may not be the best way, however, for all students to learn their facts. Such strategies often assume a logical-mathematical intelligence that may not match students' strengths. This is not to say that strategies should not be taught; rather, strategies should be part of a diverse approach designed to reach all intelligences. Possibilities for addressing students' multiple intelligences while they learn basic facts are summarized here:

Linguistic

- read a book and then make up multiplication and division story problems related to the characters in the story
- talk about fact strategies
- write poems about multiplication

Logical-Mathematical

- create fact strategies
- make generalizations (identity, zero property, commutative property)
- practice with puzzles, such as magic triangles with each side having the same product

Spatial

- find patterns on the hundreds chart
- decorate fact cards
- make triangle fact cards to connect multiplication and division
- use array models

Bodily-Kinesthetic

- dramatize story problems and fact strategies
- use counters to model problems
- play Jax to explore remainders

Musical

- create songs about facts
- relate rhythmic patterns to facts

Interpersonal

- practice with fact buddies
- discuss fact strategies in groups

Intrapersonal

- set personal fact goals
- keep a journal about fact strategies

Naturalist

- find examples in nature of things that come in fours, fives, and so on
- categorize facts that are best solved by particular strategies

Consider this third- and fourth-grade combination classroom where students are working with both multiplication and division basic facts. Among the many small groups is a cluster of three students working on computers. They are each playing a game that provides basic practice with multiplication facts. Chips, hundreds charts, and drawing materials are available for use. The game allows the user to choose the level of difficulty for each round. The less complicated levels focus on the factors zero through five and provide more time between examples. Mike has decided that he is ready for a more complicated level today, and he is excited about it.

Gil and James are writing a song about multiplication. Their words follow the melody of "ABC", a song first made popular by the Jackson 5:

> *ABC, easy as one times three.*
> *My mama is studying with me.*
> *Oo, ah, I want to know the answer to*
> *two times three.*
> *Oo, ah, I know the answer is six,*
> *because three plus three that six mix.*

The teacher is pleased to see the boys connect multiplication to repeated addition and to create a song that they are enjoying with others. She is certain that they know this fact, however, and wants to push them further without negating their hard work. After noting how pleased they seem with their song, she asks them to see if they can modify it a bit to connect to 8×3. They are beginning this new task enthusiastically as she moves to another writing group.

Brenda and Jill are among a group writing poems about multiplication facts. They have been building other facts from the square number facts that they know. Their poem follows.

> *Multiplication is really cool.*
> *It helps you at work and at school.*
> *We know our squares. They're just fine.*

Seven times seven is forty-nine.
Add one more seven to the mix.
Eight times seven is fifty-six.

As Jill describes, "It's a poem to help you. It shows how we get one fact from another." The girls return to their poem throughout the day. They change it a bit during snack time and look at it again during recess. They are quite proud of their work and ask the teacher if they may have a class bulletin board for "cool fact poems." The teacher agrees and several other poems are added over the course of the week.

Niki and Lucinda are among pairs of students who are also exploring how known facts can help to find other facts. They have pictures of arrays and a straw. When Niki chooses the 4 × 7 array, it is Lucinda's turn to place the straw in a vertical or horizontal line to separate the array into two parts. When Lucinda places the straw, two arrays result: 4 × 4 and 4 × 3. (See Figure 5–1.) The girls record the product of each new array formed and then use addition to find that 4 × 7 = 28. When they finish this example, Niki explains to Lucinda that they are using the "disbution" property.

Tina, Jared, Lori, and Tommy enjoy playing board games. Today they are playing *Multiplication Threesome* to practice their

Figure 5–1 *Array and straw result.*

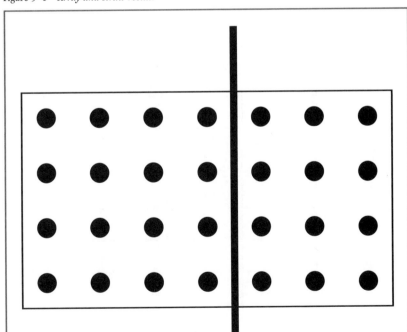

facts. The game boards are blank partial multiplication tables. The products are written on tiles and turned over. On each turn, a player picks up a tile and places it correctly on the board. The first player to place a tile that shares three complete sides with other tiles is the winner. Tina and Jared are working with factors five through nine, while Lori and Tommy focus on two through six. (See Figure 5–2.)

Janet and Casandra are connecting their multiplication and division facts. Together with their teacher, they have each identified ten facts that they want to practice. They then make their own fact cards for these examples. The teacher has shown them how to make triangle fact cards. (See Figure 5–3.) Triangle cards help students to connect the three numbers. The goal is for them to identify the correct number, no matter which one is missing. The two girls exchange fact cards and take turns covering up one of the corner numbers for their partner to recall. As the teacher checks on them she hears Janet giving Casandra a hint.

Figure 5–2 *Two levels of board games for practicing multiplication facts.*

×	2	3	4	5	6
2					
3					
4					
5					
6					

×	5	6	7	8	9
5					
6					
7					
8					
9					

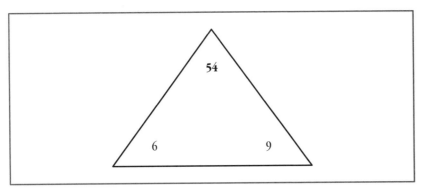

Figure 5–3   *Triangle fact card showing all three numbers in a fact family.*

"Think about ten times six," she suggests when Casandra struggles with 9×6.

Another group is working at the back table exploring number patterns on hundreds charts. Jack, Kelly, and Alysia are making connections between repeated addition and multiplication as they look for patterns. Jake volunteers immediately to count by twos and fives. Kelly said she would count by threes and fours, while Alysia quietly requests to work with six. Using colored pencils, they start their charts. Jake begins counting and shading 2, 4, 6, 8, 10, 12, 14, 16 when he realizes there is a pattern. "It's like every other one," he announces. At this point, he continues to shade without thinking about the numbers. Once he shades 50, he stops and takes a look at his chart. "Wow, this is even easier than I thought," he exclaims and proceeds to color in the rest of the five columns he has begun. He then takes another hundreds chart, and explains, "This is for counting by fives." This time he looks at the chart a bit before even picking up his pencil. When he does, he just shades the columns under five and ten.

Kelly decides to use one chart to keep track of the numbers she says when she counts by threes and fours. She starts off by shading all of the multiples of three purple, and all of the multiples of four orange. If a number is both a multiple of three and four, then she uses both colors. "Look at this," she says to Jack and Alysia. "All of the double ones march down the page to the right."

Alysia appears to be struggling a bit and somewhat distracted by Jack's quick completion. She decides to complete her chart in a similar manner. She starts at six and draws straight down her paper, finishing very quickly. Kelly, looking confused, says, "Something is wrong. Why is sixteen colored and not twelve?" Alysia shrugs her shoulders and responds meekly, "I just did what Jake did, I thought we were supposed to find all of the sixes, so I have six, sixteen, twenty-six, and thirty-six."

"Let's try it again," suggests Kelly and the three students work together to complete a chart for six. The students then place their completed charts in the middle of the table where they can all see them. Jake asks, "Well you know what we're supposed to do next. We have to ask, what do we notice?" Kelly responds, "I see that some charts have patterns up and down and some have patterns on the diagonal. I also notice that the number ninety is colored in on all of the charts."

At this point the teacher who was observing silently interjects. "Why do you think ninety is on all of the charts?" Kelly immediately raises her hand while the teacher gives the other two students a chance to think about it. She asks Jake first and he says, "Because it is even and most of the charts have even numbers on them." Alysia isn't sure and Kelly confidently states, "Well, ninety must be on all of the charts because we say ninety when we count by two, three, four, five, and six. So they are all factors of ninety, and ninety is a multiple."

The teacher asks, "What do you mean by factors and multiples?" Kelly explains, "Factors are the numbers you skip-count by and multiples are what you land on, also you can multiply all of the numbers by another number to get ninety."

The teacher turns to Alysia and asks, "What are your thoughts about what Kelly just said?" Alysia responds, "I can see that ninety is shaded on all of the charts. I'm not sure about the words *factor* and *multiples*." As the teacher works with Alysia, Kelly volunteers to write out definitions for *factor* and *multiple* to share with the group.

The teacher then takes the chart for six that Alysia helped to create and asks her to describe the patterns that she sees. She notices that all of her numbers are even, but that not all of the even numbers are shaded. The teacher responds, "Hmm, that is interesting. Tell me, would you find an odd number shaded on the twos chart?" Alysia confidently shakes her head as she looks at the pattern on Jake's chart for two and notes that all of the even numbers are colored and all of the odd numbers are blank. Jake interjects to say, "On the fives chart, all of the numbers end in zero or five."

The teacher is pleased to see that these students are beginning to make some generalizations about multiplication facts. Just before leaving she asks, "If you needed to know six times five, how would thinking about these charts help you?" Alysia offers, "I know it would be an even number because it is six times something and all of the numbers on the six chart are even." Jake adds, "I know it is thirty and I can picture the fives chart with ten, twenty, thirty, forty . . . all colored in." Kelly says, "If you had the chart, you could just count to the fifth number that was shaded."

Some of these students, such as those playing the board game, are at a similar level of learning, but some others, such as the students working on the hundreds charts, are not. The teacher likes to see students working in both configurations. She has learned that for game playing, teams need to have an even chance of winning, and thus be more similar, but in other activities, variety in abilities can lead to new possibilities. What's most important is that the students feel as if they are making progress and are enjoying gaining fact knowledge as opposed to experiencing it as an onerous task.

Engaging Multiple Senses

Being strategic and mindful of the purpose of the activities in which we ask our students to engage helps teachers to make powerful instructional choices. Having some control over their learning helps children to be more powerful learners. As we learn from the following teacher reflection, when we are trying to remember something, it is helpful to have several senses engaged.

Teacher Reflection

Last summer I read *Differentiation Through Learning Styles and Memory* by Marilee Sprenger [2003] for a course I was taking. It really made me think about memory. One part of the book that really struck me involved not being sure about whether we have turned off something. I can't remember if it was an iron or a stove in the example, but I remember the suggestion was to use all of the senses. Our eyes can see the dial move and our fingers are touching it, but we are not using our auditory memory. Just saying something like "I am turning the iron off now" can really make a difference! I began to think more about how I could improve my ability to remember things. I started looking at the key pad when I wanted to memorize a telephone number. Making a visual pattern of the numbers was much easier for me than just remembering what I heard the information operator say or what I saw in a phone book.

Next I began to think about my students and how challenging it is for some of them to learn their basic facts. I wondered if I were including enough alternative ways for them to practice their memory skills. This year I have made practice time more varied. The students have more of a choice in how they practice and I try to make sure that over time, visual, auditory, and sensory memory are involved. It seems to be helping. Just yesterday Billy asked me if we could add another practice time to our week!

As many fifth-grade teachers know, not all students master their basic facts by the end of grade 4. Such a deficit is a barrier to multiplication and division with greater numbers. As the students get older there is also more of a stigma attached to not knowing the facts. Students no longer use their fingers to count as freely as younger children do and it is much more difficult to draw models of multiplication facts than addition facts. Some teachers worry about how to attend to these students' academic needs without causing them to get further behind in other areas or without embarrassing them. One fifth-grade teacher uses a fact buddies system. She pairs students who need more work on their facts with first-, second-, or third-grade students. Students who still need work with addition and subtraction facts work with the younger children. The students begin by exploring different kinds of fact games. Then they choose one to make and play with their buddies. Many of the fifth-grade students are motivated to learn the facts for the first time. They want to be a good helper for their buddies. On days when there is indoor recess, the students can bring a game to play in their younger partners' classrooms. The students enjoy this privilege and their mathematics instruction time is preserved.

Anxiety

Anxiety can also be a barrier both to learning and to demonstrating what has been learned. Mathematics anxiety has received much attention in recent years and though early studies focused on adults, it is now recognized that it may begin early and is difficult to change once it is established. This anxiety is a major contributor to limiting the number of mathematics courses taken later in life. As a result, many people take only required mathematics courses, which can greatly limit career options. It seems essential then that we begin to address this learning anxiety in the elementary years.

While mathematics anxiety is not completely understood, experts recognize it as a specific anxiety, one that generalized anxiety alone cannot explain. Those afflicted experience a severe dread of the subject and tension that interferes greatly with their ability to work with numbers or to perform mathematical tasks in front of others. It can interfere with working memory to the point where new information cannot be stored or cannot be retrieved during a test. As one fifth-grade student explains, "I usually get a stomachache the morning of a test. I get all sweaty when the test is handed out. By the time I get my copy, my mind is totally blank."

Family attitudes, social factors, teacher judgments, and negative classroom experiences can all contribute to mathematics anxiety. Ideally, parents, teachers, and other school personnel work together to prevent its occurrence in the first place. For example, family math nights help many parents recognize that learning and doing mathematics can be enjoyable. The evenings can also be structured so that those parents who have their own mathematics anxiety are comfortable identifying themselves. Follow-up conversations can help them to understand the importance of not modeling or perpetuating negative attitudes for their children.

Schools should be sure to project a positive attitude about mathematics. Most schools have ample displays of students' writing and art work. Walls are often lined with posters related to books. Less often, we are greeted with a colorful and dynamic display related to mathematics upon entering a school building. Even a colorful bulletin board for "Numbers in the News" can help connect mathematics to the real world and make it more meaningful.

So what about our classrooms? It is clear that difficulty learning mathematics and low achievement in mathematics contribute to anxiety. Teaching mathematics in a rote, context-free manner makes it more difficult to learn and may result in more students suffering from anxiety. Providing rich contexts allows more students to relate to the subject and often suggests entry points to problems being explored. Small-group work may be less threatening than whole-class discussions, and concept building, rather than rote rules that can be forgotten easily, helps empower students' faith in their ability to do mathematics.

There are some caveats, however, to this approach. Over-emphasizing oral explanations and justifications can increase anxiety. Some students develop a great fear of doing mathematics in front of others, just as having the teacher walk near may cause some students to freeze. As one fourth-grade student put it, "I just can't do it and they all know it. How can I try it in front of them?" Students who feel this way may benefit from writing and rehearsing explanations first, and then reading them to the class. Also some students may perform better when creating explanations with a peer who will report to the group.

The following are some other ways to prevent or reduce mathematics anxiety.

- Promote self-talk in which students verbalize what they are doing with statements such as "First I am going to . . . ," in order to focus their attention and help them believe that they do know what to do. This is sometimes called *anchoring*.

• Build confidence by helping students recognize what they *can* do. Use questions such as "What do you know about this?" Keep samples of their work so that they can see their improvement over time.

• Keep number lines, hundreds charts, and calculators available so that students can use these devices to ensure accuracy.

• Use multiple sources of assessment and de-emphasize high-stakes testing. Understandably, teachers are under much pressure from all of the attention given to mandated tests. It is important not to share this pressure with the students. Test anxiety correlates highly to mathematics anxiety and vice versa.

• Have students keep a journal where they can record their feelings about mathematics. Journal prompts such as: *When we start a new topic in math I feel . . .*, *When I am asked to explain my thinking in math I feel . . .*, *When I am asked to come to the board in math class I feel. . . .* Teachers and students must be aware of these feelings in order to reduce them.

• Limit activities that are timed. Time is one more pressure that can greatly add to anxiety.

• Choose partners carefully. For some students, this may mean being in a group that works at a slower pace. For others, it may mean the need to work with the same partner throughout a unit.

• Let students set personal goals. When students set their own objectives, it gives them a greater sense of control, which in turn lessens anxiety.

• Integrate mathematics with other subject areas. Some students feel more comfortable performing mathematical tasks when they are related to an area of their strength or interest. A student interested in the Civil War may enjoy constructing a time line of that period, while a student whose favorite subject is science may be interested in collecting and analyzing data related to an experiment. Students also tend to develop more positive attitudes toward mathematics when it is perceived as connected to their world.

It is easier to prevent mathematics anxiety than it is to reduce it. If you think one of your students suffers from this affliction or appears to be developing attitudes and behaviors rooted in being anxious while learning mathematics, you may want to talk with his or her parent(s) and your school's guidance counselor. The Mathematics Anxiety Scale (Chiu and Henry 1990) can be administered to children in grades 4 through 8. In most cases classroom interventions are not sufficient. Anxiety management training usually also involves breathing exercises, visualization techniques, "I can do it" mantras, and desensitization. Working with parents and other professionals, teachers can work to prevent or lessen any future concern in this area.

Learning Challenges

The need for outside help is not limited to anxiety. Barriers, both visible and invisible, are very real for many students. The list of diagnosable learning disabilities seems to be growing by leaps and bounds as we learn more about how our brains function and what happens if an area is underdeveloped or functioning in a unique way. For many students the level of engagement and pace of learning in our elementary classrooms is overwhelming. While this is not a book about specific learning disabilities, we would be remiss not to take to heart the physical, emotional, and intellectual challenges of many students as they try to navigate the precarious terrain of mathematics. As we strive to get to know all of our students we can also recognize that no one classroom teacher can fully differentiate the mathematics curriculum for each and every student, every day. We need to be able to use all of the resources available to craft programs and meaningful experiences for each student.

In *Teaching Inclusive Mathematics to Special Learners, K–6,* Julie Sliva (2004) offers many techniques and insights that can help us meet our goal. Being able to distinguish what barriers might be present for a student is the beginning and her book offers many evaluation forms to help us make these decisions. Strategizing with colleagues and working collaboratively with assistants, tutors, remedial staff, and special educators is essential. In many ways, each educator can have a critical piece of the puzzle and together, the whole child can be seen more clearly.

As students advance in the elementary grades, parents who are able to do so sometimes seek tutors for their children. Tutors get to know our students in a different way and see them work in a different environment. Ideally, tutors are in communication with classroom teachers and insights gained from their sessions can inform classroom practice. Consider the following reflection of an experienced tutor.

Tutor Reflection

For almost twenty years, I have been working privately with math students in grades K–12. Over the years I have learned a lot about how children learn and what prevents them from learning. Most of my relationships with my students begin with a phone call from panicked parents requesting help for their children. Typically, the parent just received a report card and realizes that the child is struggling in mathematics. Nine times out of ten the child is resistant to working with me. The opportunity to receive tutoring is viewed negatively, more or less a punishment for not performing well. So my work begins with building trust and helping the student to feel comfortable with me. The goals for tutoring are to build confidence, to help the student to learn the necessary math at grade level, and to sustain the learning beyond the tutoring session.

One student I tutored was in the fifth grade when her mother called me. She described her daughter as a very social child who can memorize everyone's telephone number, but is unwilling to memorize her multiplication facts. Her daughter was failing math. Sure enough, Bea did not know her facts and she also was very weak in subtraction. As she explained, "Well, you see when I was in first grade, I was absent for two weeks and that is when the teacher taught subtraction, so I never learned it." So since first grade, Bea has carried this problem with her. Even though she had developed her own method of subtraction, she continued to view it is something that she missed and would never master. As for the multiplication facts, it turned out that Bea was unable to provide products in the speedy way she was being asked to perform in class. She actually had a good understanding of multiplication concepts, but would freeze every time the phrase *timed fact test* was mentioned. Conversations with her teacher helped to limit these tests and within a couple of months, Bea was able to retrieve the facts in a reasonable amount of time.

Another girl, Karen, struggled with algorithms for addition and subtraction. In second and third grade she spent hours learning these skills and finally mastered them on a rote level. Then fourth grade came and when she was learning how to multiply, she forgot how to add and subtract. She would get so frustrated that she would literally hit herself in the head asking for her brain to remember. Once she felt comfortable with multiplication, her addition and subtraction skills returned. Then along came long division and she forgot how to multiply.

I once heard a story that I shared with her about driving. We all can feel very comfortable driving our cars with the radio on and chatting with passengers until we hit a torrential downpour. Suddenly we need to turn off the radio and we can't talk. It takes all of our energy to concentrate on just turning the wheel and staying straight on the road, skills that are usually performed without thinking. I told Karen that I thought she needed to concentrate so hard on learning a new skill, that sometimes a skill that was once fairly rote became difficult if not impossible to remember. I think the story calmed her and made her feel less strange. She became more patient with herself and as she relaxed, she found it easier to remember previous skills. I also talked with her teacher. He agreed that while she was mastering a new skill, she could work with a partner when multiple skills were needed.

In both examples, conversations between the tutor and the student's teacher were critical. It doesn't always go so smoothly. Some students present more complex learning profiles and of course, many students don't have access to private tutoring. We need to be sure we are utilizing all school resources available to us.

In many schools Child Study Teams (CST) are formed as a venue for teachers to voice concerns about the lack of progress a student is making. Teachers are encouraged to share trepidations, raise questions, review student work, and share anecdotes about what is happening in class. In preparation, teachers often complete a form about the student's strengths or weaknesses and answer a few guiding questions for the pending conversation. Teachers may also wish to supply copies of current student work. Most teachers report a sense of relief following such meetings. As one fifth-grade teacher expressed, "More than I realized, I was worried that I was inadequate. My colleagues helped me to realize that I was making some good decisions. Just knowing that they were there to support me made me feel less isolated. I know I will bring more energy to my class now and feel more confident in the choices I make about this student."

Following the meeting, many of her colleagues checked with her to see how things were working. Their interest added to the teacher's belief that she could help this student. A special education teacher came to observe the class along with a math coach. Together, these three professionals developed an action plan and agreed to meet three weeks later.

More and more schools are looking at ways to increase instructional support in mathematics. System specialists now work more closely with teachers and students on assessment, curriculum design, implementation, and direct teaching. Some school systems are hiring assistants and tutors who focus on mathematics, and special education staff, who often have stronger backgrounds in literacy learning, are beginning to augment their skills. Many schools, however, still find that budget limitations keep all staff members from participating in professional development opportunities in mathematics or from receiving curriculum materials.

To remove barriers as successfully as possible, schools *must* provide these opportunities and materials to *all* professional staff and be committed to success in mathematics for all. Teachers must nurture open channels of communication with parents, specialists, assistants, tutors, and their students. They need to be willing to take risks, ask questions, examine their beliefs and behaviors, and make accommodations so that everyone achieves success.

Chapter 6
Scaffolding Learning

Scaffolds, a term related to architecture and construction, are temporary structures that remain in place as long as they are needed. The scaffolds are not permanent. Workers use scaffolds to get to parts of buildings that would otherwise be inaccessible; similarly, we use scaffolds to support students' learning. Training wheels are used when a child is first learning how to ride a two-wheel bike. These extra wheels allow children to ride successfully, something that would be impossible without the added support for balance. These wheels are removed when the child establishes his or her own sense of balance and is ready to ride without them.

Too often in the past our mathematics instruction has focused exclusively on students working independently, without support. Most of the time was spent working silently on the completion of seat work. Little or no assistance was given. At the end of a week or unit, each child took a test to determine what was learned. Fortunately, learning mathematics is no longer viewed as something that is done in isolation. Whole-class discussions and small-group work provide opportunities to share ideas and talk about what has been learned. These groups in and of themselves are a form of scaffolding. Many learners can do more when the classroom environment is communal. Help from a peer or collaboration with others are viewed as integral parts of the learning process.

With isolation no longer the norm, we can ask, "What can students do with support that they are not currently able to do on their own?" Another way to ask this question is, "What scaffolds can be put in place to allow students to be successful learners of mathematics?" Teaching with an emphasis on scaffolding presents a more integrated vision of teaching and learning. Teaching and learning are no longer separate, static activities, but interwoven events. The teacher develops a coaching style aimed at helping all students reach their potential. Scaffolding allows students to accomplish tasks that they would be unable to complete alone. Teaching, the act of supporting learning, is then viewed in a way more synonymous to how Vygotsky (1978) described the zone of proximal development. In this chapter we consider scaffolds that involve asking questions, focusing on strategies, having students collaborate, making connections, and using graphic organizers.

Question Strategies

One of the ways that teachers support learning in the classroom is by asking questions. It is important that our questions require students to go beyond their current comfort level and understanding. Frequently, simple questions are posed at a level of thinking that requires only recall of information, for example, "What do we call a figure that has eight sides?" By analyzing the questions we ask, we can make sure that we are inviting students to engage in more complex and deeper levels of thinking.

Though Benjamin Bloom first published his taxonomies in the 1950s, they remain helpful today. His cognitive taxonomy describes six levels of cognition: knowing, comprehension, application, analysis, synthesis, and evaluation (Bloom 1984):

> *Knowledge:* To know is to recall information that has been learned. Sample activities include telling, listing, naming, and reciting.
>
> *Comprehension:* To comprehend is to understand. Sample activities include explaining, summarizing, paraphrasing, retelling, and showing.
>
> *Application:* To apply is to use what has been learned. Sample activities include demonstrating, illustrating, solving, dramatizing, adapting, and incorporating.
>
> *Analysis:* To analyze is to examine an idea critically. Sample activities include comparing, categorizing, and deducing.

Synthesis: To synthesize means to put together in a new or different way. Sample activities include creating, inventing, formulating, transforming, and producing.

Evaluation: To evaluate is to determine the worth or value based on a set of criteria. Sample activities include making judgments, predictions, decisions, and estimates.

Since its inception, some people have viewed Bloom's taxonomy as linear and assumed that one can only move to the next level after the first levels have been mastered. Other educators see this view as problematic and believe students have been held back from potential learning opportunities because it was believed they would not be able to handle more advanced work in mathematics until they achieved less complex skills. No doubt everyone can think of students for whom the opposite was true, students who by nature engaged in analytical thinking even though they found it difficult to recall basic factual knowledge and thus did not perform well on certain types of tests. Seeing Bloom's taxonomy as more fluid can help us better challenge and serve our students.

One way to use Bloom's taxonomy is to categorize the questions we ask or tasks we provide to make sure that students are exposed to all levels. For practice, try categorizing the level of each of the following questions or tasks. The generally agreed-on levels are identified beneath the list. Note that more than six examples are listed and thus some levels will be labeled the same. This repetition is to make sure that final choices involve more than a simple process of elimination.

1. How else could you explain what Chad was saying?
2. Which estimation of the dog's weight do you think is best? Why?
3. Invent a new way to multiply these numbers.
4. What is the name of this part of the fraction?
5. Which strategy do you think is best? Why?
6. How does Sally's method compare to Janet's?
7. How many of these numbers have a 6 in the tenths place?
8. What number do you think will be next in the pattern?
9. What is a story you could dramatize for 72 ÷ 6?
10. Tell how rectangles and squares are the same.

1. comp. 2. eval. 3. synth. 4. know. 5. eval. 6. anal. 7. know. 8. eval. 9. app. 10. anal.

Although six different categories are provided, they are not necessarily discrete. For example, evaluating a pattern to predict what comes next (evaluation) requires that you first analyze the elements in the pattern that have been provided. Similarly, to dramatize a story for 72 ÷ 6 (application), one must first have knowledge and comprehension of 72 ÷ 6. Because of this overlap, it is sometimes difficult to distinguish one level from another. An additional concern is that some educators believe that synthesis, which involves creative thinking, is a more complex level of thinking than evaluation. One way to avoid these concerns is to create three categories: knowledge and comprehension, application and analysis, and evaluation and synthesis. Regardless of their exact organization, the goal is for the students to be engaged in more complex levels of thinking.

Scaffolding is one way to help students reach more sophisticated levels of cognition. It does *not* require us to start with a simple query and build up to more complex questions, as illustrated in the following sequence of questions:

- What is the name of this shape? (square)
- How would you describe a square?
- What is the name of this shape? (rectangle)
- How would you describe a rectangle?
- How is the square similar to the rectangle?
- How is the square different from the rectangle?

A more challenging approach would be to simply ask, "How are squares and rectangles alike or different?" Beginning with this question requires the students to do more of the work. They may want to draw the figures or to think about how they look. Sometimes we ask more demanding questions and then backpedal when students do not seem ready for the challenge. Too often, teachers backpedal after only two or three seconds, without giving time for students to collect their thoughts. Waiting longer can yield surprising results. There are other ways to scaffold this task than lowering its level, for example, having geometric materials always available in the classroom or asking students to first discuss their ideas with a partner.

Scaffolds are appropriate for our more ready students as well. If a task is really a challenge for them, then they too should initially need some form of support. As we see in the following reflection, until we push our more advanced students, we may not recognize their need for assistance.

I used to think my top students could just work independently no matter the task at hand. When I started to differentiate more and give them more difficult assignments, I found that they also needed my attention. It made me wonder whether I had ever been truly pushing their thinking or asking them to be in the domain of uncertainty that is often part of learning. I seem to expect that the students in my class who struggle may feel vulnerable as learners. I realized only recently that the top students may never feel this way. I now think I have viewed feeling vulnerable as weak or bad as opposed to a temporary place of discomfort that can truly help learners move on to new ideas, information, and understanding.

Focusing on Strategies

Today's reading instruction places an emphasis on reading strategies. This instructional focus asks even very young children to be aware of what is happening as they read and offers them a variety of ways to identify an unknown word as they come upon it in the printed text they are trying to comprehend. These good reader strategies are explicit. They are talked about during reading instruction and modeled by the teacher. Reminding readers of these strategies is a way to scaffold instruction. We need to make a similar cadre of strategies explicit for use when working with new mathematical content and tasks. Possible strategies, listed in the form of questions, follow. Note that the keywords *connect*, *try*, and *wonder* are used as cues to aid students as they take on this learning stance. Their use makes the learning process more transparent.

- *Connect:* What do you know about this situation?
- *Connect:* Have you ever solved a problem like this? How might that experience help you now?
- *Connect:* Are there materials in our classroom that can help you?
- *Try:* Can you make a drawing to help you?
- *Try:* Would a list or diagram help?
- *Try:* Will it help if you make an estimate?
- *Try:* Are there numbers you could put together or separate to make it easier?
- *Wonder:* What would you do if the numbers were smaller?
- *Wonder:* What might your friend do to solve this problem?

This morning I heard myself say, "What would a good reader do here?" I paused for a moment and wondered, do I have a similar phrase when a student is stuck solving a math problem?

Asking my students to think about what a good reader does has almost become a mantra in my classroom. I model good reader strategies when tackling a new word or making sense of what is happening in a story, and I have tried to make the process of reading come alive and be more accessible to the students in my class. From the first day of school my goal is to help them become proficient readers and writers and I have found it to be very effective to show them what I mean by being a good reader and writer. They are learning steps that they can rely on every time they come to an unknown word or begin to lose sight of what they are reading about. They are learning to stop, think, reread, read through the word, think about character motivation, note the significance of the setting, and much more. They know what I mean by a *strategy* and think about what sounds right, looks right, and, most important, makes sense as they read. But today I stumbled as I thought, do I give the same opportunities and models in math?

I see the strategies we use in reading and writing as a way of sharing tips that have been effective for other readers and writers that have come before. It's as though I have now given this newest group of students membership cards in the readers and writers club. Everyone gets a lifetime membership, not just some of us. Have I been this inclusive during math class if I have not made everyone aware of effective learning strategies when they run into trouble like they do in reading?

Making reading strategies a part of learning for all of my students has given all of us a common language that then allows everyone the opportunity to help each other. I love it when I hear one child turn to another and ask, "What's this word?" and the other child responds, "Remember, stop and think, what makes sense?" I'd love to hear this same type of interaction in math class.

Student collaboration

This teacher reminds us that by giving students developmentally appropriate tools and strategies, they have more opportunities to hone their skills both independently and collectively. Further, when we view every member of the classroom as a learner *and* a teacher, there are many more people in the room who can help others learn. Many teachers recognize the powerful possibilities that can arise when peers take on the teacher role. To help students engage in such behavior, teachers strategically structure situations that support peer teaching and learning.

When we engage in think/pair/share debriefings, we are using peer partnerships to scaffold learning. The thinking time may just be a few moments of silence or students might be encouraged to make a drawing, build a model, or jot down some notes before talking with their partners. Talking in pairs can help some students clarify their thinking or gain additional ideas. Sharing can happen between two sets of pairs or as a whole group.

Sometimes a simple "Turn to your neighbor and whisper your prediction" is enough to form partnerships. Direct modeling of how to work in pairs helps more efficacious peer partnerships to develop. Ideally, partners develop a sense of trust, a sense of responsibility to help one another, and a commitment to doing their best individual work. Partners also need practice in learning to strike a balance; that is, to be as helpful as possible without becoming overzealous and doing work for someone else.

Sometimes, when more independent work is preferred, teachers suggest that math partners sit across from one another rather than in the adjacent position usually preferred for reading partners. Materials can be placed between the students. The amount of shared text is much less than when reading a story, and placing written directions between them often is adequate as well. Depending on seating flexibility, you may want students to read tasks side by side first and then assume their working positions.

A variety of strategies can be adapted that foster peer collaboration. In some cases, when students are solving more than one problem, they are given one pencil and trade it between problems so that they take turns being the recorder. Pairs can also alternate recording the work (list, drawing, or computation) and the explanation. Some teachers prefer students to do the work and write their explanations separately, but then exchange their products for feedback, the same way as they might trade stories they have written. Early in the year, teachers can help students practice how to be helpful to their partners by asking such questions as "If your partner didn't know nine times eight, what hint could you give to help?" Over time a list of partner behaviors can be posted on a chart such as:

- Ask questions.
- Don't tell answers.
- Give hints.
- Respect each other.
- Listen attentively.
- Each take responsibility.

Consider this partner work at a school that is integrating its curriculum with the Winter Olympics. A specific country has been assigned to each classroom and this third-grade class is focused on Norway. Nathan and Carla are looking at the total number of events and the number of athletes planning to participate in each event. During their research they are surprised to learn that so many athletes compete in more than one event. Nathan comments, "Imagine being so good at more than one contest. That's totally cool."

Together, Nathan and Carla list all of the events and make a tally mark for each player that will be involved. As they prepare to make a bar graph of their findings, Carla says, "Oh no, now we have to write all of the events over, so that they are on the bottom!" When Nathan asks why this is so, Carla explains, "Because graphs go up and down." Nathan responds, "They can go up and down or across."

Nathan can see from Carla's expression that she doesn't think that this is the case. He decides to show her an example of a horizontal bar graph that the class constructed previously. They walk over to the "All About Us" bulletin board and Nathan points out the graph titled, "Lengths of Our Cats." Carla remembers this graph and even points out the bar that includes her cat, Beets Junior. She now agrees that their graph can "go right and left," and they return to their working area.

Nathan begins to number the horizontal bar of the graph. He has numbered up to thirty-seven when Carla asks him what he is doing. "I have to number all the way to the eighty-four. That's how many there are," he explains. Carla shakes her head and says, "I don't think so. There would never be eighty-four in one event." Nathan thinks for a bit and then says, "Oh, right, we only have to show how many in each sport. That will be a lot less."

Their teacher has been nearby during these exchanges and is pleased with the interactions. Each of the students contributed to their understanding of the task. They listened to each other's ideas and built naturally on previous knowledge. She knows that partnerships don't always work out this well, but she works hard at helping her students learn how to work together. As she put it, "I used to just direct them to work in pairs without helping them learn how to do so. Now I know better."

Making connections

The previous story also demonstrates the importance of making connections between mathematics and real-world applications. Students tend to be interested in the Olympics when they are occurring, and they provide a wealth of numerical data. Making connections is another way to scaffold learning. Students learn more easily when they connect what is to be learned to something they already know. This is one of the reasons that KWL charts are popular. By completing the K or *know* section of the chart, students are establishing their own understanding of the topic. They are also providing their teacher with pre-assessment data. By declaring what they *want to learn* (W), they are providing input into their curriculum. The final section (L) allows them to summarize what they *have learned* and reconnect to their original knowledge base by comparing the columns. An initial chart that fifth-grade students generated for geometry is shown below. Some teachers add an H, creating a KWHL chart. In section H students identify *how* they want to learn the new information.

Know	Want to Know	Learned
sides are lengths	Why names were chosen?	
2-D is flat	Who invented it?	
3-D is popping out	What shapes are used most?	
both math and art	How do all the shapes fit on a soccer ball?	
right acute, obtuse		
right is 90°	What was the first shape?	
acute is less than 90°		
obtuse is more than 90°		
90° lines are perpendicular		
parallel lines don't touch		

Making a connection or an analogy to something that is already known or is within a familiar real-world context helps students make sense of new ideas and gain access to curriculum that would otherwise be too difficult. One fifth-grade teacher, particularly concerned about the lack of connections her students are making among fractions, decimals, and percents, feels that "they are doing what I call 'school math,' but not making any connections to their own life, and therefore, not really internalizing the mathematics they are learning." She decides to work with the students to create a bulletin board about real-life connections and these topics. The bulletin board, titled "Don't be a fool, do math out of school," is in the hallway so that all of the fifth-grade classrooms can contribute. Students are given points for homework if they add an example to the board that shows how fifth graders think about fractions, decimals, and percents outside of class. Some of the items the students provide are:

- Don't be so hard on yourself if you are playing baseball and get a hit one out of every three times at bat, or about 33 percent of the time. You are doing as well as a professional baseball player.
- If you order pizza with your friends or family to be delivered to your house, you need to know decimals to figure out the money, and percent to figure out the tip. You don't want to rip off the guy delivering the pizza. He might make your food gross.
- When you leave for school, check out the weather forecast. If it is more than a 50 percent chance of rain, be ready to get wet.
- My older brother never understood decimals when he was in school. When he was getting gas the other day he didn't have enough money to pay his bill, so my mom had to talk to the gas station owner.
- It is easy for me to figure out how I do on a practice spelling test at home. I can do it in my head. For example $\frac{18}{20}$ is the same as 90 percent.

The bulletin board grows throughout the school year. Most important, students refer to it when there is an example that is relevant to their work. Further, as the students sign their contributions, each idea identifies a peer expert to contact for more information.

Graphic organizers

Graphic organizers—visual representations that provide a prompt or an organizing framework for retrieving, storing, acquiring, or applying knowledge—are also a way to scaffold learning. They are often used in the teaching of language arts, social studies, and science. They also have a prominent role in the teaching of mathematics. The more we use both linguistic and nonlinguistic representations in our classrooms, the more we can help our students learn and remember. Graphic organizers often contain both linguistic and nonlinguistic features.

Concept maps or webs are a way to graphically present relationships among ideas. The maps help students develop a framework for what they already know and provide a model that they can make more elaborate as their learning increases. Maps or webs can be developed at the beginning, in the middle, or at the end of units and they can provide important assessment data. The main concept can be written at the top or in the middle of the map. Rays or arrows then span out from that main idea. As the rays fan out, the ideas move from more general to more specific.

Students can investigate concept maps in a variety of ways. Some teachers provide a physical template for a map, with some of the topics identified. Then real objects, pictures, or words can be added to the diagram. A group of fifth-grade students were given a template for a map with some words to place in the headings. Once the words were placed, they chose their own examples to write under the remaining arrows. (See Figure 6–1.) Webs tend to be more free-flowing than concept maps and can be used to brainstorm what students know. Computer software tools are available that are designed to help K–5 students create their own graphic organizers.

One fourth-grade teacher thinks it's important that students create concept webs for themselves, rather than work from templates that have been constructed for them. She knows that the students can complete models that she offers them and that they understand the purpose of concept maps and how they are structured. Now she wants them to gain a deeper understanding of how webs are made from scratch. She thinks the best way to do this is to have students brainstorm ideas and then categorize them. Within this

Figure 6–1 *A concept map for fractions.*

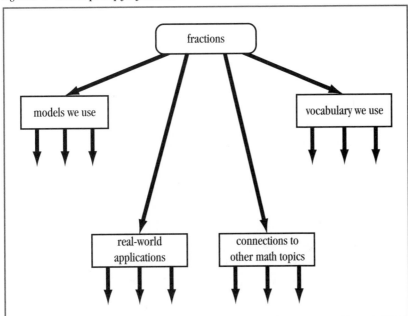

process she will be careful not to impose too many of her own ideas or organizational strategies; she hopes to encourage the students to think about what they know and how their ideas are related.

She is working with a group of six students at a table. Over the course of two days, each student in the class will participate in such a group. She prefers to work with groups rather than the whole class so that she can better access the students' thinking. She also wants to make sure that each student participates in this initial process. The students are coming to the end of their unit on fractions and the teacher is hoping that this activity will help them to solidify and connect the ideas they have explored. She comes to the table with a stack of blank index cards and a larger card with the words *What We Know About Fractions* written on it. She says, "I'd like you to think about what you know about fractions. We've been working with fractions for quite a while now and I'm curious about how you think about what you have been learning."

Jackie begins by saying, "It's about pieces of a whole." The teacher gives him an index card and asks him to write that down while Millie adds, "Like a pizza." Millie is also handed an index card to record her thinking. Nate offers, "There's a numerator and a denominator." This comment stimulates additional information about these components of a fraction and before long the following comments have also been recorded:

- The denominator is on the bottom and the numerator is on the top.
- The higher the numerator the more the pieces.
- The smaller the denominator the bigger the pieces.
- The denominator tells the number of parts.
- The parts are always equal, but they can be different shapes.
- When the numerator and denominator are the same, it's a whole.
- The numerator is the shaded part.
- It could also be about things like three of the four shirts are blue.

The teacher is pleased to see the students building on each other's thinking and doing so without her intervention. Following this burst of ideas there is a bit of a lull. The teacher waits patiently and then Dominique says, "I know that two-fourths is one-half." Once again, a flurry of similar ideas is offered. This time several students make drawings to illustrate their thinking. Before long other vocabulary is introduced including: *improper fractions, reducing fractions, mixed numbers,* and *equivalent.*

Another lull follows, but at this point the teacher decides to trigger their thinking a bit. She asks, "When do we use fractions?" There is an immediate chorus of "Pizza!" Then *musical notes*, *cooking measurements*, and *describing data* are also identified and recorded. As each idea is presented the teacher asks the student to explain his or her thinking to make sure that the other students understand the suggestion.

Now that each student has recorded six to eight ideas, the teacher decides that they are ready for the next step in the process. She asks, "How might you sort the ideas you have brainstormed? Do some of your cards go together?" Then Millie says, "I'll take the ones with pictures that show the different names for fractions." Cards are passed around and discussions are held about exactly where each one belongs. When this sorting is completed the students have placed the cards in four groups. The teacher asks them to describe each group and then to write labels for them on larger index cards. The labels *special words*, *ideas about numerators and denominators*, *ways we use them*, and *the same* are chosen. In the labeling process it's decided that they need to also write *numerator* and *denominator* on index cards so that they can be in the special words pile. Also, they move the comment about the shirts from the *numerator and denominator* group to the *ways we use them* group.

Students review the classroom's graphic software tool and discuss how labels can be created and arrows can be drawn from one to another. There are two computers in the room and the teacher sends three students to each one with the challenge of making a concept web for fractions. She tells them they can use the ideas that they have discussed already or create new ones. The students are eager to get to work. Once the teacher is confident that they are settled and comfortable with the webbing tool, she calls up another group.

Teacher Reflection

My students have made concept webs for Mexico, but I have never used this tool with a mathematical topic. With Mexico, subtopics of food, geographic features, places of interest, and so on came easily to the students. I didn't think the same would be true for the topic of fractions. So I decided to start with sorting cards before creating a web. I used to think that sorting activities were just for the primary grades. But now I realize that you really need to sort ideas before you can identify relationships and categories among them.

(Continued)

Using the cards allowed the recorded ideas to be moved without difficulty. This is a different process from brainstorming ideas in a list and then looking for ones that go together. With the cards, students could join ideas easily. They could also change their minds and move a card to a different category. I thought it was interesting that the labeling process instigated a new level of decision making. It was wonderful to hear my students brainstorming so many ideas and then working further with them.

The next time we create a web, I will give them an overall topic and suggest that they think of this as the title of the book. The next layer of categories then becomes the chapter titles they would expect to find in such a book. Below these categories are the topics or ideas they would expect to find in the particular chapters. I like to present several ways of thinking about making webs so that students realize that there is more than one approach and hopefully, find one that makes sense to them.

Venn diagrams are another example of a graphic organizer. They are often introduced in the primary grades and used to sort objects by color and shape. Although the use of Venn diagrams was traditionally limited to mathematics and science, they are now often utilized in literacy and social studies, for example, to compare two or three stories, characters, heroes, or events. Introducing these graphic organizers during math time and applying them in other subjects can help students view mathematics as a useful tool.

In the intermediate grades, terms and ideas related to number theory can be used with these diagrams. (See Figure 6–2.)

Figure 6–2 *Completing a task using a Venn diagram.*

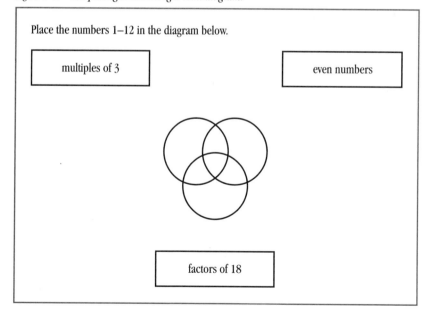

Place the numbers 1–12 in the diagram below.

multiples of 3

even numbers

factors of 18

Note that the three rings have been enclosed in a large rectangle. This helps some students better identify the region outside of all of the rings as a relevant area. Similar to other attribute games, rings can be used with numbers written on file cards, along with a variety of labels such as powers of ten, prime numbers, and common multiples of two and three. Students can then choose labels and place the number cards accordingly. They can also play "guess my label" games by having one pair of students, the leaders, choose labels and place them face down by the rings. The other students take turns giving the leaders a card to place in the diagram until they can identify the labels correctly.

Another graphic organizer that focuses on mathematical vocabulary is a word bank. When designing a task, a teacher may choose to scaffold the students' ability to explain their thinking by providing a bank of words at the bottom of the assignment sheet. (See Figure 6–3.)

Some teachers prefer to include this organizer but leave the bank empty. (See Figure 6–4.) The teacher using this format asks the students to brainstorm and record words in the bank before they begin the task. Note that this form also provides further scaffolding for questions that require students to make comparisons.

As teachers struggle with how to better help their students respond to open-ended response questions in mathematics, more teachers are considering such formats. When examining student responses, they find that too often, students lack the vocabulary to be able to adequately address the question. As we learn from the following reflection, not everyone reacts positively to the use of word banks.

Figure 6–3 *A task with accompanying word bank.*

How are a square and a cube different?
How are they the same?

Word Bank:

angle	face	three-dimensional
cube	rectangular prism	two-dimensional
degrees	side	vertices
edge	square	

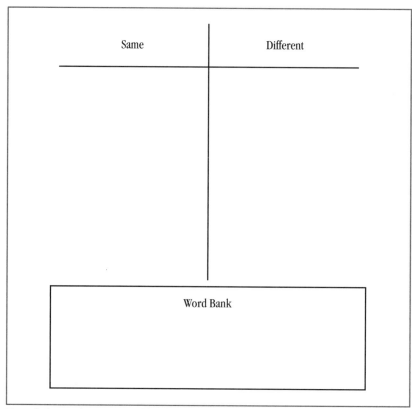

Same	Different

Word Bank

Figure 6–4 *An alternative word bank template.*

Teacher Reflection

Today was our December systemwide professional development day. The K–8 teachers all worked with our mathematics consultant. Our focus this year has been on open-ended questions. Our students have difficulty with these items. Sometimes they don't even seem to know where to begin. One thing we have worked on since September is the development of math vocabulary. One of the techniques we have explored is open-ended questions with word banks. When the consultant first suggested this technique, some of the teachers, especially at the upper grades, were really negative. One teacher even said that it was just a way to give students the answers.

I must admit I was surprised by this response. To me, it was just like using a calculator when you have to add a long list of numbers, like when we place the Scholastic book order. The calculator is just a tool. You still have to know which buttons to push, otherwise, it's useless. I have found that the quality of students' responses really improves when they have a list of related vocabulary words available to them. It jogs their memories, sure, but they still have to know what the terms mean and be able to use them correctly.

I think middle school teachers often think that we provide too much support at the elementary level. They don't believe that the students will be able to do it later without the support. I think that's because they don't see the students who used to struggle when they were first with us, but who are successful now.

What was special today was that a fifth-grade teacher came to the session all excited about a sample of student work. The student was asked the question, "Why is two the only even prime number?" No word bank had been provided, but the student drew a picture of herself with a word bubble overhead. In the word bubble were the words: *prime, even, odd, composit[e], factor.* [See Figure 6–5.] Then the student began her response on another page. The student showed just how powerful this technique can be. Because of her familiarity with word banks and the emphasis on vocabulary, she created her own word list. Her teacher told us that once the student formed her list, she was able to begin writing about her mathematical thinking. What a great connection!

Another graphic organizer is a vocabulary sheet. One third-grade teacher has students complete a sheet whenever a new term is introduced. The sheet purposely asks for the students to create and record their own definitions, rather than use one provided by

Figure 6–5   *One student's drawing suggested thinking of a word bank.*

New word: _____

My definition: _____

_____

_____

_____

_____

Examples:

Used in a sentence: _____

_____

_____

_____

Figure 6–6 *A graphic organizer used to support the learning of new mathematical terms.*

the teacher or text. This teacher believes strongly that students need to make their own connections with a term in order to internalize its meaning. Using a blank space rather than lines for the example portion of the form allows students to choose to draw pictures or to write words. (See Figure 6–6.) Students place each new sheet in the back of their mathematics binders and practice their alphabetizing skills by keeping the sheets in order. They can refer to the forms easily whenever they need to be reminded of the meaning of one of the terms. They are also encouraged to add to their pages as their understanding of the terms deepens.

Some teachers present problems in a way that graphically organizes a student's work. One example is a structured form that requires a number of steps to be completed. (See Figure 6–7.) Sometimes students just need a less-structured from with the problem presented at the top and a clearly designated place to record the answer. (See Figure 6–8.) Such graphics can scaffold students through the problem-solving process, but should not be used with all problems or be implemented for any length of time. It's important that scaffolds, even simple ones, be removed or modified as the student

There are some bicycles and tricycles.
There are 14 vehicles.
There are 34 wheels.
How many bicycles are there?
How many tricycles are there?

Facts:	Drawings:
Computation:	Answer:

Figure 6–7 *A structured scaffold.*

Massie is five years older than Kendra.
The sum of their ages is 33.
How old is Massie?
How old is Kendra?

Show your work:

Answer: _____ .

Figure 6–8 *A less-structured scaffold.*

progresses. Remember, the goal is for the problem-solving process to be organized by the student and that the student, not the teacher, take responsibility for deciding if making a drawing would be helpful and for remembering to identify the answer within the work.

Forms with spaces for multiple answers scaffold the student work. For example, if students are asked to name all possible

The Homespun Bakery sells muffins in packages of 2, 4, 6, or 8.
How can you buy a dozen muffins?
For each way you find, record how many of each package to buy.

Packs of 8	Packs of 6	Packs of 4	Packs of 2	Check total

Figure 6–9   *A scaffold for a problem with multiple responses.*

combinations, a table can be provided that indicates how the data are to be organized and provides space for the number of answers the student is to identify. (See Figure 6–9.) Again, such multiple-response scaffolds should only be used with students who would otherwise be unable to work with a more open-ended presentation. Students can use this problem (without the scaffold) as an opportunity to create their own methods for deciding if they have identified all the correct responses. But for some students this task is too overwhelming at first. The scaffold, or response template, provides a systematic way for them to give the problem a try and the structure can help students who find the empty page, or the requirement to find multiple answers, too intimidating.

The importance of providing only those scaffolds that are needed and to lessen or remove them as soon as possible cannot be overemphasized. It is also important to use scaffolds that support robust concepts. Too often students who reach the intermediate grades and still experience difficulty with choosing the correct operation to solve a word problem have been told to focus on key words. For example, words such as *take away* and *left* would be viewed as cues for subtraction, while *altogether, in all,* and *total* would cue addition. Teachers sometimes provide further scaffolding by hanging a poster in the classroom identifying key words for each operation and students might be asked to underline these words in word problems.

This approach is problematic for several reasons. For one, no list of key words can be exhaustive. For another, a term such as *total* could indicate addition or multiplication. Also, as our word problems become more realistic and less "canned," such terms may not even appear. Further, this approach assumes that subtraction would be used to solve a word problem such as:

Chad has 324 stamps from South America.
He gives 47 of them to his friend, Eduardo.
How many stamps from South America does Chad have left?

Yet some students would determine the answer by adding up from forty-seven. For these students, subtraction is not involved. So what would it mean to identify *left* as the key word that maps onto subtraction? Most important, this reductionism asks students to look for specific words, rather than the underlying conceptual meaning of the context.

Educators have identified four categories of addition and subtraction problems: *join, separate, part-part-whole,* and *compare.* Examples of word problems associated with each category include:

Join

Marietta has 289 play tickets to sell.
The play director, Nona, gives her 186 more tickets to sell.
How many tickets does Marietta have to sell now?

Separate

Marietta has 475 play tickets to sell.
She gives 186 of them to Nona to sell.
How many tickets does Marietta have to sell now?

Part-Part-Whole

Marietta is selling tickets to the upcoming play.
She has 289 adult tickets and 186 children's tickets to sell.
How many tickets does she have to sell?

Comparison

Marietta sold 289 tickets to the play.
Nona sold 186 tickets to the play.
How many more tickets did Marietta sell than Nona?
(How many fewer tickets did Nona sell than Marietta?)

Note that these examples all involve the numbers 289, 186, and 475. Often word problems are presented in the same manner; that is, the *join* stories ask about the combined total and the *separate* stories ask about the number remaining. In actuality, the questions could involve any one of the three numbers. Examples of join word problems include:

Join with Total Unknown
Lucia ran $3\frac{1}{2}$ miles and stopped for a rest.

Then she ran another $2\frac{1}{4}$ miles before she reached home.
How many miles did Lucia run?

Join with Set 2 Unknown

Lucia ran $3\frac{1}{2}$ miles and stopped for a rest.
Then she ran some more.
By the time she got home, she had run $5\frac{3}{4}$ miles.
How many miles did she run after her rest?

Join with Set 1 Unknown

Lucia ran for a bit and then stopped for a rest.
Then she ran the $2\frac{1}{4}$ miles to her home.
When she got there, she had run $5\frac{3}{4}$ miles.
How many miles did Lucia run before she stopped to rest?

While limiting initial exposure to similar problem structures may be seen as strategic planning on the part of a teacher and an appropriate scaffold, we must remember to provide appropriate challenges as well. If we don't, we are limiting the conceptual models of joining and separating that our students can build. We prefer to expose our students to a wider array of word problems and use manipulative models, dramatizations, drawings, and peer conversations to support investigations with less familiar structures. Consider the following teacher reflection about the need for continued attention to varied problem structures.

Teacher Reflection

I used to think addition and subtraction word problems were the exclusive purview of the primary years. I assumed my students had mastered these skills. By that I mean that they understood the meanings of these operations. As we explored fractions and decimals, I would just create basic addition and subtraction problems as a way for them to practice their new computational skills. Without realizing it, I was writing problems that always asked students to identify the number in all or the number that was left.

One day I was talking with my friend who teaches second grade and she mentioned how much trouble her students experienced when the first number in a word problem was missing. As she talked I began to wonder about my students. I decided to be more intentional about the kind of problems I was giving students. I created several fraction and decimal problems where the initial or second number was unknown, not the final state. All of a sudden my students were making drawings or trying to count up, or guessing and checking instead of just applying addition or subtraction. It was really an eye-opener for me. Now I am more careful to vary my problems and I see the benefit to my students.

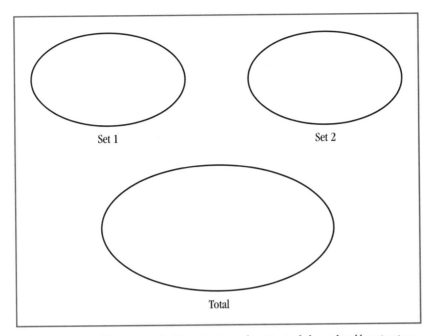

Set 1

Set 2

Total

Figure 6–10   *A graphic organizer for join, separate, and part-part-whole word problem structures.*

Graphic organizers can also be introduced to connect these problem structures. Note that while the action may vary, each type of join, separate, and part-part-whole word problem shares a similar schema in that there are two distinct sets that make up the whole. (See Figure 6–10.) Arrows can be added to the graphic to show the action of join or separate stories. (See Figure 6–11 on page 156.) Over time, students can connect problems to this graphic organizer, adding numbers or drawings to make the connection meaningful. Note that as with triangle fact cards (see Chapter 5), any one of the three numbers may be missing.

With traditional algorithms, such as addition and division, graphic organizers are used to support the series of steps in the procedures. (See Figures 6–12 and 6–13 on the following pages.) Such graphics structure the work or serve as reminders, but do not necessarily increase understanding of these algorithms. Mental computation and nontraditional algorithms require a greater flexibility with numbers and a greater familiarity with the relationships among numbers. For example, students who recognize that 396 is just four less than four hundred are able to think of 236 + 396 as 236 + 400 − 4. The traditional graphic organizer for addition does not support this type of flexible thinking.

Hundreds charts, thousands charts, and number lines are graphic organizers of our number system. The hundreds and thousands charts emphasize the way our number system is based

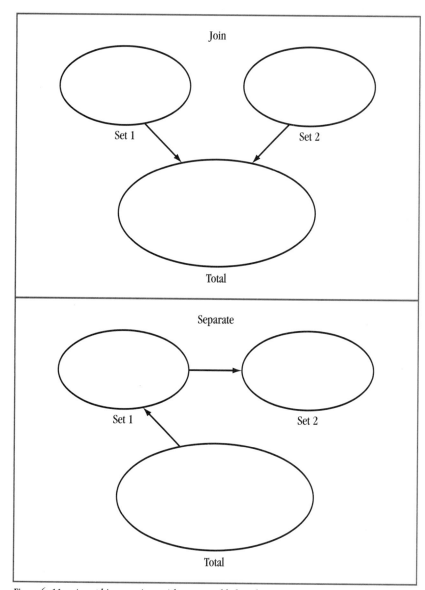

Figure 6–11   *A graphic organizer with arrows added to show action.*

hundreds	tens	ones
5	6	8
+ 2	5	7

Figure 6–12   *A graphic organizer for addition.*

on grouping by tens and can help to build number relationships. Students recognize the pattern of our counting numbers in both the ones and tens places by using the structure of the hundreds chart. The thousands chart continues the ten-to-one ratio between tens and hundreds, and hundreds and thousands. It is often assumed that students recognize these patterns by the time they have completed the primary years. For students experiencing difficulty, however, it is often these basic concepts that can be missing or not yet internalized.

Students can create a hundreds or thousands chart with a blank board and number tiles. Once created, a handful of tiles can be removed and then the missing numbers identified. A similar process could be followed using a pocket chart and files cards. (See Figure 6–14 for a more challenging task.)

Observing how a student uses a chart to find a sum or difference can provide insight into conceptual development. For example, when determining 17 + 25, some students may still place their fingers on seventeen and then count up twenty-five, touching

Figure 6–13   *A cyclical graphic for division.*

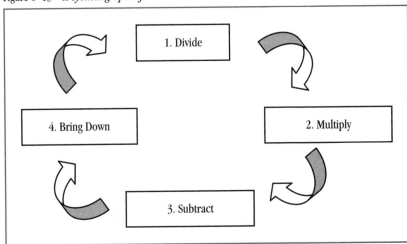

Figure 6–14   *A thousands chart challenge.*

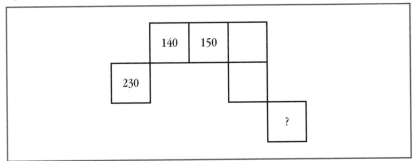

their fingers to the next numbers as they count. Others may recognize that twenty-five is composed of two tens and five ones. With this perspective, they can begin at seventeen, slide their fingers down two rows to thirty-seven, and then count on five.

Not everyone agrees how a hundreds chart should be organized. (See Figure 6–15 for three different organizations.) In the first chart, the number representing the next decade is shown at the end of each row. The number 34, for example, can be viewed as three complete rows of ten and four more in the next row. Advocates of the second model argue that this placement emphasizes the importance of zero and that the tens digit is the same throughout the row. Further, if a vertical line is drawn down the middle of the chart, numbers on the right side would round up to the next decade (when context is irrelevant) and those on the left, would round down. Critics of this format express concern for the lack of cardinality. That is, the fourth number is three, not four, and thus the starting point for students is confusing. The third model is based on the idea that it is more natural to think of numbers as growing bigger, with the numbers that are less on the bottom and the numbers that are greater on the top. These differences point out the importance of our thinking about the graphic organizers we choose to use.

A number line may emphasize grouping by tens, depending on how it is designed. One way to deepen the connection between a hundreds or thousands chart and a number line would be to cut up a chart to make the line or vice versa. Number lines illustrate the continuous nature of our number system, one to which fractions, decimals, and negative numbers can be added. In the upper elementary years it is important to extend traditional number lines so that students visualize the placement of zero, negative integers, and fractions.

Not all number lines show numbers! Open number lines are simply lines, perhaps with one or two numbers identified. They can be an excellent tool for developing a sense of the relative position or size of numbers. Tasks can provide teachers with a glimpse into students' understanding of the relative magnitude of 100 and 1,000. (See Figure 6–16.)

Number lines can also be shown with hatch marks only. Some tasks help students match a base ten or digital representation of number with a ones or linear model. When the longer hatch marks at the tens are included, they can be used to simplify the counting process. Students can use the marks to count ten at once. Such tasks help support the concept that ten is both one ten and ten ones.

Beginning with 1

1	2	3	4	5	6	7	8	9	10
11	12	13	14	15	16	17	18	19	20
21	22	23	24	25	26	27	28	29	30
31	32	33	34	35	36	37	38	39	40
41	42	43	44	45	46	47	48	49	50
51	52	53	54	55	56	57	58	59	60
61	62	63	64	65	66	67	68	69	70
71	72	73	74	75	76	77	78	79	80
81	82	83	84	85	86	87	88	89	90
91	92	93	94	95	96	97	98	99	100

Beginning with 0

0	1	2	3	4	5	6	7	8	9
10	11	12	13	14	15	16	17	18	19
20	21	22	23	24	25	26	27	28	29
30	31	32	33	34	35	36	37	38	39
40	41	42	43	44	45	46	47	48	49
50	51	52	53	54	55	56	57	58	59
60	61	62	63	64	65	66	67	68	69
70	71	72	73	74	75	76	77	78	79
80	81	82	83	84	85	86	87	88	89
90	91	92	93	94	95	96	97	98	99

Growing up

91	92	93	94	95	96	97	98	99	100
81	82	83	84	85	86	87	88	89	90
71	72	73	74	75	76	77	78	79	80
61	62	63	64	65	66	67	68	69	70
51	52	53	54	55	56	57	58	59	60
41	42	43	44	45	46	47	48	49	50
31	32	33	34	35	36	37	38	39	40
21	22	23	24	25	26	27	28	29	30
11	12	13	14	15	16	17	18	19	20
1	2	3	4	5	6	7	8	9	10

Figure 6–15   *Three organizational structures for a hundreds chart.*

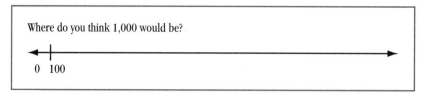

Where do you think 1,000 would be?

Figure 6–16 *A task focused on the relative magnitude of 100 and 1,000.*

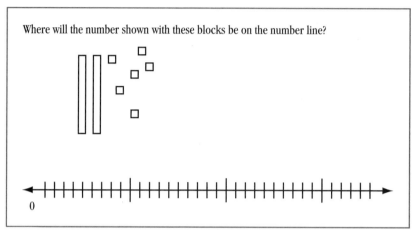

Where will the number shown with these blocks be on the number line?

Figure 6–17 *A task with number line with only hatch marks.*

Again, this is a task that we expect students to master at the primary level, but not all students do so. (See Figure 6–17.)

As can be seen from the examples of graphic organizers in this chapter, these visual tools can be powerful models for conceptual development or simple ways to illustrate a particular task or process. In the same spirit, asking questions, focusing on strategies, having students collaborate, and making connections are used to support learning by making the work more accessible for all students as they pursue tasks, make choices, and solve problems.

Chapter 7
Supporting Choice

$\mathcal{O}$ur society places value on making choices. Making choices helps us to feel autonomous, confident, and competent. Choice is highly motivating and is one way that students can take responsibility for their own learning. Making a choice involves self-expression, which is a form of creativity. We honor our students as learners by allowing them to make choices. We are also able to differentiate instruction by providing choice.

Time to make choices is a common practice in preschool and kindergarten classrooms. Often indistinguishable from play to a lay observer, children engage with classroom materials in ways that help them to develop their language, artistic, and social skills as well as motivate them to explore number, space, and scientific ideas. Though having more choices is frequently associated with growing older and being able to handle responsibilities, students often view school as a place where choice diminishes as they advance through the grades. How do we make room for and how do we structure choices for students to make in grades 3 through 5?

Many teachers in the upper grades report that there is no time in the day for the kind of choice time that is permitted in the early years. As we learn from the teacher reflection that follows, providing students with choices does not mean that anybody can do anything they want. Rather, students can be given choices among tasks, with each choice designed to support the instructional goals in the classroom.

I began my career as a kindergarten teacher. I used to marvel at the way my students focused during choice time and how activities during that time led to exciting new areas of study. These young students were used to making decisions about what materials to use, much as they did at home with toys. Choice time allowed them to do something they really cared about, to have some control of their learning environment. When I became a fourth-grade teacher I quickly realized that choice time was not something that was built into the schedule at this level. I missed the comfortable way I was able to interact with students during this time and worried that I was giving my older students the subtle message that I didn't have confidence in the decisions they would make.

In response, I decided to offer project time for the last hour of Friday afternoons. It worked well for a couple of weeks and then slowly things began to deteriorate. Too many students were getting off task and, as a result, behavior problems started to increase. After some reflection I realized that the projects weren't really connected to what we were studying. No wonder the students began to think of this time as a different kind of recess. I decided to decrease the time to 30 minutes and to make this a time for math games. Both changes helped and over time, I developed different levels of each game to be sure that student readiness was addressed.

Now that I have been teaching at this level for quite a few years, I have found a number of ways to provide choices for my students to make. I look for times when they can choose their own partners, find their own workspace, or decide which task to do first. At the beginning of the school year we spend a lot of time establishing routines and expectations for making decisions. We discuss what it means to make a good choice and they know they will be held accountable for their selections. I now incorporate choice into my curriculum on a frequent basis. In this way students recognize choice as part of our classroom practice, rather than as a sign that it is time to fool around.

This teacher offers us several key ideas to think about in terms of providing choice in our classrooms. Decision making, managing time, accountability, and building choice into the classroom practice provide us with a framework for thinking about how to design and implement choice in our classrooms. There are managerial implications around time, work habits, disposition for learning, behavior, and ways to monitor student progress that require our attention as well.

Being offered a choice implies the need for reflection and self-direction. Many children are adept at this, many are not. Childhood is a journey toward independence and self-discovery. Parents and teachers alike recognize that children need predictable structure, clear expectations, and innumerable opportunities to explore, practice, make mistakes, and learn. Teachers (and parents) also recognize that children need the time and room to practice decision making, as well as learn how to compromise. In many ways, offering choices requires more preparation than merely directing students, but the gains are worth it. Choice provides powerful opportunities for additional practice and differentiating instruction and also leads to natural extensions for learning.

There are a variety of choices we can offer our students, including:

- which topics to study;
- which tasks to complete;
- what materials to use;
- with whom to partner;
- where to work;
- how long to work;
- the order in which to complete assignments;
- how to represent and present ideas; and/or
- how to demonstrate what is understood.

Letting our students make such choices can have a positive impact on their learning and their self-esteem. The extent to which this potential impact is realized often depends on the ways in which teachers structure and organize choice in the classroom. In this chapter we consider math workshops, projects, menus, stations, Think Tac Toes, and RAFTs as ways to organize and manage classroom choice as we strive to meet individual needs.

Math Workshops

Some teachers use *main workshops* as a term to describe the kind of activity that occurs when students are given some choice in the mathematical ideas they investigate. The name, as opposed to something such as "free choice," emphasizes that everyone is expected to work. In literacy learning we have writing workshops during which students may be writing about what is important to them in the same authentic way that writers do. Such workshops may also be a time to work on specific writing skills such as elements of grammar and punctuation. Writing workshops also suggest an ongoing process, one that begins with an original draft and then continues through a revision process.

Math workshops also can be designed to support authentic mathematical investigation while providing opportunities for skill development and expectations for work of high quality. Perhaps the students are studying growing patterns, and pattern blocks, color tiles, attribute blocks, and snap cubes are available to construct models. There are a variety of ways to build choice into this workshop experience. Students could be working on the same task (for example, create a growing pattern) but choose the materials they wish to use to do so, along with the particular patterns they wish to construct. Or, teachers can assign specific students to certain materials based on readiness level. For example, a teacher may decide that the color tiles only differ by color and thus may be more accessible for less ready students to use. Conversely, as pattern blocks (color and shape) and attribute blocks (size, color, and shape) involve more than one distinguishable characteristic, these materials might provide greater challenge to other students. Snap cubes could be used in ways similar to the color tiles or more complex patterns could be made by taking advantage of the cubes' three-dimensional options. Once assigned, however, students could still choose a partner with whom to work, the types of patterns to make, and the ways in which the work would be represented.

Groups could also be assigned to specific tasks based on readiness. Some students could be expected to generate growing patterns, some to create rules for patterns that already exist, and others could be asked to generate models for specific generalizations such as "The number of total blocks is equal to four times the number in the first row, minus three." Reports of these investigations can be developed in response to open-ended questions such as "What have you learned about growing patterns?" or "What are the differences between making repeating patterns and growing patterns?" Such responses can be peer evaluated and revised, much as would be expected in process writing.

In this work with patterns, students would be choosing their own materials. Easy access to materials is one of many managerial strategies that support learning. As students learn to use mathematical materials and come to expect them to be available for use, the students are also developing the good work habits and positive behaviors that are indicative of successful, independent learners. Ironically we find primary students often have more choice in material use than upper-level students. Materials in primary classrooms are often housed in open bins or plastic tubs at a level that makes them easily accessible to young students. In upper-grade classrooms, however, materials may be stored in out-of-the-way shelves, file cabinets, or closets. We must all find places in our classrooms to store materials that suggest students are free to use them as needed. Everything should be reachable, labeled, and easy to maintain. (See Chapter 8 for a fuller discussion of classroom space.)

Projects

One way to allow our students to pursue their own interests is to involve them in projects. Projects provide students opportunities to apply concepts and skills as students wrestle with significant ideas and in-depth study. Projects usually require significant research and organizational skills, and might be better pursued during the second half of the year. Some teachers find it helpful to provide a specific time line for a project. For example, a fifth-grade class that was making math games for a third-grade class visit had specific tasks and deadlines that had to be met along the way. (See Figure 7–1.) The articulation of these tasks helped the students to break down their project into daily goals and allowed the teacher to easily identify pairs of students who were falling behind the intended schedule.

Other teachers allow for more open-ended projects and thus require students to complete a contract as to their topic and plans. (See Figure 7–2; see also Blackline Masters.)

Figure 7–1   *Checklist for project deadlines.*

Check off each task as you complete it.

Complete by Wednesday, January 5

☐ Identify the mathematical focus of your game and the name of your game.

Complete by Friday, January 7

☐ Prepare a draft of the rules of your game.

☐ Identify the materials you will need (dice, cubes, game pieces).

☐ List the parts of the game that you will make (game board, cards).

☐ List any supplies you will need.

Complete by Tuesday, January 12

☐ Submit final draft of the rules of your game.

☐ Make a sketch of game materials you will create.

Complete by Thursday, January 14

☐ Have all materials of your game ready to go for tomorrow!

Complete by Friday, January 15

☐ Play the game with your third-grade partner.

☐ Complete your reflection sheet.

1. Due date: _____
   The topic for my mathematical project is:

   This is what I want to learn:

   I will use these materials and resources:

   This is what I will create to show what I learned about mathematics:

2. Due date: _____
   This is what I have accomplished so far:

   This is what I still have to do:

3. Due date: _____
   My project is complete. The three most important things I learned about mathematics are:

   The best part of this project was:

   The most challenging part of this project was:

Figure 7–2 *A project contract.*

Some teachers provide specific projects for students to complete. Consider the following example from a third-grade teacher, whose class was working on a unit on measurement.

Teacher Reflection

For the past five years I have noticed that my students are not coming to third grade with a good understanding of measurement. As I reflected on why this might be true, I realized that children do not have the same types of experiences outside of school as they used to have. Many of my students do not have time to do arts and crafts at home and most of their activities outside of class are fairly organized. There also seems to be less time for art projects in school. As a result, students don't have many opportunities to use a ruler for their own purposes. It is as if a ruler has become just a straight edge or a tool for math class. My students are not comfortable using a ruler and don't really understand why they might need to use one.

I decided I wanted my students to have some of the arts and crafts experiences I had as a child. It started out with knitting. It was around third grade when I learned to knit. I still knit today and always have a ruler handy in my knitting bag. I began by teaching all of the students how to knit, boys and girls. They worked on making afghan squares. The students needed to keep track of their pattern and to measure the sides of their squares, either in inches or centimeters. We talked about what makes a square a square as they measured the side lengths and the perimeters of their squares. Many students began knitting on their own at home and when we had enough squares, some parent volunteers helped us put them together to make an afghan that we sent to a local children's hospital. The children were so proud of their efforts!

Next was woodworking and the students were given an opportunity to make a birdhouse. First students had to measure to make an accurate drawing of their birdhouses. Many students liked using the Internet to research what size hole they should make, depending on the birds that might be attracted to their yard. My father had some old wood he donated and he was able to work with the students to make the necessary cuts.

The last project that I introduced was string art. The students made wooden boards with nails and wrapped string around the nails to create interesting patterns. I remember doing this at camp years ago and understanding symmetry for the first time. As the students designed their boards they needed to measure the distance between the nails. This was a challenging task, but thankfully, I had my father to help out once again. Senior citizens love to work with children and to be involved in learning. I know I could have found other seniors at our town's Senior Center, if my father had not been interested. It was a wonderful way for me to share my classroom with my dad.

There are a variety of project ideas that are appropriate for students in grades 3 through 5, including:

Create a mathematics board game.

Create a poster titled, "Everything You Wanted to Know About a Million."

Design an Estimation Olympics.

Find out about number systems without a zero.

Explore toy cars and ramps.

Interview three adults about how they use mathematics at work.

Investigate mathematics and secret codes.

Investigate how mathematics helps artists.

Learn about card tricks that depend on mathematics.

Make a model of a pencil for a giant.

Make a sand clock.

Organize a group to make 1,000 origami cranes.

Pick and follow a stock portfolio.

Plan a $1,000 vacation.

Plan and plant a school garden.

Start a school store.

Summarize the life of a famous mathematician.

Tutor a younger student in mathematics.

Write your own version of *Counting on Frank*.

You may want to have students brainstorm their own ideas and then add some other ideas from this list. If your students are not familiar with mathematical projects, you might want to give them a few examples to prompt their thinking.

Projects can also be shared across grade levels. As a way to enhance vocabulary development before a statewide standardized test, one math coach helped a school create a "third through fifth grade vocabulary poster extravaganza." After a few meetings to organize the vocabulary poster event, the teachers agreed all of the classes would get together to generate a list of mathematical terms to be included. Then each student would choose a word from the list. On posters they would define the words, make illustrations, and then write about how they might use these words in real life. The work on the posters would be done in class. Each word could only be used once. At the end of the event they would have a scavenger hunt involving their posters, which were hung in the hallway, and celebrate the extravaganza with a pizza party.

After several days the teachers reconvened to talk about the project. They were pleased with the choices the students made. They felt that students chose vocabulary words they felt comfortable with and took pride in creating the definitions. Many students stretched their thinking and the teachers believed that the poster designs clearly showed new levels of understanding.

A fifth-grade student, Marco, chose the word *equal* to define. He was confident he knew the definition, but was surprised when he looked it up in a math dictionary found in his classroom. After reading he asked, "What does it mean to have the same value or meaning?" (So far he had written $7 + 3 = 10$ and $3 \times 5 = 15$ on the sketch of his poster.) He asked a classmate about this definition who explained, "Well, words can have the same meaning." So, Marco wrote "*baby = infant*" on his sketch, added "*no = shaking your head*," and then showed his sketch to his teacher. His teacher paused uncertainly, then said, "I think we better check a math dictionary." Together they found that, mathematically, *equal* refers to a relation between numbers. Marc's real-life connection was, "Sometimes in real life we use *equal* to mean *the same as*, but in math it is all about numbers!" Marc's teacher made a note to talk with her school's math coach about this new idea.

Two fourth-grade girls couldn't decide which word they wanted to define and asked if they could work together. The teacher agreed and they chose the word *polygon*. They, too, began by looking up the definition, which they wrote neatly at the top of their poster. They then made a list of all of the polygons they knew: triangle, square, rectangle, rhombus, trapezoid, pentagon, and hexagon. They drew pictures of each polygon and created a Venn diagram to show how the shapes related to each other, given the labels: "*shapes that have parallel lines*" and "*shapes that have four sides*." For their real-life connection they drew a picture of a math teacher with a talk bubble that said, "You need to know polygons if you want to be a math teacher!" Their teacher wondered, "Did this mean they didn't see a need for anyone else knowing the names of shapes?"

As the project progressed the teachers took note of misconceptions and were able to individualize instruction as well as point out common errors to their classes. The school's math coach found it particularly valuable to have a shared experience between the three grades. As she explained, "Often I see learning happening in pockets, but not as a continuum. Having all the grades working on this project demonstrated to both the teachers and the students that vocabulary would continue to be important and to be a shared responsibility across the grade levels."

Finally it is also important to remember how essential mathematics is to understanding topics in other disciplines. Projects can be vehicles for helping students to make connections between mathematics and other subject areas. For example, when studying the Boston Tea Party, making a model of how much tea was dumped and conducting an experiment to determine how long it would take to do so, helps students to better understand the risks taken in this endeavor.

Menus

Marilyn Burns suggested the use of menus to organize student choice (Burns 1987). About five activities are listed in a menu format and just as if you were in a restaurant, you can choose what to order. During the span of a week, students may be encouraged to try two or three items on the menu. For example, a class that is working with decimals may have a menu that includes:

- playing decimal concentration, a game that matches word names with written numerals
- playing the trading game *Win a One*, using base ten blocks
- solving problems in the decimal problem deck, a collection of word problems the teacher stores in an index file box
- finding baseball statistics that match statements such as "He got a hit about one out of every three times at bat."
- playing *Place Value Strategy* (see www.decimalsquares .com/dsGames/)

A special menu board can list the menu options and a recording sheet can be used to keep track of students' choices. (See Figure 7–3).

When a new item on the menu is first introduced, it might be explored with the whole class. Familiarity with menu choices may also be developed in small groups or with individual students. These students are then given the responsibility to share their menu experiences with their classmates. It is amazing how quickly an entire class can learn an interesting new game, even if it is only introduced formally to one student.

Some activities on a menu board might remain for a significant amount of time. Students, through repetition, are able to explore a certain activity over the course of weeks, months, or the year thereby creating comfort and confidence. Over time, it can also be modified by changing the size or types of numbers or by altering specific criteria for play. Having a particular choice available frequently also gives more students an opportunity to give it a try, while other activities rotate based on need. Often, teachers focus on a few menu activities for awhile, and then phase them out gradually. Rotating out some activities leaves room for new and expanded ideas to be developed, while keeping available some of the familiar choices.

How choices are organized is a reflection of a teacher's style and classroom management preferences, coupled with students' needs. Many teachers add a "have to" element to the choices offered.

Record your menu choices each day. Write a sentence to tell something you learned or practiced.

	Monday	Tuesday	Wednesday	Thursday	Friday
Concentration					
Win a One					
Problem Box					
Baseball Stats					
Strategy Place Value					

Figure 7–3 *A menu chart that students can use to record daily choices.*

Carol Tomlinson (2003a, 2003b) provides menus with required features. Main course listings must be completed, one or two side dishes must be chosen, and desserts are optional choices that students particularly interested in the topic may wish to complete.

A fourth-grade teacher wants to create such a menu. To begin, the teacher thinks about her key question for the menu and identifies it as "How is mathematics used in the real world?" She then notes the key objectives that she has for students:

- Identify ways in which mathematics is used in their daily lives.
- Identify ways in which mathematics is used in various careers.
- Collect, describe, and organize data.

She decides she will introduce the topic by reading them *Math Curse* by Jon Scieszka and Lane Smith (1995). This popular book is an amusing story of a day in the life of a young girl who wakes up and finds everything in her life to be a math problem.

The teacher then thinks about how to create a menu as a follow-up to the story. She identifies three activities that focus on her objectives and includes them within the main course section. She thinks of side dishes as ways to reinforce these ideas, so she includes six options that focus on specific applications of mathematics. Finally, she creates two desserts, activities that she thinks her students might enjoy doing, but that she doesn't think are essential. (See Figure 7–4; see also Blackline Masters.)

As needed, the teacher can easily tier the menu for less or more ready students. For example, writing only one page of an original version of *Math Curse* could be required, or a specific time of day, such as breakfast, could be identified to help students focus. For more challenge, students could interview several adults and create their own visual summaries of their data.

Figure 7–4 *A menu that requires completion of main course items, designed for fourth-grade students.*

Menu: Math All Around Us

Main Course (You must do each one.)

- For one week, keep a list of all the ways you use mathematics outside of school.
- Interview 2 adult neighbors or relatives about the ways they use mathematics when they are at work. Share your information with your team. Together, make a visual summary of your combined data.
- Create your own character. Write and illustrate your own version of *Math Curse*. Make sure your story contains at least 10 math problems and attach an answer key.

Side Orders (Complete two.)

- Write about how mathematics is used in your favorite sport.
- Read 3 stories in the newspaper. Make notes about the ways mathematics is used in the articles or how knowing mathematics helps you to understand the articles.
- Reread *Math Curse* and solve 6 of the problems in the story.
- Make a photo display of geometry in our world.
- Choose 1 of the "real-world math" websites that have been saved as favorites.
- Write 4 problems to put in our real-world problem box.

Desserts (Do one or more if you are interested.)

- Read a biography of author Jon Scieszka and coauthor/illustrator Lane Smith at www.kidsreads.com/series/series-warp-author.asp.
- Make up a song called "These Are a Few of My Favorite Uses of Math."

Think Tac Toe

Think Tac Toe is another format that can be used to structure opportunities for students to make choices. A Think Tac Toe board is a 3-by-3 matrix with nine cells, resembling the familiar tic-tac-toe game board. (See Figure 7–5; see also Blackline Masters.) Students may be asked to complete one of the tasks in each row. The tasks in the first row of this example focus on communication about ways to find products. In the second row are tasks that provide practice with multiplication and use of the guess-and-check problem-solving strategy. Making connections is the goal of the tasks in the third row. Connections are made to uses of multiplication in the real world, to a classmate's way of thinking about multiplication, and to word problems. The tasks in this type of graphic organizer can also be arranged so that students are directed to complete three tasks in a row. Further, it is possible to tier the choices, with each row containing more challenging tasks

Figure 7–5   Multiplication Think Tac Toe *example for fourth-grade students.*

Choose and complete one activity in each row.

Draw a picture that shows a model of 7×35. Make connections between your drawing and how you use paper and pencil to find the product. Discuss your ideas with a friend.	Your brother multiplied 64 by 8 and got the answer 4,832. What could you show and tell your brother to help him understand why his answer is wrong?	Write directions for two different ways to find the product of 92 and 25 when you use paper and pencil.
Place the numbers: 3, 4, 6, 15, 20, and 30, so that the product of each side is 360. Write one more problem like this one and trade it with a classmate.	Place a multiplication sign to make a number sentence that is true. $63945 = 31,970$ Write two more problems like this one and trade them with a classmate.	Which two numbers should you exchange so that the product of the numbers on each card is the same? 120 / 4 / 102 — 85 6 / 8 3 — 3 17 / 30 2 Write two more problems like this one and trade them with a classmate.
Make a collage of items that come in equal groups.	Interview a classmate about what he or she knows about multiplication. Find out as much as you can in three minutes. Write a report with suggestions for teaching.	Your friend solved a word problem by multiplying 3 by 24 and then subtracting 9. Write two interesting word problems that your friend could have solved this way.

or offering tasks that are more conducive to particular learning styles and preferences.

RAFT

A RAFT is a strategy for differentiating learning that can also provide choice for students. The acronym stands for **r**ole, **a**udience, **f**ormat, and **t**opic. To complete a RAFT activity, students create a product according to these four categories. For example, as a game designer (role) for children (audience), students might create a game (format) to practice basic facts (topic). As there is a specific purpose for each suggestion within a RAFT, this instructional strategy also helps to emphasize the usefulness of mathematics and offers students an opportunity to think about how mathematics is used beyond the classroom.

A fourth-grade teacher decides to create a RAFT about telling time. She is concerned that this topic is not included in the fourth-grade curriculum and wants to maintain her students' skills. She also recognizes that there are several students every year who do not know how to tell time on an analog clock or that cannot determine elapsed time using a digital clock. She wants students to recognize the usefulness of these skills in the real world. She tries to think about a variety of roles that might appeal to her students and different products they could create. To connect mathematics to a current topic of study, she includes a task related to the Civil War. (See Figure 7–6; see also Blackline Masters.)

RAFT: Time			
Role	**Audience**	**Format**	**Topic**
Consultant to the Principal	Principal	Report	Comparison of Schedules of First- and Fourth-Grade Classrooms
Teacher	Younger children	Math book	What You Need to Know About Telling Time
Historian	Fourth-grade students	Time line	Events Leading to the Civil War
Marketer	Consumers	Ad	Why Analog Clocks Are the Best
Self	Parent	Pie graph	I Need More (or Less) Free Time Each Week
Fill in your	choice here.	Check with me	for approval

Figure 7–6   *A RAFT chart about time.*

Learning Stations

Learning stations can be used to augment a current unit or to maintain skills from a previous one. They are particularly helpful when there are not enough materials for the whole class to engage with at the same time. For example, a learning station focused on measurement might include a trundle wheel and a weight scale, items that most classrooms would not have in multiple copies. We think of a learning station as a temporary feature in the classroom. We choose to reserve the term *center* for permanent areas in the room, such as a computer or listening center. Many teachers, however, use these terms interchangeably and that is fine.

A fifth-grade teacher decides to create a learning station for her students to use during the geometry unit. From previous experience she knows that this is an enjoyable, though challenging, unit for upper-elementary students. She realizes that students require time and repeated opportunities to make the goals related to geometry salient. They need a greater variety of examples than the classroom text provides. She also recognizes that this unit requires numerous materials, which can make some activities difficult to manage with the whole class working at the same time. She wants to design a station where a small group of students can work independently or collaboratively, while additional learning opportunities are taking place in other areas of the classroom.

Identifying the unit goals that will be supported or extended through station activities is her first step in the planning process. She wants to emphasize skills that benefit most from extended exploration with hands-on activities. She also wants the station to help students connect geometry to the real world. She decides the station will focus on the following topics explored within the unit:

- classification of two-dimensional shapes
- identification of lines of symmetry in two-dimensional shapes
- measurement of angles
- translation, rotation, and reflection of two-dimensional shapes

Her next step is to choose or design appropriate activities to meet these goals. She wants the station to allow for a variety of geometry activities, but not be so overwhelming for her students. She wants the tasks to be somewhat open-ended, but also self-sustaining, as she does not want to be called to the station too frequently while she is working with other groups. She also wants the activities to feel linked, not random to her students, so that they can make connections as they build their understanding of geometry.

She brainstorms a number of options using tangrams, pentominoes, toothpicks, patterns blocks, geoboards, mirrors, and quilting tiles, but while she is excited about all of the activities she identifies, she believes that she has too many ideas for one station. She decides to identify the following questions as a way to clarify the focus of the station and frame the different tasks that will be included there:

- How are these shapes alike and different?
- What symmetrical shapes can you build?
- What can you build with quilting tiles that includes reflections and rotations?
- How do angle measures relate to tessellations?
- Where do we find geometry in our world?

To designate space for the station the teacher moves a rectangular table alongside the bulletin board and places four chairs at the table. She hopes this arrangement will separate the station from other activities and provide a more private space to work. She usually puts a station near a bulletin board as it can provide space for sharing ideas and serve as a visual reminder of the important work there. This board works particularly well as the art materials are stored at one end of it and there are two computers at the other end.

Next she prints two copies of the five questions for the station. She tacks one copy of each question on the bulletin board and one copy of each on large shoeboxes, which she places on the table. Now it is time for her to collect the related materials and create the task cards.

She begins at the school library. She takes out several books on architecture, shapes, African art, and quilting. Then she creates the task cards and fills the shoeboxes. She puts four plastic bags in the shape box, each containing two parallelograms, rectangles, rhombuses, squares, trapezoids, and convex quadrilaterals made from cardboard. She purposely puts in two examples of each figure so that more than the most prominent image is included.

For example, she puts in two trapezoids as shown as too often she finds that students only identify the shape that is similar to the block in the pattern blocks as being a trapezoid.

She makes a task card for each question and places two laminated copies of it and the associated materials in each shoebox. In this way she hopes to allow for the students working together on the same task, working in pairs on two different tasks, or working separately on four tasks.

On the task card for the first question she writes:

1. *Choose two shapes. Describe them in your journal. Be sure to include how they are alike and how they are different.*
2. *Look at all of the shapes. In your journal, complete the following sentences about these collections of shapes. Share your ideas with a classmate. Pick your favorite observation and add it to the bulletin board under the question* How are these shapes alike and different?

   All of these shapes are . . .
   None of these shapes are . . .
   Some of these shapes have . . .
   At least five of these shapes have . . .

3. *Look at all of these shapes. Make a graphic organizer to show the relationships among them.*

The teacher believes that this task card addresses several levels of ability. She expects that everyone will be able to complete the first task and parts of the second task, many will be able to complete the entire second task, and a few will be able to complete the third task successfully.

She places the pattern blocks in the shoebox on symmetry along with four mirrors and four pattern block shape templates. Within the unit students have had the opportunity to fold shapes in order to test for lines of symmetry. The teacher wants to extend this experience by having them use mirrors to check lines of symmetry and to build figures to meet certain conditions. On the task card for the second question she writes:

1. *Consider each pattern block. How many lines of symmetry does each piece have? Use the mirror to check. Make a drawing of each shape in your journal and indicate the lines of symmetry.*

2. *Make a design for each condition. Use the pattern block template to record the designs in your journal.*

   Place four blocks so that the figure has exactly two lines of symmetry.

   Place two blocks so that the figure has no lines of symmetry.

   Place five blocks so that the figure has exactly one line of symmetry.

   Use more than six blocks to create a figure with exactly three lines of symmetry.

For the third question, "What can you build with quilting tiles that includes reflections and rotations?," the teacher gathers the books about quilts and places them in a shoebox along with the container of quilting tiles. From previous years she knows that both boys and girls enjoy manipulating these tiles, but she is always particularly pleased to think about her female students engaged in activities that will further develop their spatial relationships. She decides to write the following task card; the second item she adapts from the booklet that comes with the tiles (Cuisenaire Company of America 1995).

1. *Explore the quilt books with a partner. Choose your favorite design. Write in your journal about why you chose it.*

2. *Make a larger triangle with two red and two blue triangles. Find all the different color arrangements possible. Record your findings in your journal. An arrangement is not different if it is the mirror image of another or if the color looks exactly the same even though the triangles may be placed in somewhat different positions. So, for example, the following two designs are not different.*

3. *Make a 4" × 4" or 8" × 8" quilt design. You can use squares and triangles. Draw your design and add it to "Our Class's Quilts" book along with a description of rotations and reflections you see within your quilt.*

During the unit the students have determined interior angle measures for regular figures. The teacher wants them to apply this knowledge to determining which figures will tessellate. She puts the pattern blocks in a shoebox along with four shape templates and writes the following task card for the question "How do angle measures relate to tessellations?":

1. *A tessellation is formed when one shape can cover a flat surface without any overlaps or gaps. Which of the pattern block shapes will tessellate?*
2. *Do you think a regular pentagon will tessellate? Use the shape template to draw pentagons to check your prediction.*
3. *How might knowing interior angle measures help you to figure out if a shape will tessellate? Talk with a partner and write about your ideas in your journal.*
4. *Imagine that you have been hired to make tile patterns with the pattern blocks. Make and record some designs using more than one of the shapes. Look at the points where the blocks meet. What do you notice about the angle measures? Record your favorite pattern and place it on the bulletin board.*

For the last question, "How do we find geometry in our world?," she puts the remaining books in the last shoebox along with the following task card:

1. *Be a geometry detective at home and at school. Find examples of geometry in our world. Take a photograph or draw a picture to add to our bulletin board. Looking at these books may give you some ideas.*
2. *Go to the computer and open the Web browser. Explore the websites I have bookmarked for you in the geometry file. Write about what you learn.*

Finally, she places a hanging file organizer next to the station with a file for each student. A recording sheet is included along with several blank pieces of paper stapled together. These folders will serve as the students' portfolios. It is important that students record their work and document their station activities. This system helps the students to be independent and helps the learning station to run smoothly.

During math time the next day, the teacher spends a few minutes introducing the guiding questions for each task and the related materials. She wants her students to be aware of the purpose of the station and the goals for learning. She does not model how to complete the activities, but rather briefly describes each one making a point to show the materials available and setting out any expectations around working with a partner and how to complete the recording sheet. She emphasizes the fact that several tasks are included for each shoebox and though students may choose which ones to complete, they must complete one activity from each box. She takes time for questions and then asks if there are four people who want to open the station. She chooses four students among the volunteers. She assures the students that they will all get a turn and emphasizes that working at the station is an expectation for everyone.

Stations such as this one take time to develop and organize. In the interest of being resourceful, you might consider only making stations for those topics that will be explored in subsequent years. Ideally, station materials can be stored in a plastic tub or folder (without the related manipulatives) so that they are ready to be used again and again. Some teachers need to store stations in such ways all the time, as they need the station to be portable. This way, they can be used in different parts of the room, or even be put away for a few days, if necessary. Ample space can be a rare commodity in many classrooms. As the following teacher reflection makes clear, making strategic decisions based on availability of space, time, and amount of materials is ongoing as a teacher plans.

Teacher Reflection

I have come to value the need for setting up, maintaining, and rotating learning stations in my classroom. They have helped me be able to offer more choices to my students. In my mind this equates to more opportunities to practice and to learn. Once a station is up and running, my goal is for it to be self-sustaining. I want to be able to engage with other students at their point of need or to have a chance to sit back a bit as an observer. So, I try to design stations that do not require any teacher direction after the initial introduction.

Since I have been teaching for a few years, I have been able to reuse learning stations as a unit comes up for study in later years. Over time I have been able to test out how self-sustaining an activity may be for the majority of my students. I know I always have to be open to different learning styles and preferences. I have to give particular consideration to my ELL students and think about what they can read or write to fulfill learning expectations at any given point in the year.

I also need to consider what I use to define the space for the station. Have I given ample room? Have I separated stations from other work areas so that students are not unnecessarily distracted? Have I provided all the necessary materials for success? Do these materials need to be placed at the station or do my students know where to find them when they want them? For example, I do not put pencils and paper at my stations unless the paper is designed for a particular task. I have taught my students where to find resources around our classroom. I have set an expectation that they are the ones who know what they need at any point in time and are encouraged to act responsibly on that need.

Maintaining stations can take a lot of time. In some cases I can store all of the materials for a given activity in one box and when students have completed the work, I can store it away for another time. More typically the manipulatives used at one station are used repeatedly. I cannot store these away. For example, a manipulative like pattern blocks are used in almost every unit we study in math. I have to think about the best ways to juggle all of these things. Sometimes I have more than one station running at the same time. Then I need to think about materials. Do I have enough for my students to meet with success? Sometimes I have to borrow from another teacher or, if need be, redesign a station.

This teacher uses a word in her reflection that sounds familiar to all teachers—*juggle*. Juggling is part of the art and craft of teaching and learning. Determining what is to happen at each station and feeling confident that the activities are aligned to the curriculum must always be in the forefront of our thoughts. We must also consider the following questions:

- Who decides what materials or activities are available and when?
- Who decides if a student will engage in this work?
- How will time be managed? How long will students be given to complete a task?
- Who initiates what goes on at a station?
- How will activities at a station be assessed?

These questions are among a host of decisions that may be on our minds as we create and implement learning stations as well as the other instructional strategies for structuring choice presented in this chapter. Let's consider implications for each.

Who decides what materials or activities are available and when?

Once curriculum objectives are agreed on, teachers identify which materials are needed to help students meet those established goals. If the materials are new to students, the students need to learn how they are used and where they are stored. Once the materials are familiar, however, many can be made available to students at all times, to be used whenever needed. Of course some materials, such as thermometers, may be kept in a safe place and made available only under adult supervision. In the spirit of choice, though, we recommend that students choose materials whenever that choice does not hinder safety or greatly reduce the likelihood that learning will be successful.

Who decides if a student will engage in this work?

Often we operate from a mind-set that all students should complete every activity. This stance may stem from our desire to support inclusive and equitable classrooms. We need to balance this desire with the realization that to be equitable, each student must get what he or she needs based on readiness, interest, and learning style. Clearly there will be times when this is not exactly the same thing. All students do not need to complete every activity in order to support a classroom community. Also, we need to open our minds to the possibility that students themselves can participate in making these decisions. In fact, they can often be quite helpful. As one fifth grader explained to his teacher, "I need to work more on my division facts before I do problems like this." Conversely, sometimes a student might select a more difficult task from a RAFT option than the teacher would have assigned. When a student is motivated and supported, they often can achieve and understand more than might be expected.

How will time be managed? How long will students be given to complete a task?

Every teacher has an ongoing battle with the clock in the classroom. We can all agree there is never enough time. Part of this dilemma stems from the fact that no two students seem to work at the same pace or learn at the same rate. Many teachers plan for an average amount of time it will take most students to complete a task and then have to be flexible for those students who finish early and those who require more time. Students who finish early can be encouraged to move on to another activity or station instead of waiting for everyone to be done. Stations can also be kept up for an indefinite amount of time, if they only require a small percentage of space in the classroom. What is of most value is the recognition that students need different amounts of time at different points of learning.

Who initiates what goes on at a station?

This question begs the notion of the teachable moment. Certainly teachers make initial plans for learning stations, but we always want to be open for ideas that students offer us as a direction for learning. How we finesse these ideas, offer students permission to share their ideas, and give them time, space, and materials to follow their interests is an art. Unfortunately this seems in conflict with some current trends in our educational practices. *Coverage* of material included in curriculum guides and standardized tests seems to be of major concern, and student questions that do not immediately map onto an easily recognizable curriculum objective are sometimes viewed as unnecessary tangents. This concern has increased as school systems have adopted pacing guides, which teachers are expected to follow.

We do not want our students to think of school as a place where what they want to learn about is disregarded. Often, when we stop and think about how we can relate the topic of study to a current interest, a path can be found. For example, an interest in iPods could lead to an investigation on how size, capacity, weight, and cost may or may not be related.

How will activities at a station be assessed?

When an activity results in a product of some kind, teachers often feel that assessment is more manageable and they become more confident in their decision making. The review and reflection of student work samples is an important step in evaluating children's learning. So, too, is taking time to observe students in action and to engage students in conversations as their work is unfolding. Keeping anecdotal records is a natural strategy for capturing these moments. Digital cameras or video can be wonderful ways to document learning as well. Assessments of activities at learning stations come full circle, as do all assessments, to the learning goals that led to development of the station in the first place. Being mindful of our goals—and letting students know them—helps to focus assessment in any learning environment, whether there is a tangible product or a set of scenarios that tell the story of learning.

Answering the questions posed here can be difficult. They require that we make decisions that can be demanding of our time and our efforts. How to best make any decision is rooted in the context of our own school settings and our students' needs. We must also remember that these decisions are not set in stone. Flexibility is key; as we gather new information or learn new instructional strategies, we can revise our practice to better meet the growing needs of all of our students.

Keeping the Interest Alive

Along with empowering our students, providing choice in our classrooms helps us tap into the interests of our students. But just having choices available does not guarantee interest. Any parent who has heard the lament "There's nothing to do!" understands this well. Part of the excitement of making a choice is that it can lead to something new and exhilarating. Changing the materials that are made available to students on a regular basis adds a fresh look. Having a familiar material or activity disappear can pique curiosity, or even be a relief. Having it come back again in a few weeks or months may also be a welcome change.

Changing the format of student work also adds an element of interest that can maintain enthusiasm. Cutting recording sheets so they are in the shape of a rocket or a submarine sandwich breaks the expectation of the $8\frac{1}{2}$-by-11-inch sheet of paper. Engaging new senses, such as smell, can provide unexpected attention. Multimedia presentations can also create new interest.

Introducing topics in novel ways piques interest. Treasure maps to find a new activity, gigantic footprints across the ceiling to introduce a unit on proportional reasoning, or a set of clues to help students make guesses about a new topic add intrigue to learning. Adding a little surprise to our classrooms can be fun and helps students view mathematics in new ways, even when routines or objects are highly familiar.

Earlier in this chapter a teacher helped us consider making good choices. Helping students self-monitor this criterion is not easy. Yet, it is our role as teachers to support our students in their individual decision-making processes. Holding class meetings or individual conversations are strategies frequently used to support students' growth in this area. It is the establishment of expectations, trust, accountability, and security that can support our students as they make choices in our classrooms. As we get to know them as individuals and they get to know themselves as learners, we can encourage, direct, redirect, and applaud their efforts. All of this must happen within a full and lively classroom that changes in atmosphere and mood throughout the day and over the course of a year. Creating and maintaining learning laboratories like these presents unending questions as to how to balance the needs of the class as a whole with that of individual students. Ways to orchestrate this complex process is a challenge that teachers face every day.

Chapter 8
Managing Differentiated Instruction

*T*he role of a teacher has been compared to that of a coach or a conductor. Both lead a group of individuals with different talents and do not assume that those talents will be nurtured in the same manner. Coaches and conductors know how to motivate each member of their group and aim to develop all of the participants' strengths and work on weaknesses. Practices are held with the whole group, identified subgroups, and individuals. Each athlete or musician has slightly different tasks to perfect and yet in the end, the goal is for everyone to work together to produce a unified and masterful performance on the field or in the concert hall.

Teachers also need to develop a sense of a unified classroom while addressing the individual students' strengths and weaknesses. In a differentiated classroom where students are more likely to be engaged in multiple tasks that support their different levels of learning readiness, learning styles, and interests, it can be challenging to also develop a mathematical learning community that comes together to build, discuss, and verify ideas. Yet this is a challenge we must address. Differentiated instruction is not the same thing as individualized instruction. We do not believe that students should learn mathematics in isolation or that they should be deprived of the joy of being an active member of a well-functioning community group.

Teachers must also figure out how to manage different tasks going on at the same time. They need to distribute and collect materials in ways that do not require a lot of time and effort. They are challenged to find ways to have other students engaged in meaningful activities while they work uninterrupted with a small group. There is a necessity to create classroom spaces for noisy activities and quiet ones. Teachers need to think about the limitations of space, materials, and time as they make their plans. They must take the intricate components of classroom life and the complex needs of young learners and create a masterful learning environment.

While we do not want to promote the idea that a teacher must create a masterpiece each day in the classroom, we do believe that a well-managed classroom that supports students' learning while maintaining a sense of community is a masterpiece, one that begins its composition the moment students walk in the door on the first day of school. Right from the beginning, values, routines, and expectations need to be established that will develop an environment conducive to learning in a differentiated classroom.

Classroom Space

Ample space can be a rare commodity in many classrooms. Careful decisions need to be made about how the limited space is used so that a variety of groupings and activities can be supported. The following guidelines may be helpful.

- If you only have room for desks or tables, choose tables. In general, tables are more useful because they can accommodate individual or small-group learning and provide additional space for shared materials. Round tables are more conducive to small-group work as they allow each person's face to be seen more easily. If tables are not available, consider arranging desks in clusters to form a similar work space to support collaboration and conversation.

- Without desks, you will need to provide storage bins for students to keep their materials and belongings. Decisions will need to be made about where these bins will be housed. Keeping them in clear sight and easily accessible from the various tables in the room are just two conditions to be considered. Establishing their function and any expectations for use or boundaries around private versus communal space and supplies are also matters of importance when making your plans. Fabric bags that slip over the back of chairs also help to organize personal materials that students use frequently and keep students from needing to travel back and forth to bins on a regular basis.

- If you are asking your students to function without desks, think about doing the same yourself. While you also need ample personal storage areas, removing the teacher's desk may allow you to add an extra learning station or private space in the classroom. This may seem out of the question or unrealistic to you at first. Allowing yourself the chance to consider this option may lead to new possibilities for use of space in your classroom. It may also lead to reflecting on how space and arrangement may influence teaching and learning.

- If at all possible, designate an open area for whole-class discussions or meetings. A rug placed in the corner of a classroom can create this special space. The rug allows students to sit on the floor, rather than bringing over chairs to a meeting place, and the corner placement helps some students to focus better. Sometimes a long bench is there to provide additional seating. It is important that the meeting area be attractive and inviting and support student's sense of belonging to a community.

- Ample storage space is essential to helping classrooms be organized and efficient. As mentioned in Chapter 7, mathematics materials should be easily accessible for use and labeled to help ensure that they are returned properly. Just as with our drawers and closets at home, too many materials in too little space results in disorganization. Think about storing materials that only are used occasionally or during specific units in a supply closet or in higher cabinets in the room.

- Math manipulatives, games, and puzzles are certainly not the only tools used to learn mathematics. Along with these materials, designating a space for shared pencils, paper, scissors, glue, and a myriad of other art materials such as markers, crayons, and colored pencils also supports mathematical pursuits. Since these materials are used by all students throughout the day and across all subject matters, think about where and how to organize them; this decision is key to classroom efficiency and effectiveness. In many schools students are required to provide their own supplies of this nature. If this is the case where you teach, consider ways to make some or all of these materials more communal.

- Match features in the room to the type of work that will be done there. For example, placing the classroom library near the rug area makes sense as students like to relax when they read and there won't be other groups working in that area. Conversely, art materials should be placed away from the rug area to avoid unnecessary stains. In terms of mathematics, it makes sense to place a table adjacent to the storage area for the math materials. This placement allows one group of students to work with the materials without having to carry them too far. It also allows you and the students to place bins on a nearby tabletop when further organization or distribution of the materials is necessary.

• Consider traffic patterns. Make sure that students can travel easily from one table to another, to and from the classroom door, and to the various mathematical supplies and manipulatives in the room. Make these pathways wide enough so that you and the students can move back and forth without asking other students to move or interrupting their work.

• Designating space for other vital material such as recording sheets or packets for student work, finished-work baskets, portfolios, or other assessment-related data is an additional consideration. For example, think about the use of hanging file folders. Some teachers use these as a way to organize papers for newly assigned work. Teachers sometimes place all of the activity sheets related to a new unit in an open file box that is labeled so that students can easily get a new sheet without asking. Files of this sort can also be used for collecting student work. Many teachers put a hanging file or an open file box beside the place where they do their planning. In this way, teachers can easily access student work as they plan for the next day, prepare for student or parent conferences, or write report cards. They can also easily file students' work in portfolios or other data-type collections.

While these guidelines can help you to think about the arrangement of your room, most teachers need to find creative solutions to provide enough space for both groups and individuals to work. Consider the story of Odessa.

Odessa is a second-grade teacher who just completed her first year of teaching. Over the summer she thought about what worked during the year and what changes she wanted to make for the following year. One of the factors was the layout of the classroom. She realized that she had ample open tables and work areas where students mostly worked together, but few spaces where students could work more privately and be less distracted by what was happening around them. She remembered hearing about a simple concept called a private office where you overlap two manila folders and then staple the doubled center panel to make a trifold. The trifolds could stand up on desks or tables and provide private, separate spaces for students to work.

The following September, Odessa introduces this idea and the students are excited about having their own offices. As Seth explains, "My mom has an office at home, but I don't. Now I have one, too!" The students decorate both the outside and the inside of the folders with things you would find in an office: monthly calendars, plants (made from construction paper), and pictures of families brought from home. One girl writes, "Math is cool!" which reminds Odessa of how she puts inspirational quotes around her desk to keep her motivation high.

Sometimes she asks everyone in the class to get out their private offices. For example, during an assessment task she has the students set up their offices while they write word problems to share. She feels that this approach gives her a more accurate measure of what students are able to produce on their own. It also creates a bit of mystery and the students seem more excited about the problems they share. Spontaneously, some of the students begin to bring their "offices" to a table when they want to work independently without distractions. Over the course of the year she notices more variation in office use. A few of the students seem to use it quite often, while some only do so under direction. She is comfortable with the variety and believes that students are making appropriate choices for their learning styles.

That spring, a staff developer who understands the importance of giving teachers opportunities to share their personal success stories leads a systemwide professional development meeting for elementary teachers. The agenda is "Come share your best idea that has made a difference in how students learned this year." Odessa is excited to share her idea about creating private working spaces in her classroom. When she does so, many of her peers express interest in the idea. Colleagues from first and third grade even ask Odessa if they could visit her classroom to see how the students use their offices.

Monica decides to plan a visit. She is a third-grade teacher who is struggling with meeting her students' needs this year. The range of the students' ability levels seems broader than usual; she also has more students on individualized education plans (IEPs). She thinks the private office would help her students learn through different models and visual cues. For example, Monica knows that some of her students really need a hundreds chart on their desks to help them visualize relationships among numbers while other students have a strong preference for using a number line. Some of the students need support with vocabulary words and the word wall does not seem to be enough for them. She envisions them writing some words on sticky notes and posting them just as you might in a cubicle. One of her students still reverses the teen numbers and he can put up cues to prompt him on what to do. In their private offices the students could make decisions about what they want to put in their spaces to support their learning. She can envision helping some students create sequence cards that they could hang in their offices to remind them of specific steps that are required for success. Also, these offices would be portable, allowing the students to easily bring their supportive tools with them, wherever they work.

After the visit to Odessa's room, Monica is even more enthusiastic and decides to implement this idea. Her students are also excited about the opportunity to decorate their own spaces and with some prompting are able to make decisions about what learning tools and models to include as well. One student, Jessica, always forgets the words *numerator* and *denominator* and feels this is important to put in her office. She draws a rectangular model of three-fourths and writes $3 = numerator$ and $4 = denominator$ below the figure. Some students even make similar offices to use when they are doing homework.

Monica encourages the students to tape the tools to their folders. She wants them to be attached firmly, but she also wants tools that can be replaced as the students' learning evolves. If they wrote directly on the folders, Monica believes her students would think of the tools as more permanent, as something they would always need. The offices give the students privacy and encourage them to take ownership of their own learning. They also help Monica differentiate the scaffolding each student receives.

Respect for Differences

In order for differentiated classrooms to function well, all participants must know that respectful behavior is required. Everyone must respect others' learning needs and styles and realize that everyone has the right to have their needs met. Activities that identify and celebrate differences help students better understand why their classrooms are organized the way that they are. They also help students get to know themselves and each other better. This knowledge allows students to better support each other individually and to feel more connected as a community of learners.

One fourth-grade teacher uses the idea of multiple intelligences to help students realize that everyone has unique gifts and that we do not all learn the same way. First students look up the definition of the word *intelligence* in the dictionary and then the class talks about ways people are intelligent. Students usually identify reading, math, and writing first and then add ideas such as sports, drawing, and singing. The teacher tells them informally about Dr. Howard Gardner's research and writes the eight different intelligences on the board. The areas are named in terms the students can understand, for example, logical-mathematical is identified as "number smart." Possible career choices related to each intelligence are discussed as well. Next the students reflect on themselves in relation to these areas. For each intelligence, they write about their abilities, score themselves on a scale of one to ten, and make a bar graph to display their ratings.

Alex writes, "Pretty good for word smart, but not that good. I can speak well but I don't no [sic] how to spell." Bernie records, "I will use numbers in my job, but I will not be an accountant, scientist, or computer programmer." For "self smart" Casandra writes, "I don't like to work alone or be alone and I like to share my ideas not keep them to myself." (See Figure 8–1.) The students are engaged throughout this process and it is clear that they are learning about themselves. As Lorenzo explains, "I thought I just liked to draw, but now I know I have art and space intelligence!" They are also learning about each other. Leanna looks at her friend's work and exclaims, "I didn't know you liked nature. I've got a great place for us to explore sometime."

Once the written work is completed, each student makes a self-portrait. Then with the written work, graphs, and portraits in front of them, they each make a "brain collage." They do this by sketching an outline of their heads and filling this space with pictures found in newspapers and magazines. The students choose pictures that represent their intelligences. The students hang this work on the wall for back-to-school night. They staple their four

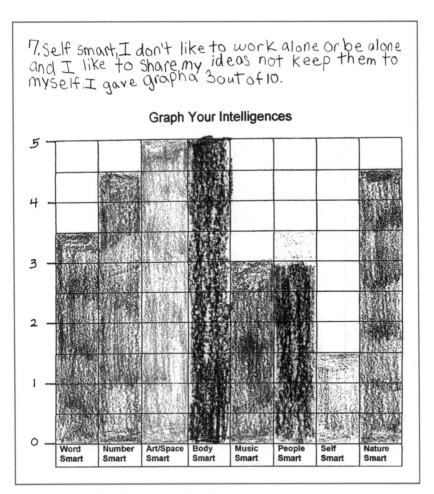

7. Self smart, I don't like to work alone or be alone and I like to share my ideas not keep them to myself. I gave grapha a 3 out of 10.

Graph Your Intelligences

Figure 8–1 *Casandra's description and graph.*

pieces of work together; the collage is on top, then the graph, the written information, and the self-portraits. Parents are challenged to identify their children's work before they see the self-portraits. From the teacher's reflection that follows we learn that not all parents do so successfully.

Teacher Reflection

I started this activity a couple of years ago when I sensed an increase in the amount of name calling going on at recess. Too often students who excelled in mathematics were being called nerds and those who were athletic were referred to as jocks. I wanted my students to view each other with more openness, to be interested in and get along with people who were different from

(Continued)

them. I felt that if I could help them understand that there is more than one way of doing things then the bullying and teasing would lessen. I also wanted them to understand their own learning styles better so that they could take more responsibility for their work and think about how they might expand their skills. I certainly didn't want them to view success with mathematics as a negative trait!

The students enjoy this activity and learn a lot. It definitely diminishes name calling and builds respect for differences. Parent's night is always interesting. The first year I was surprised to find out how many parents could not identify their children after looking at the first three pages. Some of the parents who do recognize their children's work are still surprised by the specifics. It's not unusual to hear, "When did she learn to sew?" or "I didn't know he was so interested in people." Following parent's night, we still keep the graphs on display. They provide us all with a visual reminder about our similarities and differences.

Another teacher with similar goals has students complete a survey form sometime during the first week of school. The form is called *What Matches You?* and provides twenty-five different "I statements" for students to consider. (See Figure 8–2; see also Blackline Masters.) Some of the items are general statements about learning, such as "I need quiet when I work." Other statements focus on mathematics, such as "I am better at addition than subtraction."

As we learn from the following teacher's reflection, this form can spark conversations about learning and about mathematics.

Teacher Reflection

For a couple of years I used a form like this one during the first day or two of school. It got students walking around and talking to each other and learning something about their classmates. I used to put in items such as "I like to play baseball" or "I like chocolate ice cream." This year I decided to focus more on learning. I decided that students would eventually find out about each other's recreational and food preferences, but that they might never talk about how they each learn. Also, I was hoping this activity might help them to gain an intuitive sense of why I strive to provide differentiated learning opportunities in our classroom.

The responses took somewhat longer to be formulated. They used to know right away whether they liked chocolate, but deciding if they wanted rules for solving problems required some reflection. Some students were amazed to find that everybody didn't think a digital clock was better than a face clock and others were pleased to find someone else who preferred to work alone.

After we did this activity, we talked about the differences in our classroom and how it was important to respect these different ways of learning. We made a list of what we learned. Marcus said, "I have to be quiet sometimes so that Billy can think." Jamie said, "I might want to try using a number line." Ellie said, "It's good that we are different. Otherwise, it would be boring." It felt wonderful to hear the students articulate these ideas.

Immediately following this conversation we began our first differentiated learning activity. I introduced it by saying, "Many times in our classroom we will be doing different activities from each other. Why do you think that is so?" Several hands popped up and I called on Ricardo who said, "Because we are different." I couldn't have been more pleased.

What Matches You?

Try to find two classmates to fit each description. Have them sign in the box they match. No one may sign more than three boxes on one sheet.

I learn best through hands-on experiences.	I like to solve problems.	I prefer to work alone in mathematics.	I find it helpful to write about my mathematical ideas	I sometimes get confused when others explain their thinking.
I understand fractions better than decimals.	I like to measure things.	I use drawings to understand a problem.	I learn best when the teacher writes on the board.	I find a number line more helpful than a hundreds chart.
I am better at division than multiplication.	I like rotating shapes in my mind.	I need quiet when I work.	I prefer base ten blocks to number lines.	I prefer to work with others.
I know my basic facts well.	I like digital clocks better than analog ones.	I am better at addition than subtraction.	I like reading and making maps.	I like learning different ways to solve problems.
I like to brainstorm ideas with a group and then follow up alone.	I like logic games and puzzles.	I want rules for solving problems.	I would like to use a calculator all of the time.	I read tables and graphs in the newspaper.

Figure 8–2 *A survey form for fourth graders,* What Matches You?

Routines

Routines serve several purposes in a classroom. Once students recognize ways to get into groups, distribute assignment papers, put away materials, get in line, and walk in the hallway, these activities will occur quickly and efficiently. Much of the first weeks of school are spent creating these routines and making sure that everyone can follow them. Though considerable time and effort is needed to get them launched, once established they are adhered to with minimal energy and teacher supervision. This is particularly important in a differentiated classroom where students are expected to manage themselves, more frequently and often for longer durations, while the teacher is working with other students.

Routines also instill feelings of safety and security. When the same procedures are followed on a daily or weekly basis, students understand what is expected of them and can predict what will happen next. Such regularity helps students to feel emotionally safe in our schools and thus more able to participate in the learning process. Established routines also create community. As students identify and describe the ways in which their classroom runs, they are forming their understanding of the unique culture of their classroom.

In differentiated mathematics instruction, each group of students may be working with different mathematical materials, but they need to gather and return the materials to the math storage area in the same manner. The importance of putting them away in the same way you found them is stressed as one of the ways we respect all members of the class. Figuring out how to share materials is an important aspect of developing respect.

Routines also provide common experiences that help create a sense of community. It seems all teachers, regardless of their students' ages, have some beginning-of-the-day ritual. In many classes before-school work is used to help students transition smoothly into a new day. Such work provides the time to pick up from where students left off the day before, helps to frame or launch new challenges for the day, or provides additional practice in areas of need. While students dive right in, the teacher can take care of greeting each student individually and any housekeeping chores such as attendance, lunch count, and communications from home. Some teachers ask students to be responsible for several of these housekeeping responsibilities.

Once everyone has arrived some classrooms hold a community meeting. Often there are several routines within a morning meeting, some of which are designed to build social skills and some to build academic ones. One class includes "Numbers in the News" in their morning routines. In addition to taking attendance and calling on students to share, the two morning leaders are each responsible for telling their classmates about a number in the news. It is their teacher's hope that this routine exposes students to some current events as well as supports students' number sense.

While some upper-elementary classes do not have a meeting each day, some teachers hold one on Mondays to help students transition back from the weekend. One fourth-grade teacher includes a number sense activity within this time block. From her reflection we learn that the teacher began this practice because she felt that students lost interest in numbers during their elementary school years.

Teacher Reflection

As a parent, I noticed that when my children were younger they loved numbers. They would count all the time and I would often hear them sing songs about numbers. At age four, my son's favorite number was four. If I asked him how many cookies he wanted, he would respond with an attitude that suggested he couldn't imagine why anyone would want more or less than four. Four was the perfect number for him until, of course, he turned five. This passion for numbers existed for all of my children until around second grade and then numbers became just ordinary and the passion no longer existed. When I started teaching fifth grade I noticed this same lack of interest in numbers. Personally, I love numbers. I particularly love numbers as they apply to baseball. One of my favorite numbers is 35,000. I decided to use this number to launch a weekly number routine.

The teacher writes *35,000* on the board and asks her students what this number could represent in baseball. A few suggestions are made such as the number of years baseball has existed and the total number of outs in a season. Finally, someone proposes the correct answer, the approximate number of fans that attend a game at Fenway Park in Boston, Massachusetts. The teacher explains to the students how knowing this number fact helps her to think about other numbers. For example, about 30,000 people live in her community. She can imagine all of those people being at Fenway Park and this gives her a visual image of what that number of people would look like.

Next the teacher tells the students, "Each week a student is going to share a number that means something to him or her at our Monday meeting. We will call these numbers *landmark* or *benchmark numbers* because they help us to better understand other numbers." She reminds Katley that she is meeting leader next week and that she should be sure to think of a number.

The following week Katley says her number is 100 and that she heard the number on television. Many classmates offer suggestions as to what this number could represent, such as how much money someone got for his birthday, how much money someone lost, or how much money someone found. Katley then tells her classmates that it is the amount of money a personal trainer can make in an hour. Katley also shared that she thought this was a lot of money for one hour's work and others agreed. This conversation led to other benchmark numbers that might be relevant here, such as the minimum wage and the average wage of a personal trainer. The teacher was pleased that the discussion led to a more realistic view of this career. Many of her students were of lower socioeconomic status and they were sometimes drawn to lifestyles that appeared glamorous on television.

Doreen was responsible for the next week's number and she also identified a number related to money. Doreen's number was 325, the cost of a particular Coach pocketbook. When this was identified, Jason said they should think about minimum wage again. The class figured out if you were sixteen years old working for minimum wage it would take about sixty hours to earn enough money to buy the pocketbook. The pocketbook no longer seemed such a necessity! The teacher was once again pleased at how mathematics was helping her students to develop number sense skills that could inform their choices and their understanding of the world.

As the year continues, the class's interest in this activity is maintained and they become more adapt at identifying questions related to the given numerical information. In March, Frank's number is 5,878, which is the number of neon light bulbs in the Citgo sign outside of Fenway Park. This number fact leads students to want to know other numerical data and a list of questions are created:

- How many bulbs are replaced each year because they are hit by a baseball?
- How tall is the Citgo sign and who gets to change the light bulbs?
- How big are these light bulbs?
- How long does a light bulb last before it needs to be replaced?

Some students spend snack time or indoor recess looking up answers to these questions. Most important they are engaged with numbers in ways that make sense to them and community spirit is built through this routine.

Grouping Students

Another way to maximize learning is to think critically about group work. Though whole-group teaching can be very powerful and some teachers believe it promotes equality by ensuring that all students are taught the same lessons, it is not always the most effective way to learn. As we have explored throughout this book, differentiation is focused on finding the most effective ways of meeting our students' various needs. Organizing students into groups can promote individual learning.

Grouping for differentiated instruction is different than working in groups. Group work has been long recognized as a way to break up the whole-class instructional pattern, to engage students more actively in their learning, and to provide greater opportunities for communication and social interactions. Traditionally, each group may be completing the same task. The teacher rotates among the groups, supporting their work, and informing their thinking. While a useful instructional strategy, grouping for differentiated instruction is even more intentional.

Within differentiated instruction, grouping is flexible; that is, groups are formed with a specific focus and then reconfigured when a new purpose is identified. The formation of groups may be based on readiness, learning styles, or interests and can be heterogeneous or homogenous. Groups may be formed for a day, a week, or a few weeks. The flexible grouping keeps students from being labeled and allows them to work with a variety of their peers.

It takes time and thought to group students. Thinking about why you are grouping and whether groups will be designed around a specific learning goal, learning style, interest, product, or behavior is all part of the process. Identifying the appropriate size of the groups, the amount of time the group should work together, and the composition of the group are all decisions that need to be made. Teachers also need to think about how groups and their materials will be identified and organized.

Sometimes groups are formed at random. Some teachers keep a deck of cards with stickers on them. If four groups are needed and there are twenty students in the class, five different kinds of stickers will be used. The deck is shuffled and students randomly select a card. All the like stickers form a new group. Sometimes these stickers correspond to tables or areas of the room and as students pick a card they know right away where to go to meet their new group.

Sometimes students choose their own groups or partnerships. Allowing students to make this choice is one of the ways we can share our classroom authority. Many teachers find that they are most comfortable with this option when only dyads are being formed, or when groups will be intact for a short period of time, or when partners or groups work together on the basis of interest.

More often, differentiated instruction requires teachers to form groups intentionally; that is, teachers match students specifically in ways to best meet learning needs. One teacher frequently changes student groups in her classroom. She keeps two large magnetic boards resting on the chalk tray to help her organize this process. For each board she has a set of nametags backed with magnetic tape. When she plans an activity for which new groups are required, she moves the names on the board according to her criteria. As she explains, "I used to do this on paper. When the grouping was obvious, this worked fine. Sometimes, though, I find it challenging to make groups and change my mind several times. With the board, I can try out several formations easily. Then when I am done, the list is already there for my students to see."

Many teachers keep a log of the groups that are formed during the first few weeks of school. The log can serve as a place to keep notes about groups that function particularly well together or partnerships that seem to require more supervision. A teacher can also make sure that everyone has the opportunity to work with all the other classmates during these first weeks of community building. It can also be worthwhile to note how the groups were formed so that over time, students work according to readiness, learning styles, and interests.

Though a student might become upset or feel isolated at any time, forming partners and groups can heighten such feelings. Some students may wonder why they are in one group versus another. Others may worry about being chosen or welcomed. Concern for isolation, safety, comfort, friendships, and working relationships must always be part of the grouping process. Whether in math or any other subject, it is essential to keep students' social-emotional development in mind.

Time with Individual Students

There are times when teachers and students need and want to work one on one. While some may consider this a luxury in a busy classroom, many teachers find such work to be one of the most enlightening aspects of their day. Working with an individual student can be a time for getting to know the student better, to assess a specific skill or competence, or to just dig deeper together on a problem. Sitting side by side can be rewarding and informative to both the student and teacher and can help nourish a supportive, trusting relationship so necessary to teaching and learning.

By building expectations for different learning activities to occur simultaneously, differentiated instruction supports opportunities to work with individual students. Other students do not expect the teacher to always be available to them and their ability to work independently from the teacher has been developed. Teacher-student partnerships become just one of the various configurations within the classroom. Such acceptance also supports longer individual interactions such as when interviews are conducted, some tutoring is needed, or particular follow-up to a lesson or task is required.

The image of keeping plates spinning in the air is one to which many teachers can relate. We work tirelessly to keep every child engaged and learning. Sometimes, even in our best attempts, plates fall. In these moments it is important to have time carved out in our day and our classroom to work with individual students. Sometimes we can anticipate a falter and a quick spin or adjustment will help the child get back on track. Sometimes more intensive work is needed. For example, in one fourth-grade class, students were asked to complete the following task:

> *I have four sides.*
> *Two of my sides are parallel.*
> *My other two sides are not parallel.*
> *Draw me.*

Riley was convinced that this drawing was impossible. "This is a trick question," he complained. His teacher heard his frustration and invited him to join her at the small round table in the back of the room. The teacher asked Riley to begin the task. With reluctance he agreed to do so and drew two parallel line segments:

_____

_____

"See," he began to explain, "you can't connect these lines with anything but parallel lines. And it says they can't be."

The teacher wasn't surprised by Riley's thinking; she knew many students would find this task challenging. She began by asking him, "Is there another way you could draw that first set of lines?" Riley nodded yes and drew the lines exactly the same, but in a vertical orientation. "It's still the same. This can't be done." The teacher believed a strong hint was needed and suggested that this time, he make his lines different lengths. Riley drew the line segments shown below, but was unable to complete the drawing. Instead, he announced, "I can't use these lines. They aren't parallel."

―――――

――――――――

After a few more questions to confirm, it became clear to the teacher that Riley thought that parallel lines have to be the same length. The teacher understood the tendency for most of her students to begin this task by drawing two parallel line segments of the same length, but before this conversation, never understood that they believed this to be a requirement. She checked with a couple of other students and found that they too shared this belief. She thought about the illustrations shown in the curriculum materials and realized that examples almost always show line segments that are congruent. After these conversations she knew she needed to review the definition of parallel lines with the whole class and show them drawings that would challenge their thinking. Without the time she spent individually with Riley, she never would have realized this misconception.

Sometimes teachers discover the need to meet individually with a student while they are at home looking at student work. Such was the case with a fifth-grade teacher who was examining three multiplication examples completed by Bryce, a new student in the class who had been taught the traditional algorithm for multiplication. As the teacher examines his work, she cannot diagnose his error. She isn't surprised that the first example is correct; no regrouping is required. She looks closer at the other two examples. It doesn't seem to be a basic fact error, nor does he seem to be adding in the regrouped number before he multiplies, a systematic error with which she is familiar. She recognizes that he also only seems to have difficulty when he multiplies by the tens digit, but can't figure out what he is doing. She places the paper with the other three samples that she has identified as needing follow-up conversations.

She meets with Bryce the next day and asks him to talk aloud as he explains his work. He describes the first example clearly and she is eager to hear what he will say about the second example. As she expects, he is fine until he comes to multiplying by the tens digit. He says, "I write the zero to show I am really multiplying by tens. Two times five is ten. I write the zero and trade the one. I can't multiply four numbers, but I know I have to multiply and then add, so you get eight and three and that's eleven." The teacher tries to follow his thinking, but feels lost. "Where did you get the eight and three?" she asks. "Easy," he replies. "Two times four is eight and three times one is three." The teacher thinks a bit and then looks at his last example. She sees the four numbers in his tens column and realizes he has followed the same procedure. He has multiplied each pair of numbers (5×2 and 6×4) and then added the results ($10 + 24$) to get thirty-four. (See Figure 8–3.)

The teacher knows she will have to spend more time with Bryce. His algorithm needs adjusting and she would like him to explore some alternative approaches as well as focus more on estimating products so that he can judge the reasonableness of his responses. But, she has learned that his error was systematic, which means he can follow a series of steps consistently. She is sure he will be fine with just a bit of time working with her or a peer tutor. When students have relatively simple procedural misconceptions she finds that peers can be effective teachers. This peer support also gives her more time to assess other student difficulties or work with students whose errors are not systematic.

Soon Bryce crosses off each regrouped number after he has used it and his work is basically error free. He can also connect his

Figure 8–3 *Bryce's written work.*

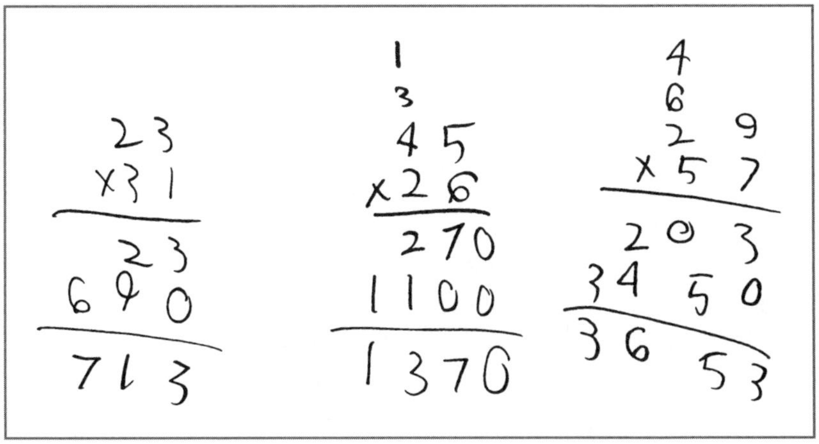

recordings to work with base ten blocks so that his procedural and conceptual knowledge are linked. When the teacher believes that Bryce is a bit more settled in his new class, she will explore alternative algorithms with him, but for now, she wants to validate his approach while helping to ensure its accuracy.

Ragged Time

When students are involved in different tasks and work at different rates, this creates what some educators refer to as *ragged time*. Helping each student transition to another appropriate activity when the assigned task is completed is not good use of a teacher's time, so it is important to have activities that students go to naturally. Such activities are sometimes known as *sponges,* as they soak up the extra time between early and late finishers. In the literacy curriculum this often translates to free reading or journal writing. It is important to have similar choices within the mathematics curriculum.

A number of options are possible and different choices may be available on different days or within different units. For example, during a geometry unit one fourth-grade teacher always sets up a jigsaw puzzle at a table in a corner of the room. Working on the puzzle is a choice during indoor recess or when their math work is completed. Over about three or four weeks the puzzle is finished by many pairs of students placing a few pieces correctly each time they visit the table. Sometimes the teacher picks out a few pieces and places them strategically so that each student can contribute. The class feels a great sense of accomplishment when the puzzle is completed.

A fifth-grade teacher launches her discussion of proof with consideration of Sudoku puzzles. She finds some examples online that are appropriate for her students. At first, many of her students respond, "I just think it should go there," when they explain the placement of a particular digit. During the course of the week, she uses these puzzles to help students understand what it means to prove that an identified digit, and only that digit, must be placed in a particular cell. Later, the teacher refers to this experience whenever she thinks her students need to be reminded about what it means to prove something. She also collects a group of puzzles that students can pursue when their work is finished. They are purposely color-coded by difficulty and students are comfortable saying, "I'm taking a yellow one, because these puzzles are new to me."

Choosing to practice basic math facts during ragged time is supported in most classrooms. Students might work in pairs with flashcards or take advantage of computer software. Some teachers set out a collection of unit-related literature books when beginning a new topic. These books can be placed in a special location and explored when the day's specific math task is completed. *Guinness Book of World Records* is also a favorite to have in the classroom. Students may also be directed to problem decks, technology, menu choices, and stations. All sponge activities don't have to be related to the current topics; in fact, bringing back some favorite choices can be a way to maintain skills. What's important is that students know what to do when they finish their work and that they continue to be involved in mathematical explorations throughout the time designated for mathematics.

Whole-Class Work

Whole-class lessons remain important. Often the notion of all of the students working on the exact same thing at the same time seems contradictory to the notion of differentiated instruction. As we have seen throughout the stories shared from various classrooms, whole-class lessons are vital. They provide common experiences and expose students to a greater array of thinking. They help develop common vocabulary and a sense of community. They offer an efficient means for introducing new content that can then be continued later working in small groups, in pairs, or individually. There is a time and a place for each form of instruction; knowing your intent and figuring out the best way to meet your goals is what is critical.

Even during the lesson, teachers have ways to support individual needs and strengths. Often a quick think/pair/share time can lead to a more successful whole-class endeavor. Many students prefer being able to stop and reflect or need the support of a partner in a larger group setting. Waiting before responses are given, encouraging several students to respond, and teaching students how to connect their comments to those of the previous speakers are all ways to support whole-class discussions.

Though differentiated instruction emphasizes meeting individual needs, we must not lose sight of the importance of the collective experience in this process. Participation in a learning community is powerful. What we learn together can far exceed what any one individual can learn alone or any single teacher can teach. Finding ways to bring a class of students together to share their experiences is an essential component of differentiated classrooms. Even when students are working on separate tasks, there needs to be designated times for students to gather and share their new knowledge, ideas, and strategies.

Whether in class meetings or debriefing sessions, students require time together to report findings, review ideas, and raise new questions. Within these discussions, students can see how others take on new challenges and make sense of new material. When students have not worked on exactly the same task, sharing can seem less important to them, to some, maybe even irrelevant or confusing. Teachers need to orchestrate these conversations in ways that build commonalities while respecting and celebrating differences.

Looking for common ground is a place to start. That's why we always identify the curriculum goal or standard before we design tasks, form groups, and make other decisions about customizing instruction. Refocusing students on the common threads of their individual learning experiences helps them to see that it makes sense to share. Sometimes simply asking students to describe one new thing they learned today, this week, or during this unit can both honor and link individual experiences. Recording personal responses in a concept web may unearth more similarity and common ground than first perceived.

Class discussions can focus on process as well as content. Sometimes, talking about how we organize our data, visualize a relationship, or represent our thinking may be more informative than sharing an answer or a solution. Further, as children learn more about each other's thinking, they are able to more authentically validate frustrations, make note of growth, and celebrate success.

As teachers gain experience with differentiated instruction, they identify their own ways to organize the classroom space, to build student awareness and respect for differences, to develop classroom routines, to form groups, to work with students individually, to provide interesting activities for students who finish early, and to lead whole-group lessons and discussions. They develop their own methods for supporting the important work of differentiation, for building the masterpiece of a well-functioning classroom that meets individual needs while maintaining classroom community.

Chapter 9

Teaching with the Goal of Differentiation
Ten Ways to Sustain Your Efforts

$\mathcal{H}$opefully, you too believe that it is essential to differentiate mathematical instruction and now have some additional ideas about what that means and how it might look in your classroom. Even with this recognition and vision, however, differentiated instruction is a long-term goal and working toward such a goal is often difficult to sustain. Just as you would require encouragement, reminders, and support to make other significant changes in behavior, you need to find ways to help your differentiation lens stay in focus, to act on your belief that students' readiness, learning styles, and interests should inform the ways in which you teach. So what can you do to keep your spirit for differentiation high? Here are ten suggestions.

1. Identify Where You Already Provide Differentiation.

It's important to remember that differentiation in mathematics is not brand new. You are already grouping students in some ways, working with students individually, and making modifications to meet students' needs. The idea is that now these decisions will be more preplanned and made with more specific needs in mind. Rather than making changes after a lesson has been problematic, you begin to make adjustments in the planning process. Sometimes just tweaking a familiar activity allows the learning experience to be more on target, to be deeper and richer for students.

Some teachers begin by thinking about the students who are the least successful with the curriculum as presented. Perhaps there are three or four students in your class who need much more support or challenge. Putting the effort into making lessons work for these students may take more time in the beginning, but the end result will be well worth it. As one teacher expressed, "Now I work more ahead of time, so I don't have to work so hard when I am teaching."

Don't lose sight of what you can do and, in fact, what you are doing already. Whether you make differentiated instruction in mathematics a priority, you still need to assess what students know and align your curriculum to national, state, and local standards. These assessment and alignment processes jump-start your goal of differentiation. It is valuable to do them anyway and they give you a secure foundation on which to base instructional decisions and to build activities that better meet individual needs. Be clear about what new work is needed and what is required already. As we learn from the following teacher reflection, this clarity is not always present.

Teacher Reflection

I spent all day Sunday getting ready for these new mathematics activities I wanted to try. I had been to a workshop on differentiated instruction and decided to do some things differently in the measurement unit we were about to begin. I had given my students a pre-assessment on Friday and spent much of Sunday morning looking at their work and rereading my school's curriculum along with a few other resources. It was a beautiful day and my husband and children were headed out for a hike. I wanted to go with them and I was feeling grouchy that my school work kept me from joining them. I was beginning to wish that I had never started this work. I complained to my husband who said, "But you always spend a Sunday working on stuff before you start a new unit. Is this like the house cleaning?"

I had to laugh at myself then. Just yesterday I had been complaining about how much work it was to have his parents to dinner. At noon we had cleaned the house and gone food shopping and hadn't even started to cook yet. My husband had been clear then, too. He reminded me that we always went food shopping and cleaned the house on Saturday mornings whether his parents were coming to dinner or not. How did I forget that? When I looked at it that way, the additional time wasn't that great and it turned out to be a lovely evening. I sometimes start out new projects with a bit of pessimism. It's important for me to remember why I am doing something and to be clear about what the actual "costs" are.

2. Recognize Where You Are Along the Journey.

Many teachers provide a task in September that students complete again sometime in November or December. The comparison of these work samples provides students and parents with concrete examples of growth. Such evidence can boost morale, particularly for students who struggled initially or who may not realize how their abilities have changed. Just as initial benchmarks help students appreciate what they have gained, teachers also benefit from learning how their teaching abilities have adapted, sharpened, broadened, or transformed. So, before you begin your new commitment to differentiated mathematics instruction, you might want to self-assess your current level of differentiation in mathematics.

We encourage you to make a copy of the "Self-Assessment of Differentiation Practices" form. (See Figure 9–1; see also Blackline Masters.) Complete it now and put it in a place where you can find it at a later date. If you keep a personal calendar, mark a date two to three months from now when you will complete this form for a second time. (You may also want to note where you are putting your original response!) Most teachers who do this find that there are significant differences between their responses. For some teachers, just knowing they are going to complete the form again encourages them to try some new instructional strategies.

3. Start Small and Build Up Your Differentiation Muscles.

Once teachers recognize the need for differentiated instruction, they sometimes feel as if they have to differentiate every lesson for every student. This would be an overwhelming task, especially if differentiated mathematics instruction is a new practice for you. Just as if you were starting a new exercise program, it's best to start slowly and extend your goals as you build your skills and experience success. Exercising too much, too soon, can result in injuries, frustration, and a sense of failure. These repercussions cause many who make an initial commitment to fitness to conclude that "exercise just isn't right for me." So, begin slowly and increase the differentiation in your mathematics teaching as your skills and confidence grow.

One way to start is to begin with the mathematics strand you believe you know the best or the one that would benefit the most from differentiation strategies. For most teachers these are one and the same: *number* and *operations*. This is the topic that gets the

Rate your agreement with each of the following statements.
1 – disagree strongly   2 – disagree somewhat   3 – agree somewhat   4 – agree strongly

I feel confident in my ability to facilitate the
learning of mathematics at my grade level.   1   2   3   4

I can challenge my most mathematically able
students.   1   2   3   4

I know how to support my least mathematically
able students.   1   2   3   4

I can meet students' individual needs in mathematics
as well as or better than I can in literacy.   1   2   3   4

I have enough knowledge of mathematics to support a variety
of models, representations, and procedures in my classroom. 1   2   3   4

Rate the likelihood of the following activities occurring within a week of mathematical instruction.
1 – very unlikely   2 – somewhat unlikely   3 – somewhat likely   4 – very likely

I work with students individually.   1   2   3   4

Students are grouped by readiness.   1   2   3   4

Students are grouped by interest.   1   2   3   4

Students are grouped by learning preferences.   1   2   3   4

Different students are working with different materials
and tasks.   1   2   3   4

Check off each instructional strategy that you have tried in your teaching of mathematics.
Give yourself two points for each checkmark.

☐ Transformation of tasks to make them more open-ended
☐ RAFT
☐ Learning station
☐ Menu
☐ Think Tac Toe
☐ Compacting
☐ Tiered task

Total Score: _____

Scores range from 10 to 54.
Are you comfortable with where you are on this continuum of change? What next step(s) do you want to take?

Figure 9–1   *Self-Assessment of Differentiation Practices.*

greatest attention in the elementary grades, and if you have been teaching for a few years, the one for which you probably have the greatest number of supplementary resources. Once you have selected a strand, you can narrow your focus to a unit, a series of lessons, or a particular outcome, for example, "fluency with whole number multiplication" (NCTM 2006, 16). Work with number and operations often yields the widest range of abilities among students. Perhaps because the skill set is so familiar to most teachers, student abilities are often apparent quickly and can be challenging to address within the same activity. This difficulty is in contrast, for example, to the way student differences seem to be addressed more easily within the data analysis and probability strand.

Most elementary teachers find that all students can easily be engaged with the same task of conducting a survey if choice is given about what data are collected and how the data are organized. Interest will influence the topic chosen. Readiness will impact how the question is stated. For example, *Did you like the school field trip or the school recital best?* is much easier to negotiate than *What did you like best about the school field trip?* Learning preferences may influence how students keep track of the data collected and make sure that everyone has the opportunity to respond. Readiness, learning styles, and interests may inform how the information is displayed and what conclusions are drawn. Most important, these differences occur naturally and do not require much teacher intervention. This is less likely to be the case with number and operations. The following reflection shows how choosing a familiar strategy and topic can be a positive way to begin.

Teacher Reflection

I decided that I would try to incorporate some of the instructional strategies I use in reading in my mathematics program. I often select books with a similar theme that span a wide range of reading levels. In this way I feel like I can place the right book in the hands of every student, books that will challenge their levels of comprehension, while being well within the instructional range of their skill levels for reading. At the same time, we can have a class discussion about themes that emerge in each story and students can be regrouped to share with those who may not have read the same book. There is usually enough commonality to sustain a dynamic conversation. If I have selected nonfiction material, students can compare details and share facts, thus allowing everyone to benefit by the different books read.

(Continued)

Trying to set up a similar dynamic for math has not been as straight-forward, but I wanted to give it a try. Focusing on number and operations I selected a word problem and then created three versions of it. The structure of each problem was the same. I created a story around a set of twins who each earned an allowance for doing chores. Within the three versions of the problem, I differentiated the amount of money each child earned, the number of times each chore was completed, and how the problem was worded. I predetermined which students would answer each problem. Students initially worked alone and then I paired them with other students who were working on the exact problem. Once I felt as though everyone had solved and compared with at least one other classmate, I grouped children in triads with one student representing each type of problem.

In this new configuration, students were asked to share their problems, answers, and solution strategies. My hope was that each student would act as the expert for the problem they were presenting to the group. Once everyone had familiarized themselves with the three problems, I wanted them to discuss what was the same or different in each problem. This seemed to work well as students made comments such as "In your problem, Julio and Rita each did the chores a lot more times." "Rita earned more money than Julio in my problem." "We all used division to get the answers."

This was a small step for me, but it was one that really worked. I could see doing something like this about once a week without too much trouble. The students were successful with their individual problems, but also were exposed to other levels of thinking. Maybe next time I could change problem settings as well, choosing contexts that I knew would appeal to different students' interests.

4. Capitalize on Anticipation.

Teachers are often thinking about what happens next. Sometimes this anticipation can be to our benefit. Sometimes it can lead to trouble. We need to think about how to use anticipation to our best advantage.

On the positive side, being able to anticipate the time and resources a specific activity will require is very helpful. Haven't we all started a lesson only to realize that we had not made enough copies of the activity packet, or that there really wasn't enough time to complete a new lesson because it took much longer to launch than expected and now the students have to be in gym class? Decisions that avoid situations like these come with experience, though even the most seasoned veteran makes similar errors in judgment from time to time. Not having quite the right resources can derail a potentially successful differentiated lesson, so it's important to make sure that manipulatives, worksheets or packets, directions and pieces for games, and any supplies or tools required are readily available. We have to consider purpose and quantity, need for replacement during completion of the task, and the mathematical implications of the types of manipulatives or technology we are offering to students.

Visualizing a future event is part of anticipation. It is important to think about how we envision a lesson unfolding. Keeping in mind our goal(s), where a given lesson falls in the learning progression, and the current levels of our students' understanding, what responses might we anticipate? What leaps in their understanding might occur? What questions might the students ask? What possible errors might they make and what misconceptions might they have? Drawing on our knowledge and past experiences can help us anticipate our responses to new insights, questions, errors, and incomplete understandings that arise. We consider what distractions or diversions may present themselves and identify key questions that we want to ask. We determine ways to scaffold learning and plan groups that will work well together and support the students in their pursuits. Basically, by trying to do as much work up front as possible, teachers reduce potential roadblocks to learning and increase the likelihood that they are available to work with a small group or support individual students once a learning activity has begun.

Establishing blocks of uninterrupted time so that students can truly dig into the task is also helpful. Check your schedule. Many teachers comment that any time they want to start a new unit or are planning a debriefing session, they want all students present. Many students receive support outside of class and it is important to be mindful of what is happening for each student as you prepare new lessons and set a schedule. Also, build in extra time for students to explore any new materials in the lesson. Captivating models and tools such as pattern blocks, geoboards, and real coins are distracting when they are first introduced.

As we anticipate, we need to be fresh and ready for new challenges and possibilities. One way that anticipation can lead us into trouble is the overanticipation of behavior. It is only natural for teachers to want to set up the most positive learning environment for students. Keeping everyone's behavior in check can be part of this mind-set. Sadly we can all describe a time in our classrooms when a student's behavior has overshadowed or impeded learning. To avoid this from happening, many teachers overly anticipate how a specific student might respond and then provide unnecessary scaffolding. Though a natural instinct, this form of anticipation can be shortsighted and limit student potential. As we strive for differentiation in our math classrooms, part of our goal is to support students in all areas of their development. Many teachers have found that when they create tailor-made assignments, negative behavior is diminished. So, for example, under new and more comfortable learning conditions, students may no longer need supportive prompts or a separate space to work. Also, even students who have had difficulty working together in the past can learn to appreciate more about each other's strengths.

Many teachers lament about how impossible it is to differentiate mathematics instruction. This attitude and worry can defeat them before they even begin. Part of anticipation is looking forward. Try and visualize how you want your students to succeed, how you want them to develop a rich understanding of and appreciation for mathematics while gaining self-confidence in their abilities. Get excited about the possibilities and visualize yourself as the key ingredient in making this happen. Change is scary, risky, and can be problematic. It also can be exciting, rewarding, and fun.

5. Expect Surprises.

Throughout the book we have presented classroom vignettes that contained surprises. Sometimes students didn't use the materials in quite the way the teacher expected, or they experienced unexpected difficulty with a representation. This happened even though experienced teachers took time to plan lessons carefully and anticipate students' needs and reactions. But instead of halting the students' work or getting frustrated, these teachers appreciated the opportunities to learn more about their students' thinking.

Sometimes we are surprised to find out that a student knows more than we thought or exhibits a more positive attitude toward mathematics than we believed possible. When choice is involved or mathematics is connected to students' interests, students are often able to make mathematical connections in new ways. For example, as one student, Jalissa, explained, "Once I learned that it takes four quarters to make a dollar, I remember that my music teacher told me about quarter notes and that it's the same. Fractions are everywhere. Even when you bake cookies you need a quarter of a cup."

Parents can also be the source of surprises. Teachers have found that when parents understand how much differentiated instruction helps their children, many ask more questions about mathematics and offer more help. They no longer make statements such as "Well, I wasn't very good at mathematics either; that's just the way it is," and recognize that their children can succeed under the right circumstances.

Teachers tell us that they have been surprised to learn that making plans for differentiated instruction is time consuming at first, but in fact saves time in the long run. Another surprise teachers have expressed is that when they differentiate instruction, they feel more creative and empowered as decision makers. Teachers are also surprised at the amount of mathematics they are learning. For example, when Thomas asked, "So why can't you divide by zero?" his teacher realized he needed to find out.

Surprises are part of the joyful mystery of teaching. They keep us interested and help us learn. They are stimulating and can help sustain our commitment to differentiated instruction.

6. Let Students Help.

Classrooms require significant management of people, paper, and materials. Differentiated instruction often requires even more organization and record-keeping skills. You will be more successful if you let your students take some of the responsibility. Students can:

- organize and distribute materials;
- review one another's work;
- keep track of their own choices and work;
- make sure a partner understands an assigned task;
- lead a routine or familiar game; and
- answer peer questions when you are working with a group.

When you encourage your students to take more responsibility for the operation of the classroom, you are fostering their confidence and helping them to be more independent. Their involvement may also increase the likelihood that differentiated activities will succeed.

Sometimes the summer months provide teachers with time to tackle projects that never seem to get accomplished during the year. One summer, Jeanette decided to create a math game library. Every year she recognized that most of her students would benefit from more practice with basic facts and mental arithmetic than she felt she had time for during the week. She decided that offering math games they could play over the weekend would give the students extra practice as well as involve their families in their learning.

Jeanette identified six basic games and then designed three levels of each by changing a few rules or the specific numbers involved. She wrote directions for each of these eighteen game versions and collected the materials such as cards and dice that were needed. She wanted four copies of each game so four students could take home the same activity. She decided to store the games in sealed plastic bags that would protect the games as they traveled back and forth to school. In each bag she put a direction sheet, a materials list, the needed supplies, and a reflection sheet that posed the questions: *How did this game help you? What did you learn while playing this game?*

In the fall she organized a storage area for the games and made additional copies of the directions, materials lists, and reflection forms for replacement. She also stored some extra packs of cards and dice in this area. She had a student teacher that fall who was given responsibility for distributing the games on Friday afternoons and checking them back in on Monday mornings. The morning process involved collecting the reflection slips, following up on any missing materials, inserting new reflection sheets, and putting the games away. Students were eager to get their "weekend game" and Jeanette noted a marked improvement in their skills.

Following the winter break, Jeanette's student teacher returned to his college campus and Jeanette took over support of this activity. She was surprised at how difficult it was to accomplish this process at the same time that so many students seemed to need her. After the second Monday morning she was certain that this ritual would need to end; she just couldn't support it. She shared her disappointment with the school's math coach who responded, "Could your students be assigned the job?"

Jeanette had to admit that she hadn't thought of this and at first didn't believe that it would work. As she thought about it throughout the day though, she decided it was worth a try. To her surprise the students became quite adept at taking over this responsibility. Students assigned to this task were listed on the class chore board along with those for the other jobs. Students were given this task for two weeks. The first week they served as assistants so that they could learn what was expected of them. During the second week they were the "math game librarians" in charge of distributing and checking in the materials, as well as training the new assistants. According to Jeanette, "I am so glad this was suggested to me. Instead of being frustrated with having to give this up, my students have taken over and it really works!"

It's worth thinking about some of the clerical and custodial tasks that you are performing. Could your students take more responsibility for them? Are there more important things you could accomplish with this time?

7. Work with Parents.

As you know, parental support can make the difference between success and failure and so it is important that your students' parents understand how your classroom works. You can begin by asking parents to help you know their children better, perhaps by completing surveys or by talking with you informally before or after school. Most parents support efforts to make sure their children's individual needs are met, once they believe that is really going to be the case. The first back-to-school meeting in the fall is also an opportunity to gain parental understanding and support.

When one teacher was on an errand she started to think about the ways she met her own children's needs. She was buying her three children socks and one child wanted high basketball socks, one wanted tennis socks so low you could hardly see them, and her youngest wanted tube socks because as he explained, "The seams hurt my feet when I have shoes on." She chuckled as she thought about how not having the "right socks" could ruin a morning for the entire family. She decided to share these thoughts at back-to-school night and to ask the parents some additional questions such as: *Do each of your children need the same amount of sleep? Enjoy the same activities? Want to eat the same food? In what ways do you adjust to meet these individual needs and interests?* She found parents enjoyed talking about these differences with others who were also trying to meet children's needs that didn't always match. It was simple to then help the parents understand that these same differences existed in the classroom and must be addressed there as well.

Evidence of their children's growth is often the most persuasive argument. Collect early work so that it can be compared to later samples at the first parent-teacher conference. Help parents see the specific concepts and skills their children have gained. Let them know how differentiated instructional strategies supported this improvement. Conferences can also be a time to address their particular concerns about the way you are teaching. Be prepared to help parents understand that:

- All learning activities are directly tied to curriculum goals and standards.
- Differentiated instruction is not a secret method for tracking the students. Groups change often and for a variety of reasons.
- They are always welcome to visit the classroom and participate in the learning activities.

Then follow up initial meetings with newsletters and notes. Newsletters, in particular, can help parents realize the common instructional threads in the classroom, which tend to lessen parental fears that their children are missing out on something.

Sometimes talking about their child's particular learning strengths and weaknesses reminds parents of their own learning profiles. Parents may also have had their own struggles in school because learning needs weren't met. Many teachers find that when they share observations with parents about their child's learning profiles, the parents sometimes ask questions that suggest they identify with what they have just heard. Comments such as "I wonder what kind of learning disability they might find for me if I were just starting out in school today?" or "I loved math class because I didn't have to read as much. But I'm worried about how much more reading my son needs to do in math class today. It seems to be turning him off."

Parents' feelings are strong and their insights about their child's learning are often profound. It is not always easy for parents to open up about their school experiences, but they often do so once a level of trust has been established with the teacher. About a month after a conference in which a teacher shared with a father that his daughter was struggling to learn the names of numbers and that perhaps this was what was making her development in counting so labored and frustrating for her, he emailed her the following note.

Parent Reflection

I had an interesting conversation with my daughter last night that I think is informative concerning her counting abilities. Lately, while playing games like hide-and-seek with her, I have been trying things such as having her start at fifteen when she counts. Naturally, she tends to hang up at the transitions between twenty to thirty to forty, etc., but she has become very upset at this, which has resulted in several teary and frustrated breakdowns. Last night I asked her how she felt about it and she confided to me that she was ashamed and upset. She went on to say that she experiences a lot of stress at school trying to hide these defects from her peers and teachers. These are my words, but her feelings. I am fairly confident that it is an accurate portrayal.

I also want you to know that I had similar learning difficulties as a child and I still have been unable to memorize half of the multiplication table. Perhaps my little one has inherited some of the same mental weaknesses.

Specific to counting, it is my opinion that Beth conceptually understands our number system, but that she just can't recall the words that represent the numbers in a timely fashion. I'm curious if this fits in with your current understanding of the situation. My game plan has been to integrate counting into as many activities as possible during our free time together to provide repetition, but to downplay the errors so that she doesn't become overly upset. I also have a large repertoire of mental tricks that I have accumulated to help me with these issues and I am trying to pass them on to her. She was visibly relieved the first time I confided to her that I, too, had problems like hers. As I am sure you are aware, she is a terribly proud child and I think her discomfort with needing help has caused her to avoid the very things that need more attention.

The teacher was honored to receive this email and knew that this parent's trust was a wonderful gift, one that would help ensure that his daughter's needs would be better met.

8. Find Sources of Professional Development.

Ideally, you are working with colleagues as you strive to further differentiate your mathematics instruction and your school system has provided you with coaches, consultants, time, and resources. Such circumstances are increasingly rare, however, and so it is more than likely that you will need to find some ways to support your efforts. Sometimes just finding one other teacher that will work with you is sufficient. Here are some activities that other teachers have engaged in with one or more colleagues:

- Use planning time or arrange coverage for your class so you can visit each other's classroom. It will help you understand how things are currently working and the challenges each of you face.
- Attend mathematics conferences in the local area to gain new ideas and connect with a wider group of teachers.
- Contact a local college library to see if they have videos on the teaching of mathematics or the general practice of differentiated instruction that you could watch together.

- Work more closely with any instructional specialists in the system. Many specialists are eager to work with teachers who want to transform their practice.
- See if your school system has a membership in the National Council of Teachers of Mathematics (NCTM) and read its journal, *Teaching Children Mathematics*, if it is available. If not, explore NCTM's website and lesson exemplars.
- Talk with your principal to find out what support might be available and if any local grants might support attendance at conferences or purchases of resource materials.
- Engage in instructional debriefing with one another about what is happening during math time.

9. Reflect on Your Journey.

When we reflect on our teaching we take the time to actively deliberate about what is working and what needs further attention. Perhaps in the evening we sift through what happened that day, maybe even replaying conversations with and among our students. Sometimes we uncover something that we didn't know was bothering us; sometimes we develop new insights and ideas. Over time, reflecting on what happens in our classrooms can help us transform as well as reaffirm aspects of our teaching habits and beliefs. Though reflecting on one's teaching is always important, it is particularly helpful when we are adjusting our practice.

Some teachers reflect with others about their teaching, some spend their commuting time mulling over the day. A few teachers reflect more intentionally, by keeping a journal. When we write our reflections, we have a record that we can return to and reread, a record that can help us identify patterns and note our changes over time. One teacher has reserved Wednesday afternoon for journal writing. Her reflection tells us about this tradition.

Teacher Reflection

Early on in my career, I found that by Wednesday, I needed to spend a bit more time working after school. By then plans made over the weekend needed more attention and my desk was a bit unorganized. Also, like many, I think of Wednesday as "hump day" and so working a bit longer on that day made sense to me.

At first, it would take me a while to get started once I returned from walking my students to the bus and pickup area. I'd come back to my desk and collapse in my chair, maybe check my email. Sometimes it would take me an hour to get back up to speed. Then I learned about journaling and how that can give you energy, help you focus. I decided to try it on Wednesdays and it really worked for me. Now when I return to my desk on Wednesdays, I immediately take out my journal and set the minute timer for fifteen minutes. It might take me a minute or two to start writing, but soon the words just begin to flow and I'm often surprised by what I write. I get so focused that I'm usually surprised when the timer goes off. Maybe it's the quiet, the focus, or the introspection, but after writing I have the energy to tackle the other things I need to do.

Some teachers prefer to take notes rather than write in prose. One teacher has a daily writing practice. She makes notes on a file card about two questions each day: *How did I address individual needs today? What did I learn about my students today that will inform what I do tomorrow?* When she comes in the next morning, she rereads the notes to help her focus on the new day. Some teachers follow a similar process, but record these notes in their plan books so that they are maintained over time. Other questions that help us to think about our practice of differentiation include:

- Did the pace of today's mathematics instruction work? For whom? Why? Why not?
- Are all students being challenged mathematically?
- How did I address students' interests this week? Did I learn anything new about an interest a student has?
- How were different types of learning styles addressed today?
- Are there students I want to meet with individually tomorrow?
- Is there a student I am worried about in terms of mathematics?
- Would some of my students be more successful using different mathematical manipulatives, representations, or recording systems?

10. Keep the Vision.

There will no doubt be times when you question the goal of differentiated mathematics instruction, or at least its viability or sustainability. Perhaps a principal will express reservations about your instructional style, a parent will complain about his or her child not doing the same work as the neighbor's child, or a colleague will suggest that you are making too much work for yourself. At these times it's important to remember the significance of the goal and what good sense it makes. Focus on what is working well in your classroom and what is best for your students. Remember that differentiated instruction is a long quest, a journey that never truly ends. It serves as a lens, however, to remind us to focus on how we can best support the individual differences among our students and provides us with a vision as to how we want our classrooms to be organized and our curriculum to be implemented. It takes courage and passion to sustain our efforts toward the goal of differentiated instruction, and the vision of all of our students becoming successful learners of mathematics.

Blackline Masters

Parent or Guardian Questionnaire

Alternative Parent or Guardian Survey

What Interests You?

Who Are You as a Learner?

What Do You Think About Mathematics?

Your Mathematics Autobiography

Robot Stepper: Red

Robot Stepper: Blue

Robot Stepper: Green

Shape Critter Card: Red

Shape Critter Card: Blue

Shape Critter Card: Green

Data Collection and Analysis: Red (Plan a Class Field Trip)

Data Collection and Analysis: Blue (Consult to a Business)

Data Collection and Analysis: Green (Plan a Lunch Party)

Arch Patterns: Red

Arch Patterns: Blue

Arch Patterns: Green

Measurement Investigation: Red

Measurement Investigation: Blue

Measurement Investigation: Green

Project Contract

Menu: Math All Around Us

Multiplication Think Tac Toe

RAFT: Time

What Matches You?

Self-Assessment of Differentiation Practices

Parent or Guardian Questionnaire

Dear Parent or Guardian:

I am always so excited about the start of the school year and a roomful of eager students. I am looking forward to getting to know each and every one of them, as well as their families. As no one knows your child as well as you do, I am hoping that you will have the time to answer these few questions. There are no right or wrong answers, just responses that will help me to better meet your child's needs when learning math. I am very interested to help children realize that math is an important part of the world, and therefore exciting to learn. I believe by connecting the learning of math to other important aspects of your child's life, I can make it more relevant and exciting. Please feel free to call me if you have any questions. Thank you.

1. What are your child's favorite hobbies, interests, pastimes, books?

2. In what ways is mathematics part of your child's life at home?

3. What, if any, concerns do you have about your child's knowledge of mathematics?

4. What is a mathematical strength that you see in your child?

5. Describe your child's experience with math homework.

Alternative Parent or Guardian Survey

Dear Parent or Guardian:

This first day has been a wonderful start to the school year. I am excited about getting to know each of my new students. I am hoping that you will help me by completing this questionnaire about mathematics. There are no right or wrong answers! Please feel free to call me if you have any questions. Thank you.

1 = agree
2 = somewhat agree
3 = somewhat disagree
4 = disagree

My child will stick with a math problem, even when it is difficult.	1	2	3	4
My child lacks confidence in mathematics.	1	2	3	4
My child has strong computational skills.	1	2	3	4
My child's favorite subject is mathematics.	1	2	3	4
My child becomes frustrated solving math problems.	1	2	3	4
My child does math homework independently.	1	2	3	4
As a parent, it is my job to help my child with math homework.	1	2	3	4
Math is talked about at home and is part of our everyday life.	1	2	3	4
I do not always understand the way my child thinks about math problems.	1	2	3	4
Math is taught better today than when I was in school.	1	2	3	4

Comments:

From *Math for All: Differentiating Instruction, Grades 3–5* by Linda Dacey and Jayne Bamford Lynch.
© 2007 Math Solutions Publications.

What Interests You?

1. What activities do you like to do after school?

2. What are your favorite sports or games?

3. What do you like to do at indoor recess?

4. If you could plan a field trip, where would the class go?

5. Who is your favorite character from a book or a video?

6. Which of these things do you like most? Put a 1 there. Which of these things do you like second best? Put a 2 there.

   ___ music   ___ reading

   ___ sports   ___ nature walks

   ___ acting   ___ drawing or art projects

   ___ being with friends   ___ building things

   ___ science experiments   ___ field trips to historical places

Who Are You as a Learner?

1. If you could learn about anything at school, what would you choose?

2. What do you know a lot about?

3. How do you work best in school?
   __ alone   __ partner   __ small group   __ large group

4. Where do you like to work at school?
   __ desk __ table __ hallway __ floor __ library area __ other

5. Do you learn best when your classroom is
   __ quiet   __ somewhat quiet   __ somewhat noisy   __ noisy

6. Do you like school work to be
   __ easy   __ somewhat easy   __ somewhat hard   __ hard

7. What else helps you to learn?

8. What makes it hard for you to learn?

From *Math for All: Differentiating Instruction, Grades 3–5* by Linda Dacey and Jayne Bamford Lynch.
© 2007 Math Solutions Publications.

What Do You Think About Mathematics?

1. Math is important to learn because . . .

2. When I am learning math I feel . . .

3. One thing I am good at in math is . . .

4. One thing I am not good at yet in math is . . .

5. This year in math I want to learn about . . .

Your Mathematics Autobiography

Directions: Write an autobiography that focuses on your experiences with mathematics. Use the following questions to guide your thinking. Be sure to explain your answers. You don't need to answer every question, but comment on at least five of them.

1. How do you feel about yourself in math classes?

2. What is your first memory of using mathematics?

3. What do you remember about learning to count or using numbers?

4. What kinds of things have your math teachers done to help you enjoy math?

5. What is your favorite area in mathematics (geometry, computation, logic, problem solving)?

6. What kind of math equipment, tools, or games do you like to use when learning mathematics? Why?

7. What are two examples of when you have used math outside of school?

8. When solving problems, do you prefer working alone or in a group? Why?

9. What area of math is a strength for you?

10. What area of math do you find the most challenging?

From *Math for All: Differentiating Instruction, Grades 3–5* by Linda Dacey and Jayne Bamford Lynch. © 2007 Math Solutions Publications.

Robot Stepper: Red

The five-stepper robot starts on the number 3 and takes a walk.

- On what numbers will the robot land when it takes fifteen steps?
- Write the numbers.

- Make a list of the patterns you see in the numbers.
- Think about:
  patterns in the ones place
  patterns in the tens place
  even and odd number patterns
  patterns in the sums of the first and second number, the third and fourth number,
  the fifth and sixth number, and so on

Start the robot at a different number.

- On what numbers will the robot land when it takes fifteen steps?
- Which patterns stay the same?
- Which patterns change?

From *Math for All: Differentiating Instruction, Grades 3–5* by Linda Dacey and Jayne Bamford Lynch.
© 2007 Math Solutions Publications.

Robot Stepper: Blue

The five-stepper robot is going for a walk.

- Pick the number on the line where the robot starts.
- On what numbers will the robot land when it takes fifteen steps?
- Pick a different start number.
- On what numbers will the robot land when it takes fifteen steps?
- Write about patterns you find in your lists. Think about:
  patterns in the ones place
  patterns in the tens place
  even and odd number patterns
  patterns in the sums of the first and second number, the third and fourth number, the fifth and sixth number, and so on

Now do the same with a four-stepper robot.

- What patterns do you find?
- Compare the patterns of these two steppers.

From *Math for All: Differentiating Instruction, Grades 3–5* by Linda Dacey and Jayne Bamford Lynch. © 2007 Math Solutions Publications.

Robot Stepper: Green

Imagine that you have several robots: a two-stepper, a three-stepper, a four-stepper, all the way to a nine-stepper.

- Pick the number on the line where the robots will start.
- Explore the walks of four different robots.
- Try at least two different start numbers for each robot.
- Write about the patterns you find in your lists. Think about:

  patterns in the ones place

  patterns in the tens place

  even and odd number patterns

  patterns in the sums of the first and second number, the third and fourth number, the fifth and sixth number, and so on
- What changes a pattern more, the stepper or the start number? Explain your thinking.

Choose a robot that you have not yet explored. Try to predict how many steps it will take for the pattern in the ones place to repeat. Explain your thinking and then check your prediction.

From *Math for All: Differentiating Instruction, Grades 3–5* by Linda Dacey and Jayne Bamford Lynch.
© 2007 Math Solutions Publications.

Shape Critter Card: Red

Each of these is a whirly do.

None of these is a whirly do.

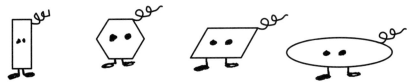

Which one of these is a whirly do?

Talk with your partner about what makes a whirly do.

Make up a name for these critters and write it in the blank.

1. Each of these is a _____.

Draw one more critter. Be sure it fits the rule.

2. None of these is a _____.

Draw one more critter. Make sure it doesn't fit the rule.

Talk with your partner about these critters.

From *Math for All: Differentiating Instruction, Grades 3–5* by Linda Dacey and Jayne Bamford Lynch.
© 2007 Math Solutions Publications.

Shape Critter Card: Blue

Each of these is a whirly do.

None of these is a whirly do.

Which one of these is a whirly do?

Describe the characteristics of a whirly do:

Make up a name for these critters and write it in the blank.

1. Each of these is a _____.

Draw one more critter. Be sure it fits the rule.

2. None of these is a _____.

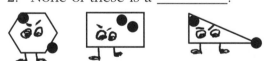

Draw one more critter. Make sure it doesn't fit the rule.

Describe the characteristics of this critter.

From *Math for All: Differentiating Instruction, Grades 3–5* by Linda Dacey and Jayne Bamford Lynch.
© 2007 Math Solutions Publications.

Shape Critter Card: Green

Each of these is a whirly do.

None of these is a whirly do.

Which one of these is a whirly do?

Describe the characteristics of a whirly do:

Make up your own critters and their characteristics.
Write their name in each blank.
Draw the pictures.
Write your rule on the back.
Trade cards with a friend and find the rules.

1. Each of these is a _____.

2. None of these is a _____.

3. Which of these are _____?

From Math for All: Differentiating Instruction, Grades 3–5 by Linda Dacey and Jayne Bamford Lynch.
© 2007 Math Solutions Publications.

Data Collection and Analysis: Red
(Plan a Class Field Trip)

1. Survey your classmates to find out the type of field trip they would like. The choices are a science museum, a historic tour, an art museum, or an aquarium.

2. Prepare a report of what you learn. In your report include:
   - the choices each person made
   - a table of your data
   - a bar graph of your data
   - your recommendation for a class trip

3. Consider the cost of the class trip. Your jobs are to:
   - brainstorm possible costs (remember four parent helpers)
   - use the computer or make calls to collect data
   - find the total cost

From *Math for All: Differentiating Instruction, Grades 3–5* by Linda Dacey and Jayne Bamford Lynch.
© 2007 Math Solutions Publications.

Data Collection and Analysis: Blue
(Consult to a Business)

The local athletic store wants to know more about students' preferences for sneakers. The owners are interested in learning more about the number, color, size, and types of sneakers that they should keep in stock. You are collecting the data for our classroom and preparing a report.

1. Make sure to include raw data, tables, and graphs in your report as well as your recommendations.

2. Investigate prices of sneakers. Based on your data, how much do you think your class will spend on sneakers this year?

Data Collection and Analysis: Green (Plan a Lunch Party)

We are going to have lunch with our kindergarten reading buddies. Use supermarket flyers to prepare possible choices.

1. Collect data about lunch preferences and activities for both classes. Make sure to include raw data, tables, and graphs in your report as well as your recommendations. At least one of your graphs must be a double bar graph representing data for both classes.

2. Analyze your menu. Use references to estimate total calories and sodium content.

3. Make a shopping list. Use the flyers to find the price of the items we will need to buy. Explain how to use the information to estimate the total cost of the lunch.

Arch Patterns: Red

Look at these arches.

It takes 4 squares, 1 rectangle that's not a square, and 4 triangles to build arch 2. So, it takes a total of 9 pieces to build arch 2.

Assume the pattern continues.

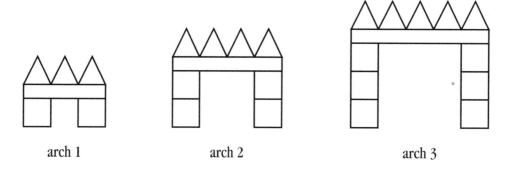

arch 1   arch 2   arch 3

1. Make sure you see the 9 pieces in arch 2.

2. Use the squares, rectangles, and triangles to build arch 4.

3. How many pieces does it take to make arch 5?

4. Draw arch 5.

5. How many squares are there in arch 6?

6. How many triangles are there in arch 7?

7. How many pieces does it take to make arch 10? Explain your thinking.

From *Math for All: Differentiating Instruction, Grades 3–5* by Linda Dacey and Jayne Bamford Lynch. © 2007 Math Solutions Publications.

Arch Patterns: Blue

Look at these arches.

It takes 4 squares, 1 rectangle that's not a square, and 4 triangles to build arch 2.
So, it takes a total of 9 pieces to build arch 2.

Assume the pattern continues.

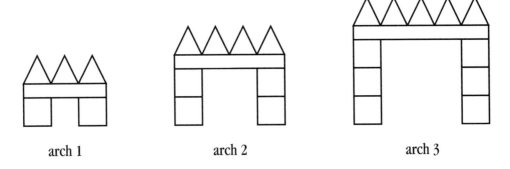

arch 1   arch 2   arch 3

1. How many pieces will it take to build arch 10? Explain your thinking.

2. In general, how can you use the arch number to find the number of triangles?

3. How many pieces will it take to build arch 40? Show your work.

Arch Patterns: Green

Look at these arches.

It takes 4 squares, 1 rectangle that's not a square, and 4 triangles to build arch 2. So, it takes a total of 9 pieces to build arch 2.

Assume the pattern continues.

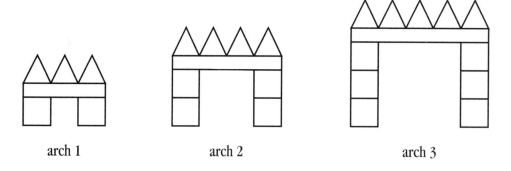

arch 1   arch 2   arch 3

1. How many pieces will it take to build arch 30? Show your work.

2. In general, how can you use the arch number to find the number of squares?

3. Rose Marie used 48 pieces to make an arch. What arch number did she make? Explain your thinking.

From *Math for All: Differentiating Instruction, Grades 3–5* by Linda Dacey and Jayne Bamford Lynch. © 2007 Math Solutions Publications.

Measurement Investigation: Red

Our class is going to make decorative boxes during art class to sell at the annual crafts fair.

Your group is going to decorate boxes that are 4-by-3-by-2 inches. You are going to cover them with the piece of wrapping paper provided. How many of these boxes can you cover? Be sure to think about different ways to put the boxes on the paper. Explain your answer.

Measurement Investigation: Blue

Our class is going to make decorative boxes during art class to sell at the annual crafts fair.

Our class is going to decorate 20 boxes that are 4-by-3-by-2 inches.

We are going to cover them with wrapping paper. You can buy the paper in a roll or in sheets (see examples). What's the least amount of paper we should buy (rolls, sheets, or rolls and sheets)? Explain your answer.

Measurement Investigation: Green

Our class is going to make decorative boxes during art class to sell at the annual crafts fair.

Our class is going to decorate boxes that have a volume of 24 cubic inches. What size boxes could we have? (Each dimension is a whole number of inches.)

We are going to cover them with wrapping paper. You can buy the paper in a roll or in sheets (see wrapping paper at the back table). What's the least amount of paper we should buy (rolls, sheets, or rolls and sheets) to cover two boxes of each size? Explain your answer.

From *Math for All: Differentiating Instruction, Grades 3–5* by Linda Dacey and Jayne Bamford Lynch. © 2007 Math Solutions Publications.

Project Contract

1. Due date: _____
    The topic for my mathematical project is:

    This is what I want to learn:

    I will use these materials and resources:

    This is what I will create to show what I learned about mathematics:

2. Due date: _____
    This is what I have accomplished so far:

    This is what I still have to do:

3. Due date: _____
    My project is complete. The three most important things I learned about mathematics are:

    The best part of this project was:

    The most challenging part of this project was:

Menu: Math All Around Us

Main Course (You must do each one.)

- For one week, keep a list of all the ways you use mathematics outside of school.

- Interview 2 adult neighbors or relatives about the ways they use mathematics when they are at work. Share your information with your team. Together, make a visual summary of your combined data.

- Create your own character. Write and illustrate your own version of *Math Curse*. Make sure your story contains at least 10 math problems and attach an answer key.

Side Orders (Complete two.)

- Write about how mathematics is used in your favorite sport.

- Read 3 stories in the newspaper. Make notes about the ways mathematics is used in the articles or how knowing mathematics helps you to understand the articles.

- Reread *Math Curse* and solve 6 of the problems in the story.

- Make a photo display of geometry in our world.

- Choose 1 of the "real-world math" websites that have been saved as favorites.

- Write 4 problems to put in our real-world problem box.

Desserts (Do one or more if you are interested.)

- Read a biography of author Jon Scieszka and coauthor/illustrator Lane Smith at www.kidsreads.com/series/series-warp-author.asp.

- Make up a song called "These Are a Few of My Favorite Uses of Math."

From *Math for All: Differentiating Instruction, Grades 3–5* by Linda Dacey and Jayne Bamford Lynch. © 2007 Math Solutions Publications.

Multiplication Think Tac Toe

Choose and complete one activity in each row.

Draw a picture that shows a model of 7 × 35. Make connections between your drawing and how you use paper and pencil to find the product. Discuss your ideas with a friend.	Your brother multiplied 64 by 8 and got the answer 4,832. What could you show and tell your brother to help him understand why his answer is wrong?	Write directions for two different ways to find the product of 92 and 25 when you use paper and pencil.
Place the numbers: 3, 4, 6, 15, 20, and 30, so that the product of each side is 360. ○ ○ ○ ○ ○ ○ Write one more problem like this one and trade it with a classmate.	Place a multiplication sign to make a number sentence that is true. 63945 = 31,970 Write two more problems like this one and trade them with a classmate.	Which two numbers should you exchange so that the product of the numbers on each card is the same? 120 4 102 | 85 6 8 3 | 3 17 30 2 Write two more problems like this one and trade them with a classmate.
Make a collage of items that come in equal groups.	Interview a classmate about what he or she knows about multiplication. Find out as much as you can in three minutes. Write a report with suggestions for teaching.	Your friend solved a word problem by multiplying 3 by 24 and then subtracting 9. Write two interesting word problems that your friend could have solved this way.

From *Math for All: Differentiating Instruction, Grades 3–5* by Linda Dacey and Jayne Bamford Lynch. © 2007 Math Solutions Publications.

RAFT: Time

Role	Audience	Format	Topic
Consultant to the Principal	Principal	Report	Comparison of Schedules of First- and Fourth-Grade Classrooms
Teacher	Younger children	Math book	What You Need to Know About Telling Time
Historian	Fourth-grade students	Time line	Events Leading to the Civil War
Marketer	Consumers	Ad	Why Analog Clocks Are the Best
Self	Parent	Pie graph	I Need More (or Less) Free Time Each Week
Fill in your	choice here.	Check with me	for approval.

What Matches You?

Try to find two classmates to fit each description. Have them sign in the box they match. No one may sign more than three boxes on one sheet.

I learn best through hands-on experiences.	I like to solve problems.	I prefer to work alone in mathematics.	I find it helpful to write about my mathematical ideas.	I sometimes get confused when others explain their thinking.
I understand fractions better than decimals.	I like to measure things.	I use drawings to understand a problem.	I learn best when the teacher writes on the board.	I find a number line more helpful than a hundreds chart.
I am better at division than multipli-cation.	I like rotating shapes in my mind.	I need quiet when I work.	I prefer base ten blocks to number lines.	I prefer to work with others.
I know my basic facts well.	I like digital clocks better than analog ones.	I am better at addition than subtraction.	I like reading and making maps.	I like learning different ways to solve problems.
I like to brainstorm ideas with a group and then follow up alone.	I like logic games and puzzles.	I want rules for solving problems.	I would like to use a calculator all of the time.	I read tables and graphs in the newspaper.

From *Math for All: Differentiating Instruction, Grades 3–5* by Linda Dacey and Jayne Bamford Lynch. © 2007 Math Solutions Publications.

Self-Assessment of Differentiation Practices

Rate your agreement with each of the following statements.
1 – disagree strongly   2 – disagree somewhat   3 – agree somewhat   4 – agree strongly

I feel confident in my ability to facilitate the learning of
mathematics at my grade level.   1   2   3   4

I can challenge my most mathematically able students.   1   2   3   4

I know how to support my least mathematically able students.   1   2   3   4

I can meet students' individual needs in mathematics
as well as or better than I can in literacy.   1   2   3   4

I have enough knowledge of mathematics to support a variety
of models, representations, and procedures in my classroom.   1   2   3   4

Rate the likelihood of the following activities occurring within a week of mathematical
instruction. 1 – very unlikely 2 – somewhat unlikely 3 – somewhat likely 4 – very likely

I work with students individually.   1   2   3   4

Students are grouped by readiness.   1   2   3   4

Students are grouped by interest.   1   2   3   4

Students are grouped by learning preferences.   1   2   3   4

Different students are working with different materials and tasks. 1   2   3   4

Check off each instructional strategy that you have tried in your teaching of mathematics. Give
yourself two points for each checkmark.

☐ Transformation of tasks to make them more open-ended
☐ RAFT
☐ Learning station
☐ Menu
☐ Think Tac Toe
☐ Compacting
☐ Tiered task

Total Score: _____

Scores range from 10 to 54.

Are you comfortable with where you are on this continuum of change? What next step(s) do
you want to take?

From *Math for All: Differentiating Instruction, Grades 3–5* by Linda Dacey and Jayne Bamford Lynch.
© 2007 Math Solutions Publications.

References

Adams, Thomasenia. 2003. "Reading Mathematics: More than Words Can Say." *The Reading Teacher* 56 (May): 786–795.

Ansell, Ellen, and Helen Doerr. 2000. "NAEP Findings Regarding Gender: Achievement, Affect, and Instructional Experiences" *Research Results from the Seventh Mathematics Assessment of the National Assessment of Educational Progress,* ed. Edward Silver and Patricia Kenney, 73–106. Reston, VA: National Council of Teachers of Mathematics.

Besser, Rusty. 2003. "Helping English-Language Learners Develop Computational Fluency." *Teaching Children Mathematics* 9 (February): 294–299.

Bley, Nancy, and Carol Thornton. 1995. *Teaching Mathematics to Students with Learning Disabilities.* 3d ed. Austin, TX: Pro-Ed.

Bloom, Benjamin, ed. 1984. *Taxonomy of Educational Objectives: Book 1 Cognitive Domain.* Reading, MA: Addison-Wesley.

Bracey, Gerald. 1999. "The Demise of the Asian Math Gene." *Phi Delta Kappan* 80 (April): 619–620.

Bray, Wendy. 2005. "Supporting Diverse Learners: Teacher Collaboration in an Inclusive Classroom." *Teaching Children Mathematics* 11 (February): 324–329.

Burns, Marilyn. 1987. *A Collection of Math Lessons: From Grades 3 Through 6.* Sausalito, CA: Math Solutions Publications.

Calkins, Lucy M., with Shelley Harwayne. 1991. *Living Between the Lines.* Portsmouth, NH: Heinemann.

Chipman, Susan, David Krantz, and Rae Silver. 2002. "Mathematics Anxiety and Science Careers Among Able College Women." *Psychological Science* 3: 292–295.

Chiu, Lian-Hwang, and Loren Henry. 1990. "Development and Validation of the Mathematics Anxiety Scale for Children." *Measurement and Evaluation in Counseling and Development* 23 (October): 121–127.

Clement, Rod. 1991. *Counting on Frank.* Milwaukee, WI: G. Stevens Children's Books.

Cole, Karen, Janet Coffey, and Shelley Goldman. 1999. "Using Assessments to Improve Equity in Mathematics: Assessment That Is Open, Explicit, and Accessible Helps All Students Achieve the Goals of Standards-based Learning." *Educational Leadership* 56 (March): 56–58.

Colen, Yong. 2006. "A Call for Early Intervention for Mathematically Gifted Elementary Students: A Russian Model." *Teaching Children Mathematics* 13 (December/January): 280–284.

Communications Division for the Office of School Education, Department of Education, Employment and Training. 2001. *Early Numeracy Interview Booklet.* State of Victoria, Australia.

Cristaldi, Kathryn. 1996. *Even Steven and Odd Todd.* New York: Scholastic.

Cuisenaire Company of America, Inc. 1995. *Quilting Tiles Resource Manual.* White Plains, NY: Cuisenaire.

Dacey, Linda, and Rebeka Eston. 2002. *Show and Tell: Representing and Communicating Mathematical Ideas in K–2 Classrooms.* Sausalito, CA: Math Solutions Publications.

Educational Development Center. 1995. *Equity in Education Series: Gender-Fair Math.* Newton, MA: Educational Development Center.

Edwards, Carol, ed. 1999. *Changing the Faces of Mathematics: Perspectives on Asian Americans and Pacific Islanders.* Reston, VA: National Council of Teachers of Mathematics.

Erwin, Jonathan. 2004. *The Classroom of Choice: Giving Students What They Need and Getting What You Want.* Alexandria, VA: Association for Supervision and Curriculum Development.

Furner, Joseph, and Mary Lou Duffy. 2002. "Equity for All Students in the New Millennium: Disabling Math Anxiety." *Intervention in School & Clinic* 4 (November): 67–74.

Gardner, Howard. 2000. *Intelligence Reframed: Multiple Intelligences for the 21st Century.* New York: Basic.

Garrison, Leslie. 1997. "Making the NCTM's Standards Work for Emergent English Speakers." *Teaching Children Mathematics* 4 (November): 132–138.

Gavin, M. Katherine, and Sally Reis. 2000. "Helping Teachers to Encourage Talented Girls in Mathematics." *Gifted Child Today* 26 (Winter): 32–44.

Ginsburg, Herbert. 1997. "Mathematics Learning Disabilities: A View from Developmental Psychology." *Journal of Learning Disabilities* 30 (January–February): 20–33.

Ginsburg, Herbert, and Arthur Baroody. 2003. *Test of Early Mathematics Ability (TEMA3).* Austin, TX: Pro-Ed.

Gregory, Gayle. 2005. *Differentiating Instruction with Style: Aligning Teacher and Learner Intelligences for Maximum Achievement.* Thousand Oaks, CA: Corwin Press.

Gregory, Gayle, and Carolyn Chapman. 2002. *Differentiated Instructional Strategies: One Size Doesn't Fit All*. Thousand Oaks, CA: Corwin Press.

Guillaume, Andrea. 2005. *Classroom Mathematics Inventory for Grades K–6: An Informal Assessment*. Boston: Pearson.

Guinness World Records. 2004. *Guinness Book of World Records 2004*. Stamford, CT: Guinness Media.

Heacox, Diane. 2002. *Differentiating Instruction in the Regular Classroom: How to Reach and Teach All Learners, Grades 3–12*. Minneapolis, MN: Free Spirit Press.

Inspiration Software. 2005. *Kidspiration 2.1*. Beavertown, OR: Author.

Isenbarger, Lynn, and Arthur Baroody. 2001. "Fostering the Mathematical Power of Children with Behavioral Difficulties: The Case of Carter." *Teaching Children Mathematics* 7 (April): 468–471.

Jennings, Lenora, and Lori Likis. 2005. "Meeting a Math Achievement Crisis." *Educational Leadership* 62: (March): 65–68.

Jensen, Eric. 2005. *Teaching with the Brain in Mind*. 2d ed. Alexandria, VA: Association for Supervision and Curriculum Development.

Jitenda, Asha. 2002. "Teaching Students Math Problem-Solving Through Graphic Representations." *Teaching Exceptional Children* 34 (March–April): 34–38.

Jones, Eric, and W. Thomas Southern. 2003. "Balancing Perspectives on Mathematics Instruction." *Focus on Exceptional Children* 35 (May): 1–16.

Kenney, Joan, Euthecia Hancewicz, Loretta Heuer, Diana Metsisto, and Cynthia L. Tuttle. 2005. *Literacy Strategies for Improving Mathematics Instruction*. Alexandria, VA: Association for Supervision and Curriculum Development.

Khisty, Lena. 2002. "Mathematics Learning and the Latino Student: Suggestions from Research for Classroom Practice." *Teaching Children Mathematics* 9 (September): 32–35.

Losq, Christine. 2005. "Number Concepts and Special Needs Students: The Power of Ten-Frame Tiles." *Teaching Children Mathematics* 11 (February): 310–315.

Lubienski, Sarah, and Mack Shelly. 2003. *A Closer Look at U.S. Mathematics Instruction and Achievement: Examinations of Race and SES in a Decade of NAEP Data*. Presented at the annual meeting of the American Educational Research Association, Chicago. ERIC Document No. ED476468. Retrieved July 17, 2004.

Malloy, Carol, and Laura Brader-Araje, eds. 1998. *Challenges in the Mathematics Education of African-American Children: Proceedings of the Benjamin Banneker Association Leadership Conference*. Reston, VA: National Council of Teachers of Mathematics.

Marzano, Robert, Debra Pickering, and Jane Pollock. 2001. *Classroom Instruction That Works: Research-Based Strategies for Increasing Student Achievement*. Alexandria, VA. Association for Supervision and Curriculum Development.

Moon, Jean, and Linda Schulman. 1995. *Finding the Connections: Linking Assessment, Instruction, and Curriculum in Elementary Mathematics*. Portsmouth, NH: Heinemann.

National Council of Teachers of Mathematics (NCTM). 2000. *Principles and Standards for School Mathematics*. Reston, VA: National Council of Teachers of Mathematics.

———. 2006. *Curriculum Focal Points for Prekindergarten Through Grade 8 Mathematics: A Quest for Coherence*. Reston, VA: National Council of Teachers of Mathematics.

Newstead, Karen. 1998. "Aspects of Children's Mathematics Anxiety." *Educational Studies in Mathematics* 36 (June): 53–71.

Ortiz-Franco, Luis, Norma G. Hernandez, and Yolanda De La Cruz, eds. 1999. *Changing the Faces of Mathematics: Perspectives on Latinos*. Reston, VA: National Council of Teachers of Mathematics.

Parish, Peggy. 1979. *Amelia Bedelia Helps Out*. New York: Greenwillow Books.

Richardson, Kathy. 2003. *Assessing Math Concepts*. Bellingham, WA: Math Perspectives.

Rotigel, Jennifer, and Susan Fello. 2004. "Mathematically Gifted Students: How Can We Meet Their Needs?" *Gifted Child Today* 27: 46–52.

Scieszka, Jon, and Lane Smith. 1995. *Math Curse*. New York: Penguin.

Silver, Harvey, Richard Strong, and Matthew Perini. 2000. *So Each May Learn: Integrating Learning Styles and Multiple Intelligences*. Alexandria, VA: Association for Supervision and Curriculum Development.

Sliva, Julie. 2004. *Teaching Inclusive Mathematics to Special Learners, K–6*. Thousand Oaks, CA: Corwin Press.

Sloan, Tina, C. J. Daane, and Judy Giesen. 2002. "Mathematics Anxiety and Learning Styles: What Is the Relationship in Elementary Preservice Teachers?" *School Science and Mathematics* 102 (February): 84–87.

Smith, Frank. 2002. *The Glass Wall: Why Mathematics Can Seem Difficult*. New York: Teachers College Press.

Snow, D. R. 2005. *Classroom Strategies for Helping At-Risk Learners*. Alexandria, VA: Association for Supervision and Curriculum Development.

Sousa, D. A. 2001. *How the Special Needs Brain Works*. Thousand Oaks, CA: Corwin Press.

Sprenger, Marilee. 2002. *Becoming a "Wiz" at Brain-Based Teaching: How to Make Every Year the Best Year*. Thousand Oaks, CA: Corwin Press.

———. 2003. *Differentiation Through Learning Styles and Memory.* Thousand Oaks, CA: Corwin Press.

Strutchens, Marilyn, Martin Johnson, and William Tate, eds. 2000. *Changing the Faces of Mathematics: Perspectives on African Americans.* Reston, VA: National Council of Teachers of Mathematics.

Tate, William. 1997. "Race-Ethnicity, SES, Gender, and Language Proficiency Trends in Mathematics Achievement: An Update." *Journal for Research in Mathematics Education* 28 (December): 652–679.

Thornton, Carol, and Graham Jones. 1996. "Adapting Instruction for Students with Special Needs K–8." *Journal of Education* 178(2): 59–69.

Tomlinson, C. A. 1999. *The Differentiated Classroom: Responding to the Needs of All Learners.* Alexandria, VA: Association for Supervision and Curriculum Development.

———. 2003a. *Differentiation in Practice: A Resource Guide for Differentiating Curriculum, Grade K–5.* Alexandria, VA: Association for Supervision and Curriculum Development.

———. 2003b. *Fulfilling the Promise of the Differentiated Classroom: Strategies and Tools for Responsive Teaching.* Alexandria, VA: Association for Supervision and Curriculum Development.

Torres-Velasquez, Diane, and Gilberto Lobo. 2004. "Culturally Responsive Mathematics: Teaching and English Language Learners." *Teaching Children Mathematics* 11 (December/January): 249–255.

U.S. Census. 2003. *Language Use and English Speaking Ability: 2000.* Retrieved January 11, 2006, from www.census.gov/prod/2003pubs/c2kbr-29.pdf

Van Luit, Johannes, and Esther Schopman. 2000. "Improving Early Numeracy of Young Children with Special Education Needs." *Remedial and Special Education* 21 (January/February): 27–40.

Vygotsky, Lev. 1978. *Mind and Society.* Cambridge, MA: Harvard University Press.

Wilkins, Michelle Muller, Jesse Wilkins, and Tamra Oliver. 2006. "Differentiating the Curriculum for Elementary Gifted Mathematics Students." *Teaching Children Mathematics* 13 (August): 6–13.

Wolfe, Pat. 2001. *Brain Matters: Translating Research into Classroom Practice.* Alexandria, VA: Association for Supervision and Curriculum Development.

Yatvin, Joanne. 2004. *A Room with a Differentiated View: How to Serve All Children as Individual Learners.* Portsmouth, NH: Heinemann.

Zaslavsky, Claudia. 2002. "Exploring World Cultures in Math Class." *Educational Leadership* 48 (October): 66–69.

Index

on communicating with parents, 59–60
on compacting, 106–7
on concept maps, 145–46
on gathering information about students, 59–60, 61
on journaling, 220–21
on learning differences activity, 193–94
on learning stations, 180–81
on love of numbers by children, 197
on materials, 88–89
on meeting the needs of all students, 82–84
on memory, 125
on models, 28–29
on open-ended tasks, 56
on pessimism for new projects, 208
on pre-assessment, 49–50
on providing special time for students, 83–84
on student-created definitions, 115
on teaching perimeter and area, 19–20
on teaching the mean, 79–80
on tiered tasks, 97–98
on use of strategies, 138
on using reading strategies with math, 211–12
on value of differentiation, 19–20
on vulnerability in learning, 137
on What Matches You? activity, 194–95
on word banks, 148–49
on word problems, 154
teachers
beliefs and actions in differentiated instruction, 3
as drowning in paperwork and information, 74–75

new skill development by, necessity of, 3–4
teaching, universal design in, 110–11
Teaching Children Mathematics (National Council of Teachers of Mathematics), 220
Teaching Inclusive Mathematics to Special Learners, K-6 (Sliva), 129
terms
dealing with problematic, 111–14, 116–17
vocabulary sheets for learning, 149–50
theory of multiple intelligences, 2, 118, 192
think/pair/share, 138–39
Think Tac Toe, 173–74
thousands charts, as graphic organizers, 155, 157, 158
tiered activities, 89–105
timelines, for projects, 165
Tomlinson, Carol, 5, 171
tracking, 54
traffic patterns in classroom, consideration of, 189
transforming tasks, 85–88

U

units, differentiation within, 5–10
universal design, 110–11

V

values, creation of different learning patterns, 3
Venn diagrams, 146–47
viewpoint, activity, 111–13
view windows, 42
visualizing, in anticipation, 213

vocabulary
development project, 168–69
sheets, 149–50
Vygotsky, Lev, 53, 133

W

Weekly Number activity, 197–99
What do you know about shapes? task, 65–74
What do you know about 100? task, 54–56
What Do You Think About Mathematics? (Blackline Master), 228
What Interests You? (Blackline Master), 226
What Matches You? activity, 194, 195
Blackline Master, 249
Who Are You as a Learner? (Blackline Master), 227
whole-class discussions, providing area for, 188
whole-class lessons, 205–6
Win a One, 170
woodworking, as arts and crafts lesson, 167
word banks, 147–48
word problems
types of, 153–54
using graphic organizers with, 154–56
word walls, 113–14
writing
mathematical autobiographies, 64, 65, 66, 67
number stories, 87

XY

Your Mathematics Autobiography (Blackline Master), 229

Z

zone of proximal development, 53, 134